STUDY GUIDE

Babu G. Baradwaj
Towson University

L. Wendell Licon
Arizona State University

AF680933

FUNDAMENTALS OF CORPORATE FINANCE

Robert Parrino
University of Texas at Austin

David S. Kidwell
University of Minnesota

WILEY

JOHN WILEY & SONS, INC.

ASSOCIATE PUBLISHER	Judith Joseph
ASSOCIATE EDITOR	Brian Kamins
EXECUTIVE MARKETING MANAGER	Amy Scholz
SENIOR PRODUCTION EDITOR	William A. Murray
COVER PHOTO	Bill Frymire/Masterfile

This book was set in Times Ten Roman by Aptara®, Inc. and printed and bound by Bind-Rite Robbinsville.

This book is printed on acid free paper. ♾

Copyright © 2009 John Wiley & Sons, Inc. All rights reserved. No part of this publication may be reproduced, stored in a retrieval system or transmitted in any form or by any means, electronic, mechanical, photocopying, recording, scanning or otherwise, except as permitted under Sections 107 or 108 of the 1976 United States Copyright Act, without either the prior written permission of the Publisher, or authorization through payment of the appropriate per-copy fee to the Copyright Clearance Center, Inc., 222 Rosewood Drive, Danvers, MA 01923, Web site: www.copyright.com. Requests to the Publisher for permission should be addressed to the Permissions Department, John Wiley & Sons, Inc., 111 River Street, Hoboken, NJ 07030-5774, (201)748-6011, fax (201) 748-6008, Web site: http://www.wiley.com/go/permissions.

To order books or for customer service please, call 1-800-CALL WILEY (225-5945).

ISBN 978-0-470-04860-3

Printed in the United States of America

10 9 8 7 6 5 4 3 2 1

CONTENTS

CHAPTER 1

The Financial Manager and the Firm

LEARNING OBJECTIVES

1. Identify the key financial decisions facing the financial manager of any business firm.
2. Identify the basic forms of business organization used in the United States, and review their respective strengths and weaknesses.
3. Describe the typical organization of the financial function in large corporation.
4. Explain why maximizing the current value of the firm's stock price is the appropriate goal for management.
5. Discuss how agency conflicts affect the goal of maximizing stockholder wealth.
6. Explain why ethics is an appropriate topic in the study of corporate finance.

I. Chapter Outline

1.1 The Role of the Financial Manager

The financial manager is responsible for making sound decisions that are in the best interest of the firm. The three fundamental decisions are capital budgeting, financing, and working capital decisions. These decisions will be made while the firm continues operating its current ongoing projects.

- A firm generates cash flows by selling the goods and services produced by its productive assets and human capital. After meeting its obligations, the firm can pay the remaining cash, called residual cash flows, to the owners as a cash dividend, or it can keep the money and reinvest the cash in the business.
  - A firm is unprofitable when it fails to generate sufficient cash flows to pay operating expenses, creditors, and taxes. Firms that are unprofitable over time will be forced into bankruptcy by their creditors.
  - In bankruptcy, the company will be reorganized, or the company's assets will be liquidated, whichever is more valuable. If anything is left after all creditor and tax claims have been satisfied, which usually does not happen, the remaining cash, or residual, is distributed to the owners.
- **The capital budgeting decision:** Which productive assets should the firm buy? This is the most important decision because they drive the firm's success or failure.
- **The financing decision:** How should the firm finance or pay for assets?
- **The working capital management decision:** How should day-to-day financial matters be managed so that the firm can pay its bills, and how should surplus cash be invested?

1.2 Forms of Business Organization

A. The three general business forms of legal organization are the sole proprietorship, the partnership and the corporation. Each has its advantages and disadvantages.

- ***A sole proprietorship*** is a business owned by one person.
  - There is also no legal distinction between personal and business income for a sole proprietor.
  - All business income is taxed as personal income.
  - A sole proprietor is responsible for paying all the firm's bills and has unlimited liability for all business debts and other obligations of the firm.
- ***A partnership*** consists of two or more owners joined together legally to manage a business.
  - A general partnership has the same basic advantages and disadvantages as a sole proprietorship.
  - When a transfer of ownership takes place, such as when a partner wants to sell out, the partnership is terminated, and a new partnership is formed.
    - The problem of unlimited liability can be avoided in a limited partnership; however, there must always be at least one general partner with unlimited liability.
- ***A corporation*** is a legal entity authorized under a state charter.
  - In a legal sense, it is a "person" distinct from its owners.
  - The owners of a corporation are its stockholders, or shareholders.
  - A major advantage of the corporate form of business is that stockholders have limited liability for debts and other obligations of the corporation.
  - A major disadvantage of the corporate organization is taxes.
    - The owners of corporations are subject to double taxation—first at the corporate level and then at the personal level when dividends are paid to them.
  - Some operate as a public corporation, which can sell their debt or equity in the public securities markets.
  - Others operate as a private corporation, where the common stock is often held by a small number of investors, typically the management and wealthy private backers.

B. ***Hybrid Forms of Business Organization***

- Limited liability partnerships (LLPs) combine the limited liability of a corporation with the tax advantage of a partnership—there is no double taxation.
- Similar forms, or hybrid organizations, include:
  - limited liability companies (LLCs)
  - professional corporations (PCs)

1.3 Managing the Financial Function

A. While it is ultimately the responsibility of the chief executive officer to manage the firm, direct responsibility for the firm's financial operations is that of the chief financial officer and the executives who report to him. The audit committee of the board of directors is responsible for hiring and firing the firm's external auditor.

B. ***The Chief Executive Officer***

- Reports directly to the board of directors, which is accountable to the company's owners.

C. ***The Chief Financial Officer***

- Has the responsibility for seeing that the best possible financial analysis is presented to the CEO, along with an unbiased recommendation.
  - **The CFO's Key Financial Reports**
    - The controller typically prepares the financial statements, oversees the firm's financial and cost accounting systems, prepares the taxes, and works closely with the firm's external auditors.
    - The treasurer looks after the collection and disbursement of cash, investing excess cash so that it earns interest, raising new capital, handling foreign exchange transactions, and overseeing the firm's pension fund managers.
    - The internal auditor is responsible for in-depth risk assessments and for performing audits of areas that have been identified as high-risk areas, where the firm has the potential to incur substantial losses.

D. *External Auditor*

- Provides an independent annual audit of the firm's financial statements.
  - o Ensures that the financial numbers are reasonably accurate, accounting principles have been consistently applied year to year and not in a manner that significantly distorts the firm's performance.

E. *The Audit Committee*

- Approves the external auditor's fees and engagement letter. The external auditor cannot be fired or terminated without the audit committee's approval.

1.4 The Goal of the Firm

A. The goal of the firm should be to maximize shareholder wealth, which is the same as maximizing the value of the firm's stock price. This is not the same as maximizing the profits of the firm. Minimizing risk or maximizing profits without regard to the other is not a successful strategy. Minimizing risk can occur without taking any risk on any projects. This will not generate cash flows for shareholders. Maximizing expected profits can occur while taking on too much risk, which can detract from the value of the firm's shares.

- To a skilled accountant, however, a decision that increases profits under one set of accounting rules can reduce it under another.
- Accounting profits are not necessarily the same as cash flows.
- Profit maximization as a goal is that it does not tell us when cash flows are to be received.
- Profit maximization ignores the uncertainty or risk associated with cash flows.

B. *Maximize the Value of the Firm's Stock Price*

- When analysts and investors determine the value of a firm's stock, they consider:
  - o the size of the expected cash flows,
  - o the timing of the cash flows, and
  - o the riskiness of the cash flows.
    - ▪ Thus, the mechanism for determining stock prices overcomes all the cash-flow objections we raised with regard to profit maximization as a goal.

C. *Can Management Decisions Affect Stock Prices?*

- Yes, management makes a series of decisions when executing the firm's strategy that affect the firm's cash flows and, hence, the price of the firm's stock.

1.5 Agency Conflicts: Separation of Ownership and Control

A. An agency relationship arises whenever one party, called the principal, hires another party, called the agent, to perform some service or represent the principal's interest. The problems associated with this relationship will occur whenever the manager, or agent, of a firm owns less than 100 percent of the firm. These costs will be borne by the shareholders of the firm.

- For large corporation, the ownership of the firm is spread over a huge number of shareholders, and the firm's owners may effectively have little control over management where management may make decisions that benefit their self-interest rather than those of the stockholders.
- Shareholders own the corporation, but managers control the money and have the opportunity to use it for their own benefit.

B. There are four tools available to help mitigate agency problems.

- **Management Compensation.** A significant portion of management compensation is tied to the performance of the firm, usually to the firm's stock price.
- **Control of the Firm.** If the interests of the manager and the firm are not aligned, then eventually the firm will underperform relative to its true potential, and the firm's stock price will fall below its maximum potential price. With its stock underpriced, the firm will become a prime target for a takeover by so-called corporate raiders or by other corporate buyers.

- **Management Labor Market.** Firms that have a history of poor performance or a reputation for "shady operations" or unethical behavior have difficulty hiring top managerial talent. The penalty for extremely poor performance or a criminal conviction is a significant reduction in the manager's lifetime earnings potential. Managers know this, and the fear of such consequences helps keep them working hard and honestly.
- **An Independent Board of Directors.** Regulators believe one of the primary reasons for misalignment between board members' and stockholders' interests is the lack of board independence.

C. Sarbanes-Oxley and other regulatory reforms that are governmental means to address agency problems include:
- Promote greater board independence
- Establish internal accounting controls
- Establish compliance programs
- Establish ethics program
- Expand audit committee's oversight powers

1.6 The Importance of Ethics in Business

A. **Business ethics** are a society's ideas about what actions are right and wrong. Studies suggest that traditions of morality are very relevant to business and to financial markets in particular. Corruption in business creates inefficiencies in an economy, inhibits the growth of capital markets, and slows the rate of economic growth in a country.

B. ***Types of Ethical Conflicts in Business***
- **Conflicts of Interest**—occur when there is a conflict between a person's personal or institutional gain and the obligation to serve the interest of another party.
- **Information Asymmetry**—occurs when one party in a business transaction has information that is unavailable to the other parties in the transaction.

  Ethicists argue, however, that laws and market forces are not enough. Despite heavy regulation, the sector has a long and rich history of financial scandals. An ethical business culture means that people have a set of principles that helps them identify moral issues and then make ethical judgments without being told what to do. In recent years, the "rules" have changed, and the legal cost of ethical mistakes can be extremely high.

II. Suggested Approach to Material

This chapter is a general survey of many of the interesting topics in corporate finance. The chapter begins with a brief discussion of the role of the financial manager and is followed by the different legal organizational forms of business. Although common organizational forms are discussed, the most common form for the purposes of the remainder of the text is the corporate form. The chapter then proceeds with the financial function of the manager and the goal of the firm, which is to maximize shareholder wealth. It is this goal that requires that we recognize its conflicts such as agency and ethical problems. Understanding the methods to help align managers and shareholders are important to understanding the decisions of financial managers.

This chapter is intended for students to begin to understand the long list of interesting problems that confront the financial manager and shareholders of the firm. It is recommended that you treat this material as groundwork for your future learning with this text. Understanding the concepts and terms in this chapter will help you understand the motivation for many of the forthcoming material in the course.

III. Chapter Glossary

Wealth	The economic value of the assets someone possesses.
Stakeholder	Anyone with a claim on the cash flows of a firm, including owners, employees, suppliers, creditors, and government.
Productive asset	The tangible and intangible assets a firm uses to generate cash flows.
Residual cash flow	The cash remaining after a firm has met operating expenses, payments to creditors, and taxes. It can be paid to the owners as a cash dividend or reinvested in the business.

Bankruptcy	Legally declared inability of an individual or a company to pay its creditors.
Capital structure	The mix of debt and equity that makes up the firm's financing.
Capital markets	Financial markets where equity and debt instruments with maturities greater than one year are traded.
Net working capital	The management of current assets and current liabilities.
Sole proprietorship	A business owned by a single individual.
Partnership	Two or more owners joined together legally to manage a business and share in its profits.
Limited liability	The legal liability of a limited partner or shareholder in a business, which extends only to the capital contributed or the amount invested.
Corporation	A legal entity authorized under a state charter. In a legal sense, it is a "person" distinct from its owners.
Public markets	Markets regulated by the Securities and Exchange Commission in which large amounts of debt and equity are publicly traded.
Privately held corporations	Corporations, whose stock is held by a small number of investors and is not traded in public markets; also called *closely held corporations.*
Limited liability partnerships (LLPs)	Hybrid business organizations that combine some of the advantages of corporations and partnerships. In general, income to the partners is taxed only as personal income, but the partners have limited liability.
Chief financial officer (CFO)	The highest-level financial manager in a company.
Agency conflicts	Conflicts of interest between a firm's owners and its management.
Agency costs	The costs of the conflict of interest between the firm's owners and its management.
Information asymmetry	The situation in which one party in a business transaction has information that is unavailable to the other parties in the transaction.

IV. Summary of Key Equations

The chapter is primarily a qualitative chapter and does not have a relevant summary of key equations.

V. True or False Questions

1. A stakeholder is anyone with an interest—financial or political—in the firm.

a. True

b. False

2. Executive compensation decisions are one of the three fundamental decisions for financial managers when running a business.

a. True

b. False

3. Working capital management is the day-to-day management of the firm's short-term assets and liabilities to ensure that the firm has enough money to pay its bills and invest any spare cash to earn interest.

a. True

b. False

4. A general partnership has the same basic advantages and disadvantages as a sole proprietorship.
   - **a.** True
   - **b.** False

5. The owners of corporations are not subject to double taxation.
   - **a.** True
   - **b.** False

6. The chief accounting officer reports directly to the audit committee of the board of directors.
   - **a.** True
   - **b.** False

7. Maximizing profits should be the goal of every financial manager.
   - **a.** True
   - **b.** False

8. Agency problems exist because the owner of a firm hires an agent to perform a service or to represent the owner's interest.
   - **a.** True
   - **b.** False

9. Management compensation is one of the methods that can align the interest of managers with that of the shareholders.
   - **a.** True
   - **b.** False

10. The Sarbanes-Oxley Act of 2002 requires firms to establish ethics programs that monitor the ethical conduct of employees.
    - **a.** True
    - **b.** False

VI. Multiple-Choice Questions

1. An underlying assumption of the text is
   - **a.** that most people who start a business do so to avoid unemployment taxes.
   - **b.** that most people who start a business do so because they want to increase their wealth.
   - **c.** that everyone starts a business to contribute to the GDP of the nation.
   - **d.** a and b

2. Which of the following are stakeholders?
   - **a.** employees
   - **b.** creditors
   - **c.** shareholders
   - **d.** all of the above

3. Which of the following is an example of an intangible asset?
   - **a.** patent
   - **b.** office building
   - **c.** widget machine
   - **d.** b and c

4. Which of the following is **NOT** a type of fundamental decision in financial management?
   - **a.** financing decisions
   - **b.** capital budgeting decisions
   - **c.** working capital management decisions
   - **d.** auditing decisions

5. Which type of organization form of business is the easiest to start?
   - **a.** limited liability partnership
   - **b.** corporation
   - **c.** partnership
   - **d.** sole proprietorship

6. Double taxation can be found in which organizational form?
   - **a.** limited liability partnership
   - **b.** corporation
   - **c.** partnership
   - **d.** sole proprietorship

7. Which type of organization provides the easiest avenue to raise capital?
   - **a.** public corporation
   - **b.** private corporation
   - **c.** partnership
   - **d.** sole proprietorship

8. Which type of organizational form is considered a hybrid form?
   - **a.** limited liability partnership
   - **b.** corporation
   - **c.** partnership
   - **d.** sole proprietorship

9. Which position within the firm has the ultimate management responsibility and decision-making power in the firm?
   - **a.** controller
   - **b.** treasurer
   - **c.** CFO
   - **d.** CEO

10. Who is responsible for approving the external auditor's fees and engagement letter?
    - **a.** controller
    - **b.** CFO
    - **c.** CEO
    - **d.** audit committee

11. Which of the following should be the goal of the firm?
    - **a.** maximize profits
    - **b.** minimize risk
    - **c.** maximize the value of shareholders' wealth
    - **d.** maximize the nearest year's cash flow

12. Which of the following is (are) a valid criticism of profit maximization as a goal for the firm?

- **a.** Accounting profits are not necessarily the same as cash flows.
- **b.** Profit maximization does not tell us when cash flows are received.
- **c.** Profit maximization ignores the uncertainty or risk associated with cash flows.
- **d.** All of the above.

13. Risk minimization, as a goal for the firm, will not be a good objective. An example of risk minimization is

- **a.** a no risk–no return policy.
- **b.** a no risk–very high return policy.
- **c.** a high risk–low return policy.
- **d.** all of the above.

14. Which of the following is true?

- **a.** A risky dollar is worth less than a safe dollar.
- **b.** A risky dollar is worth more than a safe dollar.
- **c.** A risky dollar is equivalent in value to that of a safe dollar.
- **d.** None of the above.

15. Which of the following has the greatest potential for agency problems between management and shareholders?

- **a.** Management owns 100 percent of the shares of the firm.
- **b.** Management owns 50 percent of the shares of the firm.
- **c.** Management owns 25 percent of the shares of the firm.
- **d.** Management owns no shares of the firm.

16. Which of the following would be considered an agent of the firm?

- **a.** A supplier of the firm.
- **b.** An engineer employed by the firm.
- **c.** A police officer in the same town as the firm's headquarters.
- **d.** All of the above.

17. Who generally bears the agency costs of the firm?

- **a.** employees
- **b.** debt holders
- **c.** shareholders
- **d.** IRS

18. Which of the following would best help minimize the agency costs between managers and shareholders of the firm?

- **a.** Grant the manager a compensation package of 100 percent salary.
- **b.** Grant the manager a compensation package of 50 percent salary and 50 percent bonus, which is based upon sales.
- **c.** Grant the manager a compensation package of 50 percent salary and 50 percent bonus, which is based upon the firm's stock price.
- **d.** None of the above would help reduce agency costs.

19. The situation where one contracting party has information that is unavailable to the other parties is called

- **a.** a conflict of interest.
- **b.** information asymmetry.
- **c.** information symmetry.
- **d.** none of the above.

20. Evidence that ethics are important and that laws and market forces are not enough to help markets function smoothly are
   - **a.** nonexistent as laws, and market forces are clearly enough.
   - **b.** that despite heavy regulation, the sector has a long and rich history of financial scandals.
   - **c.** irrelevant since investing is a zero-sum game.
   - **d.** irrelevant since ethics are an out-date pie-in-the-sky matter.

Answers to True or False Questions

1. b	**2.** b	**3.** a	**4.** a	**5.** b
6. b	**7.** b	**8.** a	**9.** a	**10.** a

Answers to Multiple-Choice Questions

1. b	**2.** d	**3.** a	**4.** d	**5.** d
6. b	**7.** a	**8.** a	**9.** d	**10.** d
11. c	**12.** d	**13.** a	**14.** a	**15.** d
16. b	**17.** c	**18.** c	**19.** b	**20.** b

CHAPTER 2

The Financial Environment and the Level of Interest Rates

LEARNING OBJECTIVES

1. Discuss the primary role of the financial system in the economy, and describe the two basic ways in which fund transfers take place.
2. Discuss direct financing and the important role that investment banks play in this process.
3. Describe the primary and secondary markets, and explain why secondary markets are so important to businesses.
4. Explain why money markets are important financial markets for large corporations.
5. Discuss the most important stock market exchanges and indexes.
6. Explain how financial institutions serve consumers and small businesses that are unable to participate in the direct financial markets and describe how corporations use the financial system.
7. Explain how the real rate of interest is determined in the economy, and differentiate between the real rate and the nominal rate of interest, and be able to compute the nominal or real rate of interest.

I. Chapter Outline

2.1 The Financial System

A. The financial system is competitive in that investors earn the highest rate possible while borrowers pay the lowest rate possible.

- Through the financial system, money is aggregated in small amounts and loaned in large amounts.
- Note that the people with investment opportunities are rarely the ones who have the money to lend but through the financial markets consumers, or demanders and suppliers of capital, benefit.

B. The primary concern of the financial system is funneling money from surplus spending units (SSUs) to deficit spending units (DSUs).

- If the DSU borrows directly from the SSU, then we call it a direct funds flow.
- If the borrowing takes place through an intermediary such as a commercial bank, then we call it an indirect funds flow or intermediation. Note that borrowing may take place through the sale of securities.

2.2 Direct Financing

The function of financial markets is to channel funds from people who have surplus funds (SSUs) to businesses (DSUs) that need money for capital projects.

A. Direct financial markets are wholesale markets in which the minimum transaction size is $1 million or more.
- Two types of firms generally help to facilitate these kinds of transactions.
  - Investment banks specialize in helping companies sell new debt or equity issues in the public or private security markets and money center banks are large commercial banks located in major U.S. financial centers that transact in both the national and international money markets.

2.3 Types of Financial Markets

These can be categorized by the type of securities that are traded in that market.

A. A primary market is a financial market in which new security issues are sold for the first time, whereas a secondary market is a financial market in which the owners of outstanding securities can resell them to other investors.
- Secondary markets are important to the primary market because investors are willing to pay higher prices for securities in primary markets if the securities have active secondary markets.
- The ease with which a security can be sold and converted into cash is called **marketability.**
  - Marketability depends on the cost of trading the security, physical transfer costs, and search and information costs. Therefore, the presence of a secondary market increases a security's marketability.
- Brokers are market specialists who bring buyers and seller together when a sale takes place to execute the transaction for their client.
- Dealers make markets for securities and they therefore bear risk by making a market by buying and selling from their own inventory.

B. Securities exchanges are available to trade securities.
- They can be categorized into one of two groups.
  - Organized exchanges, which provide a physical meeting place and communication facilities for members to conduct business under a specific set of rules and regulations. Only members can use the exchange, and each exchange has a limited number of seats.
    - Examples of organized exchanges are the New York Stock Exchange.
  - Over-the-counter (OTC) markets, which have no central trading location, so investors can execute OTC transactions by visiting or telephoning an OTC dealer or by using a computer-based electronic trading system linked to the OTC dealer.

C. ***Money Markets and Capital Markets***
- Money markets are global markets where short-term debt instruments, which have maturities less than one year, are sold.
- They are highly marketable in that they can be easily converted into cash, and they are issued (or sold) by economic units of the highest credit standing.
- Examples of money market instruments include U.S. Treasury bills, negotiable CDs, and commercial paper.
- ***Capital markets*** are that segment of the marketplace where capital goods, such as plant and equipment, are financed with equities or long-term debt.

D. ***Public markets*** are organized financial markets where the general public buys and sells securities through their stockbrokers.
- The SEC regulates public securities markets in the United States and is responsible for overseeing the securities industry and regulating all primary and secondary markets in which securities are traded.
- A private placement deal occurs when a company contacts an SSU directly and negotiates a deal to sell the entire security issue to the SSU. The market for private placements is not a public market, and thus, it is not subject to SEC regulations.

E. ***Futures and options markets*** trade derivative securities, which are so-called because they derive their value from some underlying asset.

- Futures contracts are contracts for future delivery of securities, foreign currencies, interest rates, or commodities.
- Options contracts call for one party (the option writer) to perform a specific act, usually to buy or sell a security at a specific price, if called upon to do so by the option buyer or owner.

2.4 The Stock Market

- The New York Stock Exchange, founded in 1792, is the oldest, largest, and best-known exchange of this kind in the United States.
  - o The common and preferred stocks of more than three thousand companies, as well as eight hundred bonds, are listed on the exchange.
  - o Collectively, the companies whose securities are traded on the NYSE have a market capitalization (total stock value) of $16 trillion.
- The NASDAQ is the world's largest electronic stock market, listing nearly four thousand companies.
  - o NASDAQ was created in 1971 by the National Association of Securities Dealers (NASD), and its odd name is an acronym for National Association of Securities Dealers Automated Quotation (NASDAQ) system.
  - o NASDAQ fits our earlier definition of an OTC market because it does not have a physical location where trading takes place.
- Stock market indexes are used to measure the performance of the stock market. For instance, the index can be used to tell whether stock prices on average are moving up or down.
  - o Dow Jones Average, which consists of 30 companies that represent about 20 percent of the market value of all U.S. stocks.
  - o Standard and Poor's 500 Index, which is regarded as the best index for measuring the performance of the largest companies in the U.S. economy.
  - o The S&P represents about 80 percent of the total market capitalization of all stocks on the New York Stock Exchange.
  - o The NASDAQ Composite Index is an example that consists of all of the common stocks listed on the NASD Automatic Quotation System of over 5,000 firms.
- ***Indirect financing***—when a financial intermediary such as a commercial bank or insurance company stands between the SSU and the DSU.

2.5 Financial Institutions and Indirect Financing

o ***Indirect financing*** occurs when a financial intermediary repackages securities between lender-savers and borrower-spenders.

A. ***Commercial Banks*** are the most prominent and largest financial intermediaries in the economy and offer the widest range of financial services to businesses. Their major sources of funds are consumers: checking accounts, savings accounts, and a variety of time deposits.
- Banks accumulate these funds and make a variety of loans to consumers, businesses, and governments. They also do a significant amount of equipment lease financing.

B. ***Life and Casualty Insurance Companies***
- Life insurance companies obtain funds by selling life insurance policies that protect individuals against the loss of income from a family member's premature death.
- Casualty insurance companies sell protection against loss of property from fire, theft, accidents, and other predictable causes.
- With the funds from these delayed liabilities, they provide funding to public corporations through the purchase of stocks and bonds in the direct credit markets and to closely held corporations through direct placement financing.

C. ***Pension Funds*** provide retirement programs for businesses as part of their employee benefit programs.
- They obtain money from employee and employer contributions during the employee's working years, and then provide monthly payments upon retirement.

D. ***Investment Funds*** sell shares to investors and use the funds to purchase a wide range of direct and indirect financial instruments.

E. ***Business Finance Companies*** sell short-term IOUs, called *commercial paper,* to investors in the direct credit markets, where these funds are used to make a variety of short- and intermediate-term loans and leases to small and large businesses.

2.6 The Determinants of Interest Rate Levels

A. ***The Real Rate of Interest.*** This is a long-term interest rate determined in the absence of inflation.
- The determinants of the real rate are a firm's return on investment as well as the time preference for consumption.

B. ***Money, Inflation, and Purchasing Power.*** The value of money is its purchasing power, which means that there is an inverse relationship between changes in price level and the value of money.

C. ***Inflation and Loan Contracts.*** The real rate of interest ignores inflation, and this means that lenders must incorporate anticipated inflation into lending contracts. Otherwise they may lose purchasing power when the loan is repaid.

D. ***Inflation Premiums.*** Lenders can incorporate protection against changes in buying power due to anticipated inflation in a loan contract.
- The relationship between inflation and the rate charged in loans, or the nominal rate is:

$$\text{Nominal Rate} = \text{Real Rate of Interest} + \text{Expected Changes in Commodity Prices}$$

E. ***Interest Rates: The Business Cycle and Inflation.*** Interest rates tend to follow the business cycle.
- During periods of economic expansion, interest rates tend to rise while during a recession, the opposite tends to take place. This also suggests that inflationary expectations have a major impact on interest rates.

II. Suggested Approach to Material

Chapter 2 provides information that will serve as a useful background for the material later in the course. While much of the material will be covered once again later in the text, it is offered at this point to make the later chapters more accessible.

The chapter begins with a discussion of why financial markets exist; that is, they facilitate the efficient distribution of capital. A distinction is made between markets for where capital is initially raised versus where the securities are bought and sold after the initial sale. A brief survey is then presented concerning the legal and regulatory rules affecting financial markets, followed by a list of the financial market participants and their role. A list of the different types of markets, by the type of security in which they specialize, is presented and is followed by a brief listing of the major institutions in the financial marketplace. Finally, since interest rates are such an important component of an efficient capital market, the chapter introduces the major determinants of interest rates.

If the student has already covered this material in a previous course, then the chapter will serve as a review for the later parts of the chapter. In that case, the student may want to cover the material briefly before proceeding to the next chapter. If the student is covering the material for the first time, a more in-depth study of the chapter is warranted and, in fact, will be necessary.

III. Chapter Glossary

Investment banks	Firms that specialize in helping companies sell new debt or equity issues in the public or private security markets and that also provide a variety of broker-dealer services for businesses and consumers.
Money center banks	Large commercial banks located in major U.S. financial centers that transact in both the national and international money markets.
Primary market	A financial market in which new security issues are sold by companies directly to investors.
Secondary market	A financial market in which the owners of outstanding securities can sell them to other investors.
Marketability	The ease with which a security can be sold and converted into cash.

Liquidity	The ability to convert an asset into cash quickly without loss of value.
Brokers	Market specialists who bring buyers and sellers together in secondary markets. They execute transactions for their clients and are compensated with a commission.
Money market	A collection of markets trading in short-term financial instruments.
Capital markets	Markets where equity and debt with maturities greater than one year are traded.
Public markets	Wholesale markets where securities registered with the SEC are sold.
Private placement	The sale of security directly to an investor, such as an insurance company.
Financial intermediation	Conversion of securities with one set of characteristics into securities with another set of characteristics.
Initial public offering (IPO)	A corporation's first offering of its stock to the public.
Real rate of interest	The interest rate that would exist in the absence of inflation.
Nominal rate of interest	The market rate of interest, that is, unadjusted for inflation.

IV. Summary of Key Equations

Equation	Description	Formula
2.1	Fisher effect	$i = r + \Delta P_e$

V. True or False Questions

1. The financial system is important because a complex industrial economy like that of the United States could not exist without an efficient financial system.

a. True
b. False

2. Investment banks are large commercial banks located in major U.S. financial centers that transact in both the national and international money markets.

a. True
b. False

3. A primary market is any financial market in which the owners of outstanding securities can resell them to other investors.

a. True
b. False

4. Brokers are market specialists that bear risk for compensation.

a. True
b. False

5. The capital markets are a segment of the marketplace where capital goods, such as plant and equipment, are financed with equities or long-term debt.

a. True
b. False

6. Intermediation financing is the same thing as indirect financing.

a. True

b. False

7. Casualty insurance companies obtain funds by selling life insurance polices that protect individuals against the loss of income from a family member's premature death.

a. True

b. False

8. A mutual fund is a type of investment fund.

a. True

b. False

9. The real rate of interest is the price of borrowing money for the use of its purchasing power.

a. True

b. False

10. If inflation is anticipated to be very high over the next year, then we would expect that nominal interest rates would also be high.

a. True

b. False

VI. Multiple-Choice Questions

1. Markus has decided to save funds this period in order to be able to consume more next period. Markus is

a. a deficit spending unit (DSU).

b. a balanced budget unit (BBU).

c. a surplus spending unit (SSU).

d. none of the above.

2. In an economy, all economic units can be classified as

a. a household.

b. a business firm.

c. a government.

d. any of the above.

3. When a DSU borrows directly from a an SSU in a financial market by selling a security, that is called

a. reverse financing.

b. direct financing.

c. indirect financing.

d. none of the above.

4. Another name for a security is

a. a financial instrument.

b. a derivative.

c. a future.

d. a or b

5. Which of the following are presently allowed to provide security underwriting services for their clients?

a. investment banks

b. all commercial banks

c. money center banks

d. a and c

6. An initial public offering is an example of a(n) ____________transaction.

a. primary market

b. secondary market

c. electionary market

d. a and b

7. Which of the following is responsible for establishing the U.S. Securities and Exchange Commission?

a. the Securities Act of 1933

b. the Securities Exchange Act of 1934

c. the Glass-Steagall Act of 1933

d. the Financial Services Modernization Act of 1999

8. Which of the following broke the barrier between commercial and investment banks?

a. the Securities Act of 1933

b. the Securities Exchange Act of 1934

c. the Glass-Steagall Act of 1933

d. the Financial Services Modernization Act of 1999

9. Which of the following is not subject to SEC regulation?

a. IPO

b. a private placement of debt securities

c. a public placement of equity securities

d. a and c

10. Which of the following can "make a market" in a security?

a. a broker

b. a dealer

c. a loan officer

d. a and b

11. The New York Stock Exchange is an example of

a. an organized stock exchange.

b. an over-the-counter market.

c. a regional exchange.

d. a and b

12. The money markets are dependent on

a. a different location to trade at everyday.

b. being able to trade at a portion of the NYSE cost.

c. telephone links in order to communicate.

d. a and b

13. Which of the following is not a money market instrument?

a. U.S. Treasury bill

b. negotiable CD

c. commercial paper

d. corporate bond

14. Which of the following derives its value from an underlying asset?
   a. a future
   b. U.S. Treasury bill
   c. negotiable CD
   d. a and b

15. Another name for indirect financing is
   a. intermediate financing.
   b. intermediation financing.
   c. multidirectional financing.
   d. private issue financing.

16. ______________ are the most prominent and largest financial intermediaries in the economy and offer the widest range of financial services to business.
   a. Investment banks
   b. Commercial banks
   c. Life insurance companies
   d. Finance companies

17. _____________ sell shares to investors and use the funds to purchase direct financial instruments.
   a. Investment banks
   b. Investment funds
   c. Life insurance companies
   d. Finance companies

18. The fundamental determinants of interest rates are
   a. the firms that invest in capital projects.
   b. the individual's time preference for consumption.
   c. the Federal Reserve and the U.S. Treasury.
   d. a and b

19. ___________ is a long-term interest rate determined in the absence of inflation.
   a. The nominal rate
   b. The real rate
   c. The prime rate
   d. None of the above

20. If the real rate of interest for a one-year investment is 8 percent and the expected rate of inflation is 3 percent, then what should the nominal rate of interest be for a one-year investment?
   a. 8 percent
   b. 11 percent
   c. 24 percent
   d. None of the above

Answers to True or False Questions

1. a	2. b	3. b	4. b	5. a
6. a	7. b	8. a	9. b	10. a

Answers to Multiple-Choice Questions

1. c	**2.** d	**3.** b	**4.** a	**5.** d
6. a	**7.** b	**8.** d	**9.** b	**10.** b
11. a	**12.** c	**13.** d	**14.** a	**15.** b
16. b	**17.** b	**18.** d	**19.** b	**20.** b

CHAPTER 3

Financial Statements, Cash Flows, and Taxes

LEARNING OBJECTIVES

1. Discuss generally accepted accounting principles (GAAP) and their importance to the economy.
2. Know the balance sheet identity, and explain why a balance sheet must balance.
3. Describe how market-value balance sheets differ from book-value balance sheets.
4. Identify the basic equation for the income statement and the information it provides.
5. Explain the difference between cash flows and accounting income.
6. Explain how the four major financial statements discussed in this chapter are related.
7. Discuss the difference between the average and marginal tax rates.

I. Chapter Outline

3.1 Financial Statements and Accounting Principles

A. ***Annual Reports***

- The annual report is a vehicle for management to communicate with the firm's shareholders and members of the public.
- The annual report has three sections—financial summary related to the past year's performance; information about the company, its products, activities, and audited financial statements including historical financial data.

B. ***Generally Accepted Accounting Principles (GAAP)***

- These principles are accounting rules and standards that companies need to adhere to when they prepare financial statements and reports.
- GAAP is prepared by the Financial Accounting Standards Board (FASB) and is authorized by the SEC.
- It is founded on basic principles such as **the assumption of arm's-length transaction, the cost principle, the realization principle, the matching principle, and the going concern assumption**.
- Critics feel that GAAP is too complicated and detail-oriented, leaving no room for accountants to use their judgment, and can easily be circumvented by sharp financial managers and accountants.

C. ***International GAAP***

- The International Accounting Standards Board promotes uniform accounting rules and procedures, and European Union firms were expected to comply with International Accounting Standards (IAS) by 2007.
- The SEC does not recognize IAS and requires foreign firms listed on U.S. stock exchanges to use U.S. GAAP.

3.2 The Balance Sheet

A. This financial statement identifies all the assets and liabilities of a firm at a point in time.

- The liabilities of the firm represent the funds that the firm has borrowed from both creditors and shareholders.
- The assets represent what the firm owns and uses to generate revenues.
- In addition to the amount borrowed from suppliers and other creditors, the balance sheet also lists the capital raised from its shareholders.
- While assets are listed in their order of their liquidity, the liabilities are listed in the order in which they must be paid.
- Shareholders of the firm's common equity are listed last as they will be paid with whatever remains after paying all other suppliers of funds.

B. ***Current Assets and Liabilities***

- Short-term assets are called current assets. These include cash and marketable securities, accounts receivables, and inventory.
- Short-term liabilities like bank loans and other borrowings with less than a year's maturity, accounts payables, accrued wages, and taxes are current liabilities.
- The difference between the amount of current assets and current liabilities is called net working capital.
- Inventory is reported in one of two different ways on the balance sheet—FIFO and LIFO.
- Firms may switch from one to another only under extraordinary circumstances and not frequently.

C. ***Long-Term Assets***

- These include land, buildings, plant and equipment, and intangible assets such as goodwill, patents, and copyrights.
- All long-term real assets are depreciated while intangible assets are amortized. Depreciating assets allow a firm to lower taxable income and reduce taxes.

D. ***Long-Term Liabilities and Equity***

- These consist of the long-term debt of the company, including bank loans, mortgages, and bonds that have a maturity of one year or longer.
- There are two sources of equity funds—common equity and preferred equity—representing ownership of the firm.
- Retained earnings result from the funds that the firm has reinvested in the firm.
- The treasury stock account reflects the value of the shares that the firm repurchased from investors.
- The other source of equity capital is preferred stock. It has features that are a combination of a fixed income security and an equity security.

3.3 Market Value versus Book Value

Traditionally, all assets are reported at their historical cost.

- The balance sheet does not reflect the current market value of the assets, only their acquired cost.
- Adopting a marking to market approach—that is, reporting assets at their current market value—provides better information to management and investors.
- The downside is the difficulty in estimating the market values of assets.

3.4 The Income Statement and the Statement of Retained Earnings

A. ***The Income Statement***

- The basic identity is shown in Equation 3.3.
- Revenues represent the value of the products and services sold by the firm and include both cash and credit sales.
- Expenses range from the cost of producing goods for sale and asset utilization costs such as depreciation or amortization.
- Net income is the difference between the firm's revenues and expenses.

B. ***Depreciation, Amortization, and Other Income Statement Accounts***

- Depreciation is the cost of writing off any physical asset like plant or machinery over its lifetime. This is a noncash expense. It reduces the taxable income for a firm and increases the cash flow available to shareholders.
- Amortization expenses are related to the writing off of the value of intangible assets like goodwill, patents, and licenses. It is also a noncash expense like depreciation.
- Nonrecurring expenses are associated with the closing down of unprofitable operations or the restructuring of a firm's operations.

- Extraordinary items refer to income or expenses associated with events that are not expected to happen on a regular basis.

C. ***Bottom-Line Accounts***
- The first bottom-line income figure that would be of interest to shareholders and creditors is **earnings before interest, taxes, depreciation and amortization (EBITDA),** which is the earnings generated from operations prior to the payment of expenses not directly connected to the production of the goods and services.
- After netting out the expenses related to depreciation and amortization, we arrive at **earnings before interest and taxes (EBIT)**.
- The next important income line is **earnings before taxes (EBT),** and it represents the taxable income for the period.
- Finally, subtracting taxes from EBT yields **net income,** or net income after taxes.

D. ***Statement of Retained Earnings***
- This financial statement shows the changes in this account from one period to the next.
- This account will show changes whenever a firm reports a loss or profit and when a cash dividend is declared.

3.5 Cash Flows

A. ***Net Cash Flow versus Net Income***
- Whereas accountants focus on net income, shareholders are more interested in net cash flows. Net cash flow and net income are not the same because of the presence of noncash revenues and expenses.
- Equation 3.4 shows how we can derive the net cash flows from operating activities (NCFOA) from net income.

B. ***The Statement of Cash Flows***
- The statement of cash flows helps to measure cash outflows and cash inflows generated during any period.
- It has three parts: the cash flows resulting from operating activities, investing activities, and financing activities.
  - Operating activities: Cash flows result from producing and selling goods and services.
  - Investing activities: Cash inflows and outflows arise out of the acquisition and selling of real assets necessary to operate the business.
  - Financing activities: Cash flows are related to raising funds or payments to creditors and shareholders.

3.6 Tying the Financial Statements Together

The role of the balance sheet includes the following:
- The balance sheet brings all the financial statements together, summarizing the financing and investment activities of the firm at a point in time.
- It recognizes the changes in the company's financial position since the last reporting period that result from new activities or discontinued activities.
- It identifies to shareholders the impact on owners' equity account of all the transactions that the firm was involved in since the last reporting period and that are recognized in the income statement and statement of retained earnings.

3.7 Federal Income Tax

A. ***Corporate Income Tax Rates***
- The federal income tax schedule for the year 2007 is shown in Exhibit 3.6.

B. ***Average versus Marginal Tax Rates***
- The average tax rate is the total taxes paid divided by taxable income for the period, while the marginal tax rate is the tax rate that is paid on the last dollar earned or the next dollar earned.

C. ***Tax Treatment of Dividends and Interest Payments***
- The current tax code in the United States allows interest payments on debt issued by firms to be tax deductible, but dividends paid on the firm's preferred stock or common stock are not deductible for tax purposes and are paid from after-tax income.

II. Suggested Approach to Material

This chapter provides a foundation for topics that will be covered throughout the course. In this chapter, you review the basic financial statements—balance sheet, income statement, statement of cash flows—which would have been studied in detail in the basic accounting courses. In some schools, this material is not reviewed in the first finance course, and it is assumed that students have previous knowledge of the material. In other schools, the material will be reviewed to varying degrees. Regardless of whether or not the material is covered in the course, it is important for a student to understand these basic financial statements. The following is one approach that will help a student of finance to develop a solid foundation.

To recognize the key concepts in this chapter, you should learn the individual items that go on the balance sheet, income statement, and statement of cash flows., as well as identify and understand the firm's sources of funds (liabilities) and the accounts that represent the uses of funds (assets). You also need to recognize which assets and liabilities are short-term and which are long-term, and understand the differences between book-value accounting and market-value accounting and the implications of using market-value accounting for the various stakeholders of the firm—management, creditors, and shareholders. Study carefully how an income statement is constructed. Equation 3.3 is the basic identity that you need to recognize.

Read Section 3.4 for its discussion of the income statement. What are the expense items, and how do they affect the different earnings measures such as EBITDA, EBIT, EBT, and net income after taxes? Also, study the concept of cash flows given in Section 3.5. This concept represents a major difference in approach from accounting. In finance, we use cash flows as the basis for valuation, whereas in accounting the bottom-line figure everyone focuses on is profit after tax. Finally, you need to understand how the various financial statements are connected to each other as well as learn what the marginal tax rate is.

III. Chapter Glossary

Annual report	A report prepared annually by a corporation, as required by law, to provide shareholders with information about the corporation's operating and financial performance over the past year.
Generally accepted accounting principles (GAAP)	A set of widely agreed-upon rules and procedures that define how companies are to maintain financial records and prepare financial reports.
Book value	The value of an asset as carried on the company's financial accounts, generally based on the asset's historical cost.
Balance sheet	A financial statement that represents a firm's financial position at a particular point in time.
Net working capital	The difference between total current assets and total current liabilities.
Depreciation	Allocation of the cost of an asset over its estimated life to reflect the wear and tear on the asset as it is used to produce the firm's goods and services.
Treasury stock	Stock that the firm has repurchased from investors.
Market value	The price at which an item can be sold.
Income statement	A financial statement that reports on the profits or losses of a firm over some period of time—usually a month, a quarter, or a year.
Earnings per share (EPS)	Net income divided by the number of common shares outstanding. EPS measures how much a firm has earned (or lost) for each share of stock outstanding.
Net cash flow	A firm's actual cash receipts less cash payments.
Statement of cash flows	A financial statement that shows a firm's cash inflows (receipts) and cash outflows (payments) for a period of time.
Average tax rate	Total taxes paid divided by taxable income.
Marginal tax rate	The tax rate paid on the last dollar of income earned.

IV. Summary of Key Equations

Equation	Description	Formula
3.1	Balance sheet identity	Total assets = Total liabilities + Total stockholders' equity
3.2	Net working capital	Net working capital = Total current assets − Total current liabilities
3.3	Income statement identity	Net income = Revenues − Expenses
3.4	Net cash flow from operating activities	NCFOA = Net income − Noncash revenues + Noncash expenses
3.5	Net cash flow from operating activities	NCFOA = Net income + Depreciation and amortization

V. True or False Questions

1. GAAP principles determine the rules for how a company maintains its accounting system and how it prepares financial statements.

a. True

b. False

2. The balance sheet informs the shareholders of the firm about the revenues and expenses the firm has earned over the last fiscal period.

a. True

b. False

3. The net cash flow from operating activities (NCFOA) is another term for net income.

a. True

b. False

4. The largest noncash charges are depreciation and amortization expenses.

a. True

b. False

5. The statement of cash flows shows the company's cash inflows (receipts) and cash outflows (payments) for a period of time.

a. True

b. False

6. A company using the LIFO method assumes the sale of a product is from the newest, highest-cost inventory.

a. True

b. False

7. Goodwill appears in the accounting statements only if the firm is acquired for a price in excess of the fair market value of its net assets.

a. True

b. False

8. Depreciation allocates the cost of an asset over its estimated life to better match the cost of the asset with the market value of the asset.

a. True

b. False

9. The treasury stock account represents stock that the firm has purchased back from managers who left the firm.

a. True

b. False

10. The company takes more depreciation under accelerated depreciation methods than under the straight-line method over the life of the asset.

a. True

b. False

VI. Multiple-Choice Questions

1. Annual reports are prepared by a firm's management to

a. communicate to shareholders the firm's failures in the previous year.

b. provide an overview of the firm's financial and operating performance.

c. highlight the performance of its chief competitors.

d. provide a forecast of the economy in the coming years.

2. The matching principle calls for the accountant of a firm to

a. identify an asset with each liability of the firm.

b. associate the revenue generated from a sale to the costs incurred to produce the product.

c. match each item of inventory with the historical cost at which it was acquired.

d. none of the above.

3. Accounting principles and procedures for U.S. firms are put together by the

a. Securities and Exchange Commission.

b. Federal Reserve Bank.

c. Accounting Principles National Committee.

d. Federal Accounting Standards Board.

4. The assumption of arm's-length transaction states that

a. both parties to a transaction can act independently of each other and make economically rational decisions.

b. both parties to a transaction have to have had previous transactions.

c. one of the parties to the transaction is a bank that has full knowledge of your creditworthiness.

d. none of the above.

5. The major criticism of U.S. GAAP is that

a. it gives no directions to auditors on how to deal with various situations a firm may encounter.

b. it gives explicit instructions to auditors for every situation that FASB has anticipated.

c. it favors the large publicly held firms only.

d. none of the above.

6. The basic balance sheet identity is stated as follows:

a. Total assets + Total liabilities = Total stockholders' equity.

b. Total assets = Total liabilities − Total stockholders' equity.

c. Total assets + Total stockholders' equity = Total liabilities.

d. Total assets − Total liabilities = Total stockholders' equity.

7. When prices are falling, valuing inventory using the LIFO method rather than FIFO gives

a. inventory a higher value but lowers net income.

b. inventory a lower value and also lowers net income.

c. both inventory and net income a higher value.

d. inventory a lower value and net income a higher value.

8. All but ***one*** of the following are basic rights of ownership associated with common stock:

a. the right to vote to elect the firm's board of directors

b. the right to receive cash dividends if they are paid

c. the right to buy additional shares of the firm's stock if a new issue is made so as to avoid dilution of ownership

d. the right to be repaid the full value of their investment in the company prior to preferred stockholders if it fails

9. Market-value accounting is better because

a. it provides a truer picture of the firm's financial condition.

b. it improves the ability of management to make better economic decisions.

c. it limits management's ability to conceal a failing business or hide unrealized gains on assets.

d. All of the above are advantages of market-value accounting.

10. Which ***one*** of the following is **NOT** true for a corporation?

a. Interest paid on bonds issued last year is tax deductible.

b. Common-stock dividends to be paid this year are not tax deductible.

c. Common-stock dividends to be paid this year will be tax deductible if the firm has a net loss for the year.

d. Preferred stock dividends to be paid this year are not tax deductible.

11. Maddux, Inc., has completed its fiscal year and reported the following information. The company had current assets of $153,413, net fixed assets of $412,331, and other assets of $7,822. The firm also has current liabilities worth $65,314, long-term debt of $178,334, and common stock of $162,000. How much retained earnings does the firm have?

a. $405,648

b. $243,648

c. $167,918

d. $573,566

12. Prime Corp. has completed its fiscal year and reported the following information. The company had current assets of $413,776, net fixed assets of $1,372,331, and other assets of $37,711. The firm also has current liabilities worth $275,425, long-term debt of $387,334, and common stock of $500,000. How much retained earnings does the firm have?

a. $885,634

b. $773,725

c. $1,161,059

d. $661,059

13. Teakap, Inc., has current assets of $1,456,312, and total assets of $4,812,369 for the year ending September 30, 2006. It also has current liabilities of $1,041,012, common equity of $1,500,000, and retained earnings of $1,468,347. How much long-term debt does the firm have?

a. $1,844,022

b. $2,303,010

c. $1,844,022

d. $803,010

14. Tre-Bien Bakeries generated net income of $233,412 this year. At year end the company had accounts receivables of $47,199, inventory of $63,781, and cash of $21,461. It also had accounts payables of $51,369, and notes payables of $11,417 and accrued taxes of $6,145. The net working capital of the firm is

a. $68,931.

b. $63,510.

c. $69,655.

d. none of the above.

15. Centennial Brewery in 2006 produced revenues of $1,145,227. It has expenses (excluding depreciation) of $812,640, depreciation of $131,335, and interest expense of $81,112. It pays a marginal tax rate of 34 percent. What is the firm's net income after taxes?

a. $120,140

b. $248,475

c. $79,292

d. $40,848

16. Radical Treatments in 2008 produced revenues of $645,366. It has expenses (excluding depreciation) of $321,554, depreciation of $53,444, and interest expense of $52,324. It pays a marginal tax rate of 34 percent. What is the firm's net income after taxes?

a. $178,443

b. $143,909

c. $79,292

d. $140,848

17. Trident Manufacturing Company's treasurer identified the following cash flows during this year as significant. It had repaid existing debt of $425,110, while raising additional debt capital of $750,000. It also repurchased stock in the open markets for a total of $63,250. It paid dividends to its shareholders to the tune of $233,144. What is the net cash provided by financing activities?

a. $28,496

b. $91,746

c. −$28,496

d. −$91,746

18. Security Corp's treasurer identified the following cash flows during this year as significant. It had repaid existing debt to the tune of $205,110, while raising additional debt capital of $300,000. It also issued stock in the open markets for a total of $75,000. It paid dividends of $150,365 to its shareholders. What is the net cash provided by financing activities?

a. $19,525

b. $224,635

c. −$19,525

d. −$185,585

19. Gentle Bedding provided the following financial information for the quarter ending September 30, 2008:

Depreciation and amortization = $412,650   Net income = $1,212,060

Increase in receivables = $221,610   Increase in inventory = $111,447

Increase in accounts payables = $182,322

Decrease in marketable securities = $29,725.

What is the cash flow from operating activities generated during this quarter by the firm?

a. $2,169,814

b. $920,420

c. $1,503,700

d. $879,003

20. Princeton Corp. announced that in the year ended June 30, 2008, its earnings before taxes amounted to $13,231,445. Calculate its taxes using the following table.

Tax Rate	Taxable Income
15%	$0 to $50,000
25	50,001–75,000
34	75,001–100,000
39	100,001–335,000
34	335,001–10,000,000
35	10,000,001–15,000,000
38	15,000,001–18,333,333
35	More than $18,333,333

a. $4,498,691
b. $4,531,006
c. $4,631,006
d. None of the above

Answers to True or False Questions

1. a **2.** b **3.** b **4.** a **5.** a
6. a **7.** a **8.** b **9.** b **10.** b

Answers to Multiple-Choice Questions

1. b **2.** b **3.** d **4.** a **5.** b
6. d **7.** c **8.** d **9.** d **10.** c
11. c **12.** d **13.** d **14.** b **15.** c
16. b **17.** a **18.** a **19.** c **20.** b

Solutions to Multiple-Choice Questions

11. Solution:

Total assets = $153,413 + $412,331 + $7,822 = $573,566
Total liabilities = $65,314 + $178,334 = $243,648
Total stockholders' equity = Total assets − Total liabilities
= $573,466 − $243,648 = $329,918
Retained earnings = Stockholders' equity − Common stock
= $329,918 − $162,000 = **$167,918**

12. Solution:

Total assets = $413,776 + $1,372,331 + $37,711 = $1,823,818
Total liabilities = $275,425 + $387,334 = $662,759
Total stockholders' equity = Total assets − Total liabilities
= $1,823,818 − $662,759 = $1,161,059
Retained earnings = Stockholders' equity − Common stock
= $1,161,059 − $500,000 = **$661,059**

13. Solution:

Stockholders' equity = \$1,500,000 + \$1,468,347 = \$2,968,347

Long-term debt = Total assets − Current liabilities − Stockholders' equity
= \$4,812,369 − \$1,041,012 − \$2,968,347 = **\$803,010**

14. Solution:

Total current assets = \$21,461 + \$47,199 + \$63,781 = \$132,481

Total current liabilities = \$51,369 + \$11,417 + \$6,145 = \$68,931

Net working capital = \$132,481 − \$68,931 = **\$63,510**

15. Solution:

Earnings before taxes = \$1,145,227 − (\$812,640 + \$131,335 + \$81,112) = \$120,140

Net income = \$120,140 (1 − 0.34) = **\$79,292**

16. Solution:

Earnings before taxes = \$645,366 − (\$321,554 + \$53,444 + \$52,324) = \$218,044

Net income = \$218,044 (1 − 0.34) = **\$143,909**

17. Solution:

Cash inflows from financing activities = \$750,000

Cash outflows from financing activities = \$425,110 + \$63,250 + \$233,144 = \$721,504

Net cash flows from financing activities = \$750,000 − \$721,504 = **\$28,496**

18. Solution:

Cash inflows from financing activities = \$300,000 + \$75,000 = \$375,000

Cash outflows from financing activities = \$205,110 + \$150,365 = \$355,475

Net cash flows from financing activities = \$375,000 − \$355,475 = **\$19,525**

19. Solution:

2008 Statement of Cash Flows (\$ thousands)

Operating Activities	
Net income	\$1,212,060
Additions (sources of cash)	
Depreciation and amortization	412,650
Increase in accounts payable	182,322
Decrease in marketable securities	29,725
Subtractions (uses of cash)	
Increase in accounts receivable	(221,610)
Increase in inventories	(111,447)
Net cash provided by operating activities	\$1,503,700

20. Solution: Earnings before tax = \$13,231,445.00

Tax rate	Income	Tax
15%	\$0 to \$50,000	\$ 7,500.00
25	50,001–75,000	6,250.00
34	75,001–100,000	8,500.00
39	100,001–335,000	91,650.00
34	335,001–10,000,000	3,286,100.00
35	10,000,001–15,000,000	1,131,005.75
38	15,000,001–18,333,333	
35	More than \$18,333,333	
	Total taxes payable	\$4,531,005.75

CHAPTER 4

Analyzing Financial Statements

LEARNING OBJECTIVES

1. Explain the three perspectives from which financial statements can be viewed.
2. Describe common-size financial statements, explain why they are used, and be able to prepare and use them to analyze the historical performance of a firm.
3. Discuss how financial ratios facilitate financial analysis, and be able to compute and use them to analyze a firm's performance.
4. Describe the DuPont system of analysis and be able to use it to evaluate a firm's performance and identify corrective actions that may be necessary.
5. Explain what benchmarks are, describe how they are prepared, and discuss why they are important in financial statement analysis.
6. Identify the major limitations in using financial statement analysis

I. Chapter Outline

4.1 Background for Financial Statement Analysis

A. The analysis of a firm's financial statements can be conducted from the perspective of multiple stakeholders of the firm. Each of the three major stakeholders—management, shareholders and creditors—is looking for information that is specific to their objectives. Sometimes their perspectives are overlapping, and sometimes they are divergent.

- The shareholders' focus centers on the value of the stock they hold.
  - o Their interest in the financial statements is to evaluate the cash flows that the firm will generate from operations, which allows them to determine the firm's profitability, their return for that period, and the dividend they are likely to receive.
- Management's interest in the firm's financial statement is somewhat similar to that of shareholders.
  - o A good performance by the firm will keep management in the firm, while a poor performance can cost them their jobs.
  - o In addition, management gets feedback on their investing, financing, and working capital decisions by identifying trends in the various accounts that are reported in the financial statements.
- Creditors or lenders are primarily concerned about getting their loans repaid and receiving interest payments on time, which causes them to focus on:
  - o Amount of debt the firm has.
  - o Firm's ability to meet short-term obligations.
  - o Firm's ability to generate sufficient cash flows to meet all legal obligations first and still have sufficient cash flows to meet debt repayment and interest payments.

B. ***Guidelines for Financial Statement Analysis***

- Identify whose perspective you are using to analyze a firm—management, shareholder, or creditor.
- Use only audited financial statements if possible.
- Perform analysis over a three- to five-year period—**trend analysis.**
- Compare the firm's performance to that of its direct competitors—that is, firms that are similar in size and offer similar products.
- Perform a **benchmark** analysis. This involves comparing the firm to one or more of the most relevant competitors—American Air with Delta or United Airlines.

4.2 Common-Size Financial Statements

A common-sized balance is created by dividing each asset or liability by a base number such as total assets or sales. Such common-size or standardized financial statements allow one to compare firms that are different in size.

A. ***Common-Size Balance Sheets***

- Each asset and liability item on the balance sheet is standardized by dividing it by **total assets,** which results in these accounts being represented as percentages of total assets.

B. ***Common-Size Income Statements***

- Each income statement item is standardized by dividing it by the dollar amount of **sales,** making each income statement item to be projected as a percentage of sales.

4.3 Financial Statement Analysis

A. ***Overview***

- A ratio is computed by dividing one balance sheet or income statement item by another.
- A variety of ratios can be computed to focus on specialized aspects of the firm's performance.
- The choice of the scale determines the story that can be garnered from the ratio.
- Different ratios can be calculated based on the type of firm being analyzed or the kind of analysis being performed.
- Ratios may be computed to measure liquidity, efficiency, leverage, profitability, or market value performance.

B. ***Liquidity Ratios***

- Liquidity ratios measure the ability of the firm to meet short-term obligations with short-term assets without putting the firm in financial trouble.
- There are two commonly used ratios to measure liquidity—current ratio and quick ratio.
  - o **Current ratio** tells how many dollars of current assets the firm has per dollar of current liabilities. The higher the number, the more liquid the firm and the better its ability to pay its short-term bills.
  - o **Quick ratio** or **acid test** tells us how many dollars of liquid assets the firm has per dollar of current liabilities; the higher the number, the more liquid the firm and the better its ability to pay its short-term bills.

C. ***Efficiency Ratios***

- This set of ratios, sometimes called asset turnover ratios, measures the efficiency with which a firm's management uses the assets to generate sales.
- While management can use these ratios to identify areas of inefficiency that require improvement, creditors can use some of these ratios to determine the speed with which inventory can be converted to receivables, which can then be converted to cash and help the firm to meet its debt obligations.
- These efficiency ratios focus on inventory, receivables, and the use of fixed and total assets.
  - o **Inventory turnover ratio** measures how many times the inventory is turned over into saleable products. The more times a firm can turn over the inventory, the better.
  - o Another ratio that builds on the inventory turnover ratio is the **days' sales in inventory,** which measures the number of days the firm takes to turn over the inventory. The fewer the days, the faster the firm is turning its inventory and the more efficient it is.
  - o **Accounts receivables turnover ratio** measures how quickly the firm collects on its credit sales. The higher the frequency of turnover, the quicker it is converting its credit sales into cash flows.
  - o **Days' Sales Outstanding** measures in days the time the firm takes to convert its receivables into cash. The fewer the days it takes the firm to collect on its receivables, the more efficient the firm is.

  - **Total asset turnover ratio** measures the level of sales a firm is able to generate per dollar of total assets. The higher the total asset turnover, the more efficiently management is using total assets.
  - **Fixed asset turnover ratio** measures the level of sales a firm is able to generate per dollar of fixed assets. The higher the fixed asset turnover, the more efficiently management is using its plant and equipment.

D. ***Leverage Ratios***

- The ability of a firm and its owners to use their equity to generate borrowed funds is reflected in the leverage ratios.
- **Financial leverage** refers to the use of long-term debt in a firm's capital structure. The use of debt increases shareholders' returns thanks to the tax benefits provided by the interest payments on debt.
- Debt ratios that quantify the use of debt in the capital structure are as follows.
  - The first ratio, **total debt ratio,** measures the level of debt (including current liabilities) per dollar of total assets. The higher the amount of debt, the higher the firm's leverage, and the more risky it is.
  - A second leverage ratio is the **debt-to-equity ratio,** which measures the amount of debt per dollar of equity.
  - The third leverage ratio, the **equity multiplier** or **leverage multiplier,** tells us the amount of assets that the firm has for every dollar of equity. It serves as the best measure of the firm's ability to leverage shareholders' equity with borrowed funds.
- Coverage ratios that measure the ability of the firm to meet its debt obligations are as follows.
  - **Times interest earned** measures the number of dollars in operating earnings the firm generates per dollar of interest expense. The higher the number, the greater the ability of the firm to meet its interest obligations.
  - The second ratio, the **cash coverage ratio,** measures the amount of cash the firm has to meet its interest payments.

E. ***Profitability Ratios***

- These ratios measure the financial performance of the firm.
  - **Gross profit margin** measures the amount of gross profit generated per dollar of net sales, while **operating profit margin** measures the amount of operating profit generated by the firm for each dollar of net sales. **Net profit margin** measures the amount of net income after taxes generated by the firm for each dollar of net sales.
- While management and creditors are likely to focus on these profitability measures, shareholders are likely to concentrate on two others.
  - **Return on assets (ROA)** ratio measures the amount of net income per dollar of total assets.
  - A variation of this ratio, called the **EBIT return on assets,** is a powerful measure of return because it tells us how efficiently management utilized the assets under their command, independent of financing decisions and taxes. This measures the amount of EBIT per dollar of total assets.
  - The **return on equity (ROE)** ratio measures the dollar amount of net income per dollar of shareholders' equity.

F. ***Market-Value Indicators***

- The ratios that follow tell us how the market views the company's liquidity, efficiency, leverage, and profitability.
- **Earnings per share (EPS)** ratio measures the income after taxes generated by the firm for each share outstanding.
- The **price-earnings (P/E)** ratio ties the firm's earnings per share to price per share and reflects investors' expectations that the firm's earnings will grow in the future.

4.4 The DuPont System: A Diagnostic Tool

A. ***An Overview***

- The DuPont system is a set of related ratios that links the balance sheet and the income statement.
- It is based on two equations that relate a firm's ROA and ROE.

B. ***The ROA Equation***

- Return on assets can be broken down into two components—profit margin and total assets turnover ratio. See Equation 4.21.
- The net profit margin measures management's ability to generate sales and efficiently manage the firm's operating expenses and is a measure of *operating efficiency*.
- Total asset turnover looks at how efficiently management uses the assets under its command—that is, how much output can be generated with a given asset base. Thus, asset turnover is a measure of *asset use efficiency*.
- The ROA equation says that if management wants to increase the firm's ROA, it can increase the profit margin, asset turnover, or both.

- By the same token, management can examine a poor ROA and determine whether operating efficiency or asset use efficiency is the problem.

C. ***The ROE Equation***

- This equation is simply a restatement of Equation 4.18. Reorganization of the terms allows ROE to be restated as a product of the ROA and the equity multiplier.
- A firm with a small ROA can magnify it by using a higher leverage to get a higher ROE.

D. ***The DuPont Equation***

- Substituting the ROA into the ROE equations gives us the Du Pont equation, as shown in Equations 4.23 and 4.24.
- The DuPont equation shows that a firm's ROE is determined by three factors: (1) net profit margin, which measures the firm's operating efficiency, (2) total asset turnover, which measures the firm's asset use efficiency, and (3) the equity multiplier, which measures the firm's financial leverage.
- If operational efficiency is the area of weakness, then it calls for a closer look at the firm's income statement items. If asset turnover or leverage is the problem area, then the focus shifts to the balance sheet.

E. ***ROE as a Goal***

- The issue of whether maximizing ROE is equivalent to maximizing shareholders' wealth has both detractors and supporters.
- Those who do not agree that they are the same identify three key weaknesses.
  - The first weakness with ROE is that it is based on after-tax earnings, not cash flows. Second, ROE does not consider risk. Third, ROE ignores the size of the initial investment as well as future cash flows.
- Those who believe that they are consistent propose that:
  - ROE allows management to break down the performance and identify areas of strengths and weaknesses. ROE is highly correlated with shareholder wealth maximization.

4.5 Selecting a Benchmark

- A ratio analysis becomes relevant only if it can be compared against a benchmark.
- Financial managers can create a benchmark for comparison in three ways: through trend analysis, industry average analysis, and peer group analysis.

A. ***Trend Analysis***

- This benchmark is based on a firm's historical performance and allows management to examine each ratio over time and determine whether the trend is good or bad for the firm.

B. ***Industry Analysis***

- Firms in the same industry are grouped by size, sales, and product lines in order to establish benchmark ratios.
- One way of identifying industry groups is the **Standard Industrial Classification (SIC) System.**

C. ***Peer Group Analysis***

- Instead of selecting an entire industry, management may choose to identify a set of firms that are similar in size or sales, or that compete in the same market.
- The average ratios of this peer group would then be used as the benchmark.

4.6. Using Financial Ratios

Limitations of ratio analysis include the following:

- Ratio analysis depends on accounting data based on historical costs.
- There is no theoretical backing in making judgments based on financial statement and ratio analysis.
- When doing industry or peer group analysis, you are often confronted with large, diversified firms that do not fit into any one SIC code.
- Time-trend analysis could be distorted by financial statements affected by inflation.

II. Suggested Approach to Material

The chapter begins with an overview of how different stakeholders—management, shareholders, and creditors—will view the financial statements of a firm and what their focus will be. Following this overview is a discussion of the the common-size balance sheet and income statement. Then, a comprehensive coverage of various financial ratios is provided. The DuPont system of equations is developed in detail, thus allowing students to understand how this tool can be used to diagnose the strengths and weaknesses of the firm being analyzed. The chapter concludes with a review of the shortcomings of ratio analysis.

While many of you may already have had a preview of this material in your basic accounting course, you will extend your understanding of this material in this course. You will not only be calculating these ratios but will learn to interpret the ratios. This will give you a better understanding of the firm that you are analyzing. This material will serve you well beyond your college years.

One way that you can reinforce the learning of this material is to pick a firm that you are interested in, obtain its financial statements from online sources, and do a ratio analysis along the lines covered in this chapter. Then compare your analysis with what analysts say on the net about the firm.

III. Chapter Glossary

Financial statement analysis	The use of financial statements to evaluate a company's overall performance and assess its strengths and shortcomings.
Trend analysis	Analysis of financial data based on financial statements that cover three to five years or more to see how various ratios are increasing, decreasing, or staying constant over time.
Benchmark	A standard against which performance is measured.
Common-size financial statement	A financial statement in which each number is expressed as a percentage of a base number, such as total assets or total revenues.
Financial ratio	A number from a financial statement that has been scaled by dividing by another financial number.
Insolvency	The inability to pay debts when they are due.
Liquidity	The extent to which an asset can be converted to cash quickly without a loss of value.
Financial leverage	The extent to which debt is used to finance a firm.
Default risk	The risk that a firm will not be able to pay the debt as it comes due.
Standard Industrial Classification (SIC) System	A numerical system developed by the U.S. government to classify businesses according to the type of activity they perform.
North American Industry Classification System (NAICS)	A classification system for businesses introduced to refine and replace the older SIC codes

IV. Summary of Key Equations

Equation	Description	Formula
4.1	Liquidity ratios	$\text{Current Ratio} = \dfrac{\text{Current asstes}}{\text{Current liabilities}}$
4.2		$\text{Quick Ratio} = \dfrac{\text{Current assets} - \text{Inventory}}{\text{Current liabilities}}$

(Continued)

Equation	Description	Formula
4.3	Efficiency ratios	$\text{Inventory Turnover} = \dfrac{\text{Cost of goods sold}}{\text{Inventory}}$
4.4		$\text{Day's Sales in Inventory} = \dfrac{\text{365 Days}}{\text{Inventory turnover}}$
4.5		$\text{Accounts Receivable Turnover} = \dfrac{\text{Net sales}}{\text{Accounts receivable}}$
4.6		$\text{Day's Sales Outstanding} = \dfrac{\text{365 Days}}{\text{Account receivable turnover}}$
4.7		$\text{Total Asset Turnover} = \dfrac{\text{Net sales}}{\text{Total assets}}$
4.8		$\text{Fixed Asset Turnover} = \dfrac{\text{Net sales}}{\text{Net fixed assets}}$
4.9	Leverage ratios	$\text{Total Debt Ratio} = \dfrac{\text{Total debt}}{\text{Total assets}}$
4.10		$\text{Debt} - \text{Equity Ratio} = \dfrac{\text{Total debt}}{\text{Total equity}}$
4.11		$\text{Equity Multiplier} = \dfrac{\text{Total assets}}{\text{Total equity}}$
4.12		$\text{Times Interest Earned} = \dfrac{\text{EBIT}}{\text{Interest expense}}$
4.13		$\text{Cash Coverage} = \dfrac{\text{EBIT} + \text{Depreciation}}{\text{Interest expense}}$
4.14	Profitability ratios	$\text{Gross Profit Margin} = \dfrac{\text{Net sales} - \text{Cost of goods sold}}{\text{Net sales}}$
4.15		$\text{Operating Profit Margin} = \dfrac{\text{EBIT}}{\text{Net sales}}$
4.16		$\text{Net Profit Margin} = \dfrac{\text{Net income}}{\text{Net sales}}$
4.17		$\text{EBIT Return on Assets (EROA)} = \dfrac{\text{EBIT}}{\text{Total assets}}$
4.18		$\text{Return on Assets (ROA)} = \dfrac{\text{Net income}}{\text{Total assets}}$
4.19		$\text{Return on Equity (ROE)} = \dfrac{\text{Net income}}{\text{Common equity}}$
4.20	Market value ratios	$\text{Earnings per share} = \dfrac{\text{Net income}}{\text{Shares outstanding}}$
4.21		$\text{Price to Earnings Ratio} = \dfrac{\text{Price per share}}{\text{Earnings per share}}$
4.22	DuPont identity	$\text{ROA} = \text{Net profit margin} \times \text{Total asset turnover}$
4.23		$\text{ROE} = \text{ROA} \times \text{Equity multiplier}$
4.24		$\text{ROE} = \text{Net profit margin} \times \text{Total asset turnover} \times \text{Equity multiplier}$
4.25		$\text{ROE} = \dfrac{\text{Net income}}{\text{Sales}} \times \dfrac{\text{Sales}}{\text{Total assets}} \times \dfrac{\text{Total assets}}{\text{Common equity}}$

V. True or False Questions

1. The three perspectives from which we can view financial statement analysis are those of shareholders, management, and employees.
   - **a.** True
   - **b.** False

2. Audited financial statements are not critical for performing ratio analysis on a firm.
   - **a.** True
   - **b.** False

3. One approach to construct a common size income statement is by dividing all items in an income statement items by sales.
   - **a.** True
   - **b.** False

4. When a firm disposes its assets very quickly at whatever price it can get, the firm is said to be liquid.
   - **a.** True
   - **b.** False

5. The higher the inventory turnover ratio, the more inefficient the firm is in managing its inventory.
   - **a.** True
   - **b.** False

6. Service industry firms are more likely to have low fixed asset turnover ratios than manufacturing firms.
   - **a.** True
   - **b.** False

7. Return on assets represents the total return on the net investment in the firm.
   - **a.** True
   - **b.** False

8. The DuPont equation relates the ROA of a firm to its net profit margin and total asset turnover ratio.
   - **a.** True
   - **b.** False

9. Time-trend analysis uses historical ratios as a benchmark for comparing a firm's performance in any period.
   - **a.** True
   - **b.** False

10. Ratio analysis is not hampered by any weaknesses or limitations.
    - **a.** True
    - **b.** False

VI. Multiple-Choice Questions

1. A firm's management analyzes financial statements so that:
   - **a.** they can get feedback on their investing, financing, and working capital decisions by identifying trends in the various accounts that are reported in the financial statements.
   - **b.** similar to shareholders, they can focus on profitability, dividend, capital appreciation, and return on investment.

- **c.** they can get more stock options.
- **d.** a and b.

2. All but ***one*** of the following is true of common-size income statements.

- **a.** Each income statement item is standardized by dividing it by total assets.
- **b.** Income statement accounts are represented as percentages of sales.
- **c.** Each income statement item is standardized by dividing it by sales.
- **d.** Common-size financial statement analysis is a specialized application of ratio analysis.

3. Which ***one*** of the following does **NOT** change a firm's current ratio?

- **a.** The firm collects on its accounts receivables.
- **b.** The firm purchases inventory by taking a short-term loan.
- **c.** The firm pays down its accounts receivables.
- **d.** None of the above.

4. One of the following statements is **NOT** true of asset turnover ratios.

- **a.** Asset turnover ratios measure the level of sales per dollar of assets that the firm has.
- **b.** The fixed asset turnover ratio is less significant for equipment-intensive manufacturing industry firms than the total assets turnover ratio.
- **c.** The higher the total asset turnover, the more efficiently management is using total assets.
- **d.** All of the above are true.

5. If Firm A has a higher equity ratio (equity to total assets) than Firm B, then

- **a.** Firm A has a lower equity multiplier than Firm B.
- **b.** Firm B has a lower equity multiplier than Firm A.
- **c.** Firm B has lower financial leverage than Firm B.
- **d.** None of the above.

6. Which one of the following statements is **NOT** correct?

- **a.** The **gross** profit margin is the amount of gross profit generated per dollar of net sales.
- **b.** The **operating** profit margin measures the amount of earnings before taxes (EBT) generated by the firm for each dollar of net sales.
- **c.** The **net** profit margin measures the amount of net income after taxes generated by the firm for each dollar of net sales.
- **d.** All of the above statements are correct.

7. For a firm that has both debt and equity,

- **a.** ROE $>$ ROA.
- **b.** ROE $<$ ROA.
- **c.** ROE $=$ ROA.
- **d.** None of the above.

8. The DuPont equation ____________

- **a.** is a set of related ratios that links the balance sheet and the income statement.
- **b.** is based on two equations that relate a firm's ROA and EPS.
- **c.** is used by creditors to understand why a firm is unable to meet its debt obligations.
- **d.** is used by investors to assess the price-to-earnings performance of a firm.

9. Which one of the following is **NOT** an advantage of using ROE as a goal?

- **a.** ROE is highly correlated with shareholder wealth maximization.
- **b.** ROE allows management to break down the performance and identify areas of strengths and weaknesses.

c. ROE does not consider risk.

d. All of the above are advantages of using ROE as a goal.

10. Limitations of ratio analysis include all but

a. Ratios depend on accounting data based on historical costs.

b. Differences in accounting practices like FIFO versus LIFO make comparison difficult.

c. Time-trend analysis could be distorted by financial statements affected by inflation.

d. All of the above are limitations of ratio analysis.

11. Geo Traders has a current ratio of 1.67, current liabilities of $233,845, and inventory of 165,347. What is the firm's quick ratio?

a. 0.72

b. 0.96

c. 1.92

d. None of the above

12. Trident Manufacturing Company is required by its bank to maintain a current ratio of at least 2.0, and its current ratio now is 2.25. The firm plans to acquire additional inventory to meet an unexpected surge in the demand for its products, and it will pay for the inventory with short-term debt. How much inventory can the firm purchase without violating its debt agreement if its total current assets equal $2.75 million?

a. $0

b. $305,556

c. $1.33 million

d. None of the above

13. If Grayton Corp. has accounts receivables of $1,154,122 and net sales of $6,444,672, what is its accounts receivable turnover?

a. 0.18 times

b. 1.65 times

c. 5.58 times

d. None of the above

14. Gateway Corp. has an inventory turnover ratio of 5.6. What is the firm's days' sales in inventory?

a. 65.2 days

b. 64.3 days

c. 61.7 days

d. 57.9 days

15. Laurel Electrical Supplies has sales of $1,272,435, and a gross profit margin of 71.7 percent. What is the firm's cost of goods sold?

a. $360,099

b. $275,200

c. $912,336

d. None of the above

16. Secund Corp. has an EBIT of $3,667,346 and interest expense of $632,250. Its depreciation for the year is $1,734,530. What is its cash coverage ratio?

a. 5.4 times

b. 7.3 times

c. 8.5 times

d. None of the above

17. What will be a firm's equity multiplier given a debt ratio of 0.45?

a. 1.82

b. 1.28

c. 2.22

d. None of the above

18. Genome Pharma has total assets of $5,232,288, total debt of $2,512,000, and net sales of $8,335,456. Their net profit margin for the year is 16.5 percent. What is Genome's ROA?

a. 25.6%

b. 18%

c. 26.3%

d. None of the above

19. GenTech Pharma has reported the following information:

Sales/Total assets = 2.89; ROA = 10.74%; ROE = 20.36%.

What are the firm's profit margin and equity multiplier?

a. 7.1%; 0.53

b. 7.1%; 1.90

c. 3.7%; 0.53

d. 3.7%; 1.90

20. Andrade Corp has debt of $2,834,950, total assets of $5,178,235, sales of $8,234,121, and net income of $812,355. What is the firm's return on equity?

a. 7.1%

b. 34.7%

c. 28.1%

d. None of the above

Answers to True or False Questions

1. b	**2.** b	**3.** a	**4.** b	**5.** b
6. b	**7.** a	**8.** a	**9.** a	**10.** b

Answers to Multiple-Choice Questions

1. d	**2.** a	**3.** a	**4.** b	**5.** a
6. b	**7.** a	**8.** a	**9.** c	**10.** d
11. b	**12.** b	**13.** c	**14.** a	**15.** a
16. c	**17.** a	**18.** c	**19.** d	**20.** b

Solutions to Multiple-Choice Questions

11. **Solution:**

Current ratio = 1.67

Current liabilities = $233,845

Inventory = $165,347

$$\text{Current ratio} = \frac{\text{Current assets}}{\text{Current liabilites}}$$

$$1.67 = \frac{\text{Current assets}}{\text{Current liabilites}}$$

$$\text{Current assets} = 1.67 \times \$233{,}845 = \$390{,}521$$

$$\text{Quick ratio} = \frac{\text{Current assets} - \text{Inventory}}{\text{Current liabilities}}$$

$$= \frac{390{,}521 - \$165{,}347}{\$233{,}845}$$

$$= \mathbf{0.96}$$

12. Solution:

Let X represent the additional borrowing against the firm's line of credit (which also equals the addition to current assets).

We can solve for that level of X which forces the firm's current ratio to be at 2.0

$2,750,000/ Current liabilities = 2.25

Current liabilities = $1,222,222

2.0 = ($2,750,000 + X) / ($1,222,222 + X)

(2 * $1,222,222) + 2X = $2,750,000 + X

X = $2,750,000 − $2,444,444

X = $305,556

13. Solution:

Accounts receivables = $1,154,122

Net sales = $6,444,672

$$\text{Accounts receivables turnover} = \frac{\text{Net sales}}{\text{Accounts receivables}}$$

$$= \frac{\$6{,}444{,}672}{\$1{,}154{,}122}$$

$$= \mathbf{5.58\ times}$$

14. Solution:

$$\text{Days' sales in inventory} = \frac{365}{5.6} = \mathbf{65.2\ days}$$

15. Solution:

Sales = $1,272,435

Gross profit margin = 71.7%

$$\text{Gross profit margin} = \frac{\text{Sales} - \text{Cost of goods sold}}{\text{Sales}}$$

$$0.717 = \frac{\$1{,}272{,}435 - \text{Cost of Goods Sold}}{\$1{,}272{,}435}$$

$$\text{Cost of goods sold} = \$1{,}272{,}435 - (0.717 * \$1{,}272{,}435)$$

$$= \mathbf{\$360{,}099}$$

16. Solution:

Depreciation = $1,734,530

Interest expenses = $632,250

EBIT = $3,667,346

$$\text{Cash coverage rates} = \frac{\text{EBITDA}}{\text{Interest expense}} = \frac{\text{EBIT} + \text{Depreciation}}{\text{Interest expense}}$$
$$= \frac{\$3{,}667{,}346 + \$1{,}734{,}530}{\$632{,}250}$$
$$= \mathbf{8.5\ times}$$

17. Solution:

$$\text{Equity multiplier} = \frac{\text{Total assets}}{\text{Equity}} = \frac{1}{\text{Equity/Total assets}}$$
$$= \frac{1}{1 - \text{Debt/Total assets}} = \frac{1}{1 - 0.45}$$
$$= \mathbf{1.818}$$

18. Solution:

Total assets = \$5,232,288; Total debt = \$2,512,000

Net sales = \$8,335,456; Net profit margin =16.5%

$$\text{Net profit margin} = \frac{\text{Net income}}{\text{Sales}}$$
$$\text{Net income} = 0.165 * \$8{,}335{,}456$$
$$= \mathbf{\$1{,}375{,}350}$$
$$\text{ROA} = \frac{\text{Net income}}{\text{Total assets}} = \frac{\$1{,}375{,}350}{\$5{,}232{,}288} = \mathbf{26.3\%}$$

19. Solution:

Total assets turnover = 2.89

ROA = 10.74%

ROE = 20.36%

ROA = Profit margin × Total assets turnover

$$\text{Profit margin} = \frac{\text{ROA}}{\text{Total assets turnover}} = \frac{0.1074}{2.89} = \mathbf{3.7\%}$$

ROE = ROA × Equity multiplier

$$\text{Equity multiplier} = \frac{\text{ROE}}{\text{ROA}} = \frac{0.2036}{0.1074} = \mathbf{1.90}$$

20. Solution:

$$\text{Debt ratio} = \frac{2{,}834{,}950}{5{,}178{,}235} = 0.55$$

Equity ratio = 1 − 0.55 = 0.45

$$\text{Equity multiplier} = \frac{1}{0.45} = 2.21$$

ROE = PM × TATO × EM

$$= \frac{\text{Net income}}{\text{Sales}} \times \frac{\text{Sales}}{\text{Total assets}} \times \text{EM}$$
$$= \frac{\$812{,}355}{\$8{,}234{,}121} \times \frac{\$8{,}234{,}121}{\$5{,}178{,}235} \times 2.21$$
$$= 0.09866 \times 1.590 \times 2.21$$
$$= \mathbf{34.7\%}$$

CHAPTER 5

The Time Value of Money

LEARNING OBJECTIVES

1. Explain what the time value of money is and why it is so important in the field of finance.
2. Explain the concept of future value, including the meaning of *principal amount, simple interest,* and *compound interest,* and be able to use the future value formula to make business decisions.
3. Explain the concept of present value and how it relates to future value, and be able to use the present value formula to make business decisions.
4. Discuss why the concept of compounding is not restricted to money, and be able to use the future value formula to calculate growth rates.

I. Chapter Outline

5.1 The Time Value of Money

- A basic problem faced by managers in financial decision making is to determine the value of a series of future cash flows, whether paying for an asset or evaluating a project.
- The question that is being raised is: What is the value of the stream of future cash flows today?
- We refer to this value as *time value of money*.

A. ***Consuming Today or Tomorrow***
- People prefer to consume goods today rather than wait to consume similar goods in the future—that is, a positive time preference.
- The **time value of money** is_based on the belief that people have a positive time preference for consumption.
- Money has a time value because a dollar in hand today is worth more than a dollar to be received in the future. The dollar in hand could be either invested to earn interest or spent today.
  - o The value of a dollar invested at a positive interest rate grows over time, and the further in the future you receive a dollar, the less it is worth today.

B. ***Time Lines as Aids to Problem Solving***
- A time line is a horizontal line that starts at time zero (today) and shows cash flows as they occur over time. See **Exhibit 5.1.**

C. ***Future Value versus Present Value***
- Financial decisions are evaluated on either a future value basis or a present value basis.
- ***Future value*** measures what one or more cash flows are worth at the end of a specified period, while ***present value*** measures what one or more cash flows to be received in the future will be worth today (at $t = 0$).
- The process of converting an amount given at the present time into a future value is called ***compounding***, while ***discounting*** is the process of converting future cash flows to what its present value is.

5.2 Future Value and Compounding

A. ***Single-Period Investment***

- We can determine the value of an investment at the end of one period (whether it is a month, quarter, or year) if we know the interest rate to be earned by the investment.
- If you invest for one period at an interest rate of i, your investment, or principal, will grow by $(1 + i)$ per dollar invested.
- The term $(1 + i)$ is the ***future value interest factor***—often called simply the ***future value factor***.

B. ***Two-Period Investment***

- When more than one period is considered, interest accrues on both the original investment (principal) and the interest earned in the preceding periods.
- The **principal** is the amount of money invested.
- **Simple interest** is the amount of interest paid on the original principal amount only.
- With compounding, you are able to earn **compound interest,** which consists of both simple interest and interest-on-interest.

C. ***The Future Value Equation***

- Equation 5.1 gives us the general equation to find the future value after any number of periods.
- The term $(1 + i)^n$ is the future value factor.

D. ***Compounding More Frequently Than Once a Year***

- The more frequently the interest payments are compounded, the larger the future value of $1 for a given time period. See Equation 5.2.
- When interest is compounded on a continuous basis, we can use Equation 5.3.

5.3 Present Value and Discounting

- Present value calculations involve bringing a future amount back to the present; this process is called **discounting,** and the interest rate i is known as the **discount rate.**
- The **present value (PV)** is often called the *discounted value of future cash payments***.**
- The *present value factor* is more commonly called the *discount factor.*
- Equation 5.4 gives us the general equation to find the present value after any number of periods.
- The further in the future a dollar will be received, the less it is worth today.
- The higher the discount rate, the lower the present value of a dollar.

5.4 Additional Concepts and Applications

A. ***Finding the Interest Rate***

- In Finance, a number of situations will require you to determine the interest rate (or discount rate) for a given stream of future cash flows.
- For an individual investor or a firm, it may be necessary:
  - o to determine the return on an investment.
  - o to determine the interest rate on a loan.
  - o to determine a growth rate.

B. ***The Rule of 72***

- The Rule of 72 can be used to determine the amount of time it takes to double an investment.
- The **Rule of 72** says that the time to double your money (TDM) approximately equals $72/i$, where i is expressed as a percentage.
- The rule is fairly accurate for interest rates between 5 and 20 percent.

C. ***Compound Growth Rates***

- Compound growth occurs when the initial value of a number increases or decreases each period by the factor (1 + growth rate).
- Such changes over time include the population growth rate of a city, or the sales or earnings growth rate of a firm.

II. Suggested Approach to Material

This chapter begins with a discussion of the time value of money. The chapter then focuses on the concept of the future value of a single cash flow, which is achieved through the process of compounding. The chapter also discusses the determination of the future value of an investment over multiple periods. The idea of an investment earning interest over periods shorter than a year is also discussed. A similar process is adopted in the chapter to discuss the idea of present value. Finally, related issues like the Rule of 72, compound growth rates, and the determination of the term or interest rate of an investment are discussed.

This chapter and Chapter 6 discuss what may be considered the most significant concept in finance—***time value of money.*** These concepts will play a significant role in the later chapters. It is very important to understand these ideas of present and future values of a cash flow. In the next chapter, the authors deal with multiple cash flows. The processes—discounting and compounding—are significant for both individuals and businesses, allowing the decision maker to value securities and determine the financial feasibility of investments. These and other concepts incorporating the time value of money are covered in the chapters that follow.

III. Chapter Glossary

Time value of money	The difference in value between a dollar in hand today and a dollar promised in the future. A dollar today is worth more than a dollar in the future.
Future value (FV)	The sum to which an investment will grow after earning interest for one or more periods.
Principal	The amount of money on which interest is paid.
Simple interest	Interest earned on the original principal amount only.
Interest on interest	Interest earned on interest that was earned in previous periods.
Compounding	The process by which interest earned on an investment is reinvested so that in future periods, interest is earned on the interest as well as the principal.
Compound interest	Interest earned both on the original principal amount and on interest previously earned
Discounting	The process of finding the present value of future cash flows.
Discount rate	The interest rate used in the discounting process to find the present value of future cash flows.
Present value (PV)	The current value of future cash flows discounted at the appropriate discount rate; often called the *discounted value of future cash payments*.
Rule of 72	A rule proposing that the time required to double money invested (TDM) approximately equals $72/i$, where i is expressed as a percentage.
Compound annual growth rate (CAGR)	The average annual growth rate over a specified period of time.

IV. Summary of Key Equations

Equation	**Description**	**Formula**
5.1	Future value of an n-period investment with annual compounding	$FV_n = PV \times (1 + i)^n$
5.2	Future value with compounding more than annually	$FV_n = PV \times (1 + i/m)^{m \times n}$
5.3	Future value with continuous compounding	$FV_\infty = PV \times e^{i \times n}$

Equation	Description	Formula
5.4	Present value	$PV = \frac{FV_n}{(1+i)^n}$
5.5	Rule of 72	$TDM = \frac{72}{i}$
5.6	Future value with general growth rate	$FV_n = PV \times (1+g)^n$

V. True or False Questions

1. The time value of money is based on the belief that people have a positive time preference for consumption.

a. True

b. False

2. The sooner in the future you receive a dollar, the less it is worth today.

a. True

b. False

3. The present value technique uses *compounding* to find the present value of each cash flow at the beginning of the project.

a. True

b. False

4. The future value technique uses *discounting* to find the future value of each cash flow at the end of the project's life.

a. True

b. False

5. Compound interest consists of both simple interest and interest-on-interest.

a. True

b. False

6. The less frequently the interest payments are compounded, the larger the future value of $1 for a given time period.

a. True

b. False

7. If Bank A pays interest on a monthly basis and Bank B pays the same interest rate on a daily basis, then investing $1,000 in Bank B will lead to a higher future value than investing the same amount in Bank A.

a. True

b. False

8. The Rule of 72 allows one to calculate the return earned on an investment over six years.

a. True

b. False

9. The present value of an investment of $2,000 to be received in three years at a discount rate of 8 percent is $1,587.66.

a. True

b. False

10. The lower the discount rate, the lower the present value of a future cash flow.
    a. True
    b. False

VI. Multiple-Choice Questions

1. Which one of the following statements is **NOT** true?
    a. The time value money refers to what the value of the stream of future cash flows today is.
    b. A dollar received today is worth more than a dollar received tomorrow.
    c. A dollar received tomorrow is worth less than a dollar received today.
    d. A dollar received today is worth less than a dollar received tomorrow.

2. Future value measures
    a. what one or more cash flows are worth at the end of a specified period.
    b. what one or more cash flows that are to be received in the future will be worth today.
    c. both a and b
    d. none of the above

3. The process of converting future cash flows to its present value is
    a. time value of money
    b. discounting
    c. compounding
    d. None of the above

4. Which one of the following statements is **NOT** true?
    a. Present value calculations involve bringing a future amount back to the present.
    b. The future value is often called the discounted value of future cash payments.
    c. The present value factor is more commonly called the discount factor.
    d. The higher the discount rate, the lower the present value of a dollar.

5. The Rule of 72
    a. is a rule that can be used to determine the amount of time it takes to double an investment.
    b. is fairly accurate for interest rates between 25 and 50 percent.
    c. states that the time to double your money (TDM) approximately equals $72/i$, where 72 represents the years it takes to double your investment.
    d. None of the above describes the Rule of 72.

6. Using higher discount rates will
    a. not affect the future value of the investment.
    b. increase the future value of any investment.
    c. decrease the future value of any investment.
    d. None of the above.

7. Using lower discount rates will
    a. decrease the future value of any investment.
    b. increase the future value of any investment.
    c. will not affect the future value of the investment.
    d. None of the above,

8. Ning Gao is planning to buy a house in five years. She is looking to invest $35,000 today in an index mutual fund that will provide her a return of 11 percent annually. How much will she have at the end of five years? Round to the nearest dollar.
   a. $45,000
   b. $28,000
   c. $58,977
   d. None of the above

9. Carlos Sanchez is looking to invest for the next three years. He is looking to invest $8,500 today in a bank CD that will earn interest at 6.75 percent annually. How much will he have at the end of three years? Round to the nearest dollar.
   a. $10,340
   b. $8,000
   c. $9,681
   d. None of the above

10. Normandy Textiles had a cash inflow of $2 million, which it needs for a long-term investment at the end of one year. It plans to deposit this money in a bank CD that pays daily interest at 2.75 percent. What will be the value of the investment at the end of the year? Round to the nearest dollar.
    a. $2,211,375
    b. $2,000,103
    c. $2,037,500
    d. $2,055,761

11. John Botti wants to invest $5,000 today in a money market fund that pays quarterly interest at 5.5 percent. He plans to fund a scholarship with the proceeds at his alma mater, Towson University. How much will John have at the end of six years? Round to the nearest dollar.
    a. $7,091
    b. $6,548
    c. $6,939
    d. $5,075

12. Joachim Noah is investing $5,000 in an account paying 6.75 percent annually for three years. What is the interest-on-interest if interest is compounded?
    a. $1,012.50
    b. $1,082.38
    c. $82.38
    d. $69.88

13. Dat Nguyen is depositing $7,500 in an account paying an annual interest rate of 8.5 percent compounded monthly. What is the interest on interest after six years?
    a. $3,825.00
    b. $11,325.00
    c. $1,142.25
    d. $1,092.48

14. Jack Robbins is saving for a new car. He needs to have $21,000 for the car in three years. How much will he have to invest today in an account paying 8 percent annually to achieve his target? (Round to nearest dollar.)
    a. $22,680
    b. $26,454
    c. $16,671
    d. $19,444

15. Your friend Jackson is asking to borrow today with a promise to repay $6,665 in four years. If you could earn 7.45 percent annually on the any investment you make today, how much will you be willing to lend Jackson today? (Round to nearest dollar.)

   a. $5,000
   b. $4,035
   c. $4,500
   d. $5,150

16. You need to have $15,000 in five years to pay off a home equity loan. You open an account that pays 5.75 percent compounded quarterly. How much will you have to invest today to attain your target in five years? (Round to nearest dollar.)

   a. $4,903
   b. $11,275
   c. $14,184
   d. $12,250

17. Ray Seo has $5,000 to invest in a small business venture. His partner has promised to pay him back $8,200 in five years. What is the return earned on this investment?

   a. 9.3%
   b. 8.7%
   c. 11.1%
   d. 10.4%

18. Trayne Rice has $3,000 to invest for three years. He wants to receive $5,000 at the end of the three years. What *i* rate would his investment have to earn to achieve his goal? (Round to the nearest percent.)

   a. 19%
   b. 21%
   c. 13%
   d. 16%

19. Cleargen, a detergent manufacturer, has announced this year's net income as $832,500. It expects its net earnings to grow at a rate of 15 percent per year for the next two years, before dropping to 12 percent for each of the following two years. What is the firm's net income after four years? (Round to the nearest dollar.)

   a. $1,381,071
   b. $1,266,128
   c. $1,233,099
   d. $1,072,260

20. Fahrenheit Opticals announced that its sales were $1,335,450 this year. The company forecasts a growth rate of 18 percent for the foreseeable future. How long will it take the firm to produce earnings of $3 million? Use a financial calculator to solve this problem. (Round to the nearest year.)

   a. 7 years
   b. 5 years
   c. 8 years
   d. 6 years

Answers to True or False Questions

1. a	**2.** b	**3.** b	**4.** b	**5.** a
6. b	**7.** a	**8.** b	**9.** a	**10.** b

Answers to Multiple-Choice Questions

1. d	**2.** a	**3.** b	**4.** b	**5.** a
6. b	**7.** a	**8.** c	**9.** a	**10.** d
11. c	**12.** d	**13.** c	**14.** c	**15.** a
16. b	**17.** d	**18.** a	**19.** a	**20.** b

Solutions to Multiple-Choice Questions

8. **Solution:**

Present value of the investment = PV = $35,000

Return on mutual fund = i = 11%

No. of years = n = 5.

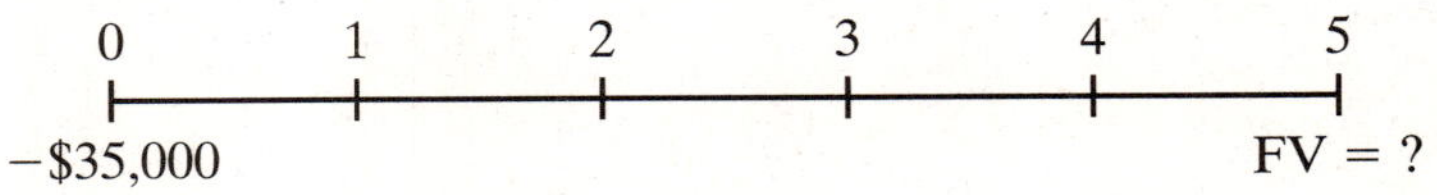

$$FV_5 = PV \times (1 + i)^n = \$35{,}000 \times (1.11)^5$$
$$= \mathbf{\$58{,}977.04}$$

9. **Solution:**

Present value of the investment = PV = $8,500

Interest rate on CD = i = 6.75%

No. of years = n = 3.

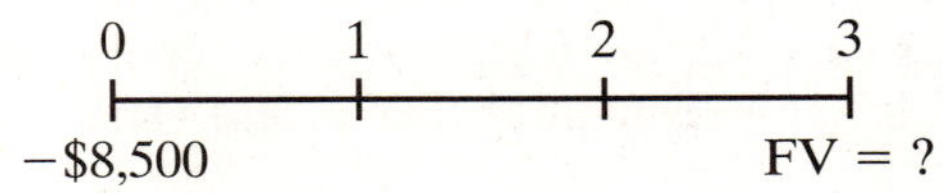

$$FV_3 = PV \times (1 + i)^n = \$8{,}500 \times (1.0.0675)^3$$
$$= \mathbf{\$10{,}340.05}$$

10. **Solution:**

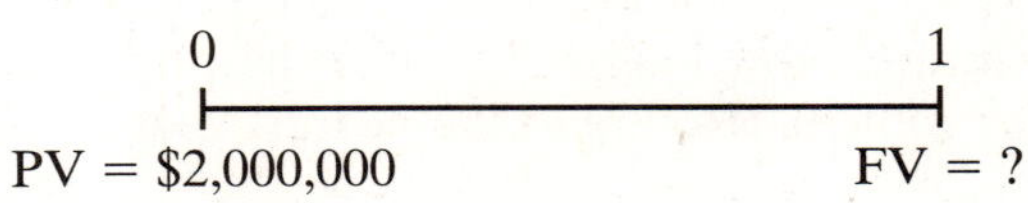

Amount invested today = PV = $2,000,000

Interest rate on CD = i = 2.75%

Duration of investment = n = 1 year

Frequency of compounding = m = 365

Value of investment after 1 year = FV_1

$$FV_1 = PV \times \left(1 + \frac{i}{m}\right)^{mn} = \$2{,}000{,}000 \times \left(1 + \frac{0.0275}{365}\right)^{365 \times 1}$$
$$= \$2{,}000{,}000 \times (1.000075342)^{365}$$
$$= \mathbf{\$2{,}055{,}761.10}$$

11. Solution:

$$\begin{array}{lcr} 0 & & 7 \\ \vdash\!\!\!\text{———————————}\!\!\!\dashv \\ PV = \$5{,}000 & & FV = ? \end{array}$$

Amount invested today = PV = \$5,000

Interest rate on money market account = i = 5.5%

Duration of investment = n = 6 years

Frequency of compounding = m = 4

Value of investment after 6 years = FV_6

$$FV_6 = PV \times \left(1 + \frac{i}{m}\right)^{mn} = \$5{,}000 \times \left(1 + \frac{0.055}{4}\right)^{4\times 6}$$

$$= \$5{,}000 \times (1.01375)^{24}$$

$$= \mathbf{\$6{,}939.22}$$

12. Solution:

Deposit today = PV = \$5,000

Interest rate = i = 6.75%

No. of years = n = 3

Future value with simple interest:

Simple interest per year = \$5,000 (0.0675) = \$337.50

Simple interest for 3 years = \$337.50 × 3 = **\$1,012.50**

Future value with compound interest:

$FV_3 = \$5{,}000\ (1 + 0.0675)^3 = \$6{,}082.38$

Simple interest = \$1,012.50

Interest on interest = \$6,082.38 − \$5,000 − \$1,012.50 = **\$69.88**

13. Solution:

Deposit today = PV = \$7,500

Interest rate = i = 8.5%

No. of years = n = 6

Frequency of compounding = m = 12

Future value with simple interest:

Simple interest per year = \$7,500 (0.085) = \$637.50

Simple interest for 6 years = \$637.50 × 6 = **\$3,825**

Future value with compound interest:

$$FV_6 = PV \times \left(1 + \frac{i}{m}\right)^{mn} = \$7{,}500 \times \left(1 + \frac{0.085}{12}\right)^{12\times 6}$$

$$= \$7{,}500 \times (1.0007083)^{72}$$

$$= \mathbf{\$12{,}467.25}$$

Simple interest = \$3,825

Interest-on-interest = \$12,467.25 − \$7,500 − \$3,825 = **\$1,142.25**

14. Solution:

$$\begin{array}{lcr} 0 & & 3 \text{ Years} \\ \vdash\!\!\!\text{———————————}\!\!\!\dashv \\ PV = ? & i = 8\% & FV = \$21{,}000 \end{array}$$

Value of investment after 7 years = FV_3 = \$21,000

Return expected from investment = i = 8%

Duration of investment $= n = 3$ years

Amount to be invested today = PV

$$PV = \frac{FV_n}{(1+i)^n} = \frac{\$21,000}{(1.08)^3} = \mathbf{\$16,670.48}$$

15. Solution:

0 —————————————— 4 Years

PV = ? $i = 7.45\%$ FV = \$6,665

Loan repayment amount after 4 years $= FV_4 = \$6,665$

Return expected from loan $= i = 7.45\%$

Duration of loan $= n = 4$ years

Amount to be loaned today = PV

$$PV = \frac{FV_n}{(1+i)^n} = \frac{\$6,665}{(1.0745)^4} = \mathbf{\$5,000}$$

16. Solution:

0 —————————————— 5 Years

PV = ? $i = 5.75\%$ FV = \$15,000

Return expected from investment $= i = 5.75\%$

Duration of investment $= n = 5$ years

Frequency of compounding $= m = 4$

Target investment proceeds in 5 years $= FV_5 = \$15,000$

Present Value of amount = PV

$$PV = \frac{FV_n}{\left(1+\frac{i}{m}\right)^{mn}} = \frac{\$15,000}{\left(1+\frac{0.0575}{4}\right)^{5\times 4}} = \frac{\$15,000}{(1.014375)^{20}}$$

$$= \mathbf{\$11,275.10}$$

17. Solution:

0 —————————————— 5 Years

PV = \$5,000 FV = \$8,200

Amount being invested = PV = \$5,000

Amount to be paid back after 5 years = FV = \$8,200

Interest rate on investment $= i = ?$

Duration of investment $= n = 5$ years.

Present value of investment = PV

$$PV = \frac{FV_n}{(1+i)^n}$$

$$\$5,000 = \frac{\$8,200}{(1+i)^5}$$

$$(1+i)^5 = \frac{\$8,200}{\$5,000} = 1.6400$$

$$(1+i) = (1.6400)^{1/5} = 1.103999$$

$$i = \mathbf{10.4\%}$$

18. Solution:

0 — 3 Years

PV = −$3,000 — FV = $5,000

Amount being invested = PV = $3,000
Amount to be paid back after 3 years = FV = $5,000
Interest rate on investment = i = ?
Duration of investment = n = 3 years.
Present value of investment = PV

$$PV = \frac{FV_n}{(1+i)^n}$$
$$\$3{,}000 = \frac{\$5{,}000}{(1+i)^3}$$
$$(1+i)^3 = \frac{\$5{,}000}{\$3{,}000} = 1.66667$$
$$(1+i) = (1.6667)^{1/3} = 1.1856$$
$$i = \mathbf{18.6\%}$$

19. Solution:

0 — 4 Years

$g_{1-2} = 15\%$ $g_{3-4} = 12\%$

PV = $832,500 — FV = $?

Current net income = PV = $832,500
Expected net income four years from now = FV
To calculate the expected net earnings, we set up the future value equation.

$$FV_4 = PV \times (1+g_1)^2(1+g_2)^2$$
$$= \$832{,}500(1.15)^2(1.12)^2$$
$$= \$1{,}381{,}070.88$$

20. Solution:

Enter

4.89	**18%**		**−$1,335,450**	**$3,000,000**
N	**g (i)%**	**PMT**	**PV**	**FV**

Answer: **5 years**

CHAPTER 6

Discounted Cash Flows and Valuation

LEARNING OBJECTIVES

1. Explain why cash flows occurring at different times must be discounted to a common date before they can be compared, and be able to compute the present value and future value for multiple cash flows.
2. Describe how to calculate the present value of an ordinary annuity and how an ordinary annuity differs from an annuity due.
3. Explain what a perpetuity is and how it is used in business, and be able to calculate the value of a perpetuity.
4. Discuss growing annuities and perpetuities, as well as their application in business, and be able to calculate their value.
5. Discuss why the effective annual interest rate (EAR) is the appropriate way to annualize interest rates, and be able to calculate EAR.

I. Chapter Outline

6.1 Multiple Cash Flows

A. ***Future Value of Multiple Cash Flows***

- Solving future value problems with multiple cash flows involves drawing a time line to make sure that each cash flow is placed in the correct time period, calculating the future value of each cash flow for its time period, and finally adding up the future values.

B. ***Present Value of Multiple Cash Flows***

- Many situations in business call for computing the present value of a series of expected future cash flows. This could be to determine the market value of a security or business, or to decide whether a capital investment should be made.
- The process is similar to determining the future value of multiple cash flows.

6.2 Level Cash Flows: Annuities and Perpetuities

- There are many situations in which both businesses and individuals would be faced with either receiving or paying a constant amount for a length of period.
- When a firm faces a stream of constant payments on a bank loan for a period of time, we call that stream of cash flows an annuity.

- Individual investors may make constant payments on their home or car loans, or invest a fixed amount year after year to save for their retirement.
- If the cash flow payments continue forever, the contract is called a **perpetuity**.
- Constant cash flows that occur at the end of each period are called **ordinary annuities**.

A. ***Present Value of an Annuity***

- We can calculate the present value of an annuity the same way as we calculated the present value of multiple cash flows. However, if the number of payments were to be very large, then this process would be tedious.
- Equation 6.1 can be used to calculate the present value of an annuity.

$$
\begin{aligned}
PVA_n &= CF \times \text{Present value factor for an annuity} \\
&= CF \times \left[\frac{(1 - \text{Present value factor})}{i}\right] \\
&= CF \times \left[\frac{1 - \dfrac{1}{(1+i)^n}}{i}\right]
\end{aligned}
$$

- In addition to using this annuity equation to solve for the present value of an annuity, financial calculators and spreadsheets may be used. Present value and annuity tables created with the help of Equation 6.1 have limited use outside of a classroom setting.
- One problem that is widely solved using a financial calculator is finding the monthly payment on a car loan or home loan.

B. ***Preparing a Loan Amortization Schedule***

- **Amortization** refers to the way the borrowed amount (principal) is paid down over the life of the loan.
- The monthly loan payment is structured so that each month a portion of the principal is paid off and at the time the loan matures, the loan is entirely paid off. All of the payments are prescheduled to be the same amount.
- A loan **amortization schedule** is just a table that shows the loan balance at the beginning and end of each period, the payment made during that period, and how much of that payment represents interest and how much represents repayment of principal.
- Amortization schedules are best done on a spreadsheet (see Exhibit 6.5).

C. ***Finding the Interest Rate***

- The annuity equation (Equation 6.1) can also be used to find the interest rate or discount rate for an annuity.
- Other than using a trial-and-error approach, it is easier to solve for the interest rate with a financial calculator.

D. ***Future Value of an Annuity***

- Future value annuity calculations usually involve finding what a savings or an investment activity is worth at some point in the future.
- Equation 6.2 represents the future value annuity equation.

$$
\begin{aligned}
FVA_n &= CF \times \text{Future value factor for an annuity} \\
&= CF \times \frac{\text{Future value factor} - 1}{i} \\
&= CF \times \left[\frac{(1+i)^n - 1}{i}\right]
\end{aligned}
$$

- As with present value annuity calculations, future value calculations are made easier when financial calculators or spreadsheets are used, especially when lengthy investment periods are involved.

E. ***Perpetuities***

- A **perpetuity** is a constant stream of cash flows that goes on for an infinite period.

$$
\begin{aligned}
PVA_\infty &= CF \times \text{Present value factor for an annuity} \\
&= CF \times \left[\frac{1 - \dfrac{1}{(1+i)^\infty}}{i}\right] = CF \times \frac{(1-0)}{i} \\
&= \frac{CF}{i}
\end{aligned}
$$

- In the stock markets, preferred stock issues are considered to be perpetuities, with the issuer paying a constant dividend to holders.

F. *Annuity Due*

- When you have an annuity with the payment being incurred at the beginning of each period rather than at the end, the annuity is called an **annuity due**.
- Rent or lease payments are typically made at the beginning of each period rather than at the end of each period.
- The annuity transformation method (Equation 6.4) shows the relationship between the ordinary annuity and the annuity due.
  Annuity due = Ordinary annuity value $\times$ $(1 + i)$

6.3 Cash Flows That Grow at a Constant Rate

- In addition to constant cash flow streams, one may have to deal with cash flows that grow at a constant rate over time.
- These cash flow streams are called **growing annuities** or **growing perpetuities**.

A. *Growing Annuity*

- Business may need to compute the value of multiyear product or service contracts with cash flows that increase each year at a constant rate.
- These are called **growing annuities**.

B. *Growing Perpetuity*

- When the cash flow stream features a constant growing annuity forever, it is called a **growing perpetuity**.
- This can be derived from Equation 6.5 when n tends to infinity and results in Equation 6.6.

6.4 The Effective Annual Interest Rate

- Interest rates can be quoted in the financial markets in a variety of ways.
- The most common quote, especially for a loan, is the **annual percentage rate (APR)**.
- The APR is a rate that represents the simple interest accrued on a loan or investment in a single period. This is annualized over a year by multiplying it by the appropriate number of periods in a year.

A. *Calculating the Effective Annual Interest Rate (EAR)*

- The correct way to compute an annualized rate is to reflect the compounding that occurs. This involves calculating the effective annual rate (EAR).
- The EAR is the true cost of borrowing and lending.
  $\text{EAR} = (1 + \text{Quoted rate}/m)^m - 1$

B. *Consumer Protection Acts and Interest Rate Disclosure*

- Congress passed the **Truth-in-Lending Act** in 1968 to ensure that the true cost of credit was disclosed to consumers so that they could make sound financial decisions.
- Similarly, another piece of legislation called the **Truth-in-Savings Act** was passed to provide consumers an accurate estimate of the return they would earn on an investment.
- These two pieces of legislation require by law that the APR be disclosed on all consumer loans and savings plans and that it be prominently displayed on advertising and contractual documents.

II. Suggested Approach to Material

The authors begin the chapter by describing calculations of future and present values for multiple cash flows. They then examine some situations in which future cash flows are level over time: these involve annuities, in which the cash flow stream goes on for a finite period, and perpetuities, in which the stream goes on forever. Next, annuities and perpetuities in which the cash flows grow at a constant rate over time are discussed. These cash flows resemble common cash flow patterns encountered in business. Finally, the discussion focuses on the effective annual interest rate, which is compared with the annual percentage rate (APR), a rate that is used to describe the interest rate in consumer loans.

The chapter builds on the concepts of compounding and discounting that were introduced in Chapter 5. The analysis of annuities and perpetuities, both constant and growing, shows the variety of cash flow streams that individuals and businesses can encounter and have to value. The importance of using an appropriate rate to do present and future value calculations is also highlighted.

III. Chapter Glossary

Annuity	A series of equally spaced and level cash flows extending over a finite number of periods.
Perpetuity	A series of level cash flows that extend forever.
Ordinary annuity	An annuity in which payments are made at the ends of the periods.
Present value of an annuity (PVA)	The present value of the cash flows from an annuity, discounted at the appropriate discount rate.
Amortized loan	A loan for which each loan payment contains some payment of principal and some payment of interest based on the remaining principal to be repaid.
Amortization schedule	With regard to a loan, a table that shows the loan balance at the beginning and end of each period, the payment made during that period, and how much of that payment represents interest and how much represents repayment of principal.
Future value of an annuity (FVA)	The value of an annuity at some point in the future.
Annuity due	A type of annuity in which payments are made at the beginnings of each period.
Growing annuity	An annuity in which the cash flows increase at a constant rate.
Growing perpetuity	A cash flow stream that grows at a constant rate forever.
Annual percentage rate (APR)	The simple interest rate charged per period multiplied by the number of periods per year.
Effective annual interest rate (EAR)	The annual interest rate that reflects compounding within a year.
Quoted interest rate	A simple annual interest rate, such as the APR.
Truth-in-Lending Act	A federal law requiring lenders to fully inform borrowers of important information related to loans, including the annual percentage rate charged.
Truth-in-Savings Act	A federal law requiring institutions offering consumer savings vehicles, such as certificates of deposits (CD), to fully inform consumers of important information about the savings vehicles, including the annual percentage rate paid.

IV. Summary of Key Equations

Equation	Description	Formula
6.1	Present value of an ordinary annuity	$\mathrm{PVA}_n = \frac{\mathrm{CF}}{i} \times \left[1 - \frac{1}{(1+i)^n}\right]$ $= \mathrm{CF} \times \frac{1 - 1/(1+i)^n}{i}$ $= \mathrm{CF} \times \frac{1 - \text{Present value factor}}{i}$ $= \mathrm{CF} \times \text{PV annuity factor}$

(Continued)

Equation	Description	Formula
6.2	Future value of an ordinary annuity	$\text{FVA}_n = \frac{\text{CF}}{i} \times [(1+i)^n - 1]$ $= \text{CF} \times \frac{(1+i)^n - 1}{\text{i}}$ $= \text{CF} \times \frac{\text{Future value factor} - 1}{i}$ $= \text{CF} \times \text{FV annuity factor}$
6.3	Present value of a perpetuity	$\text{PVA}_\infty = \text{CF}/i$
6.4	Value of an annuity due	Annuity due value = Ordinary annuity value × (1 + i)
6.5	Present value of a growing annuity	$\text{PVA}_n = \frac{\text{CF}_1}{i - g} \times \left[1 - \left(\frac{1+g}{1+i}\right)^n\right]$
6.6	Present value of a growing perpetuity	$\text{PVA}_\infty = \frac{\text{CF}_1}{i - g}$
6.7	Effective annual interest rate	$\text{EAR} = \left[1 + \frac{\text{Quoted rate}}{m}\right]^m - 1$

V. True or False Questions

1. In computing the present and future value of multiple cash flows, each cash flow is discounted or compounded at the same rate.
   - **a.** True
   - **b.** False

2. The future value of multiple cash flows is greater than the sum of those cash flows.
   - **a.** True
   - **b.** False

3. In the text, the perpetual British government war bonds were referred to as *consols*.
   - **a.** True
   - **b.** False

4. When you pay the same amount every month as your insurance premium for a term life policy for a period of five years, the stream of cash flows is called a perpetuity.
   - **a.** True
   - **b.** False

5. The present value of a perpetuity is the promised constant cash payment divided by the interest rate (i).
   - **a.** True
   - **b.** False

6. In an annuity due, cash flows occur at the beginning of each period.
   - **a.** True
   - **b.** False

7. The rent paid for an apartment is an example of an ordinary annuity.
   - **a.** True
   - **b.** False

8. The present value of an annuity due is equal to the present value of an ordinary annuity.
   - **a.** True
   - **b.** False

9. Trey Hughes opened a pizza place last year. He expects to increase his revenue from last year by 7 percent every year for the next 10 years. This is an example of a growing annuity.
   - **a.** True
   - **b.** False

10. The APR is the annualized interest rate using compound interest.
    - **a.** True
    - **b.** False

11. The APR is the true cost of borrowing and lending.
    - **a.** True
    - **b.** False

12. Only the APR or some other quoted rate should be used as the interest rate factor for present or future value calculations.
    - **a.** True
    - **b.** False

VI. Multiple-Choice Questions

1. To solve future value problems with multiple cash flows involves which of the following steps?
   - **a.** First, draw a time line to make sure that each cash flow is placed in the correct time period.
   - **b.** Second, calculate the future value of each cash flow for its time period.
   - **c.** Third, add up the future values.
   - **d.** All of the above are necessary steps.

2. Calculating the present and future values of multiple cash flows is relevant
   - **a.** for businesses only.
   - **b.** for individuals only.
   - **c.** for both individuals and businesses.
   - **d.** None of the above.

3. In computing the present and future value of multiple cash flows,
   - **a.** earlier cash flows are discounted at a lower rate.
   - **b.** each cash flow is discounted or compounded at the same rate.
   - **c.** earlier cash flows are discounted at a higher rate.
   - **d.** None of the above.

4. If your investment pays the same amount at the end of each year for a period of six years, the cash flow stream is called
   - **a.** a perpetuity.
   - **b.** an ordinary annuity.
   - **c.** an annuity due.
   - **d.** None of the above.

5. Cash flows associated with annuities are considered to be
   a. an uneven cash flow stream.
   b. a constant cash flow stream.
   c. a mix of constant and uneven cash flow stream.
   d. None of the above.

6. Which **ONE** of the following statements is true about amortization?
   a. Amortization refers to the way the borrowed amount (principal) is paid down over the life of the loan.
   b. With an amortized loan, each loan payment contains some payment of principal and an interest payment.
   c. A loan amortization schedule is just a table that shows the loan balance at the beginning and end of each period, the payment made during that period, and how much of that payment represents interest and how much represents repayment of principal.
   d. All of the above are true.

7. The annuity transformation method is used to
   a. transform a present value annuity to a future value annuity.
   b. transform a present value annuity to a future value annuity.
   c. transform an ordinary annuity to an annuity due.
   d. transform a perpetuity to an annuity.

8. A firm receives a cash flow from an investment that will increase by 10 percent annually for an infinite number of years. This cash flow stream is called
   a. an annuity due.
   b. a growing perpetuity.
   c. an ordinary annuity.
   d. a growing annuity.

9. The true cost of borrowing is the
   a. annual percentage rate.
   b. effective annual rate.
   c. quoted interest rate.
   d. periodic rate.

10. Which one of the following statements is **NOT** true?
    a. The **Truth-in-Lending Act** was passed by Congress to ensure that the true cost of credit was disclosed to consumers.
    b. The **Truth-in-Savings Act** was passed to provide consumers an accurate estimate of the return they would earn on an investment.
    c. These two pieces of legislation require by law that the APR be disclosed on all consumer loans and savings plans.
    d. All of the above are true statements.

11. Stiglitz, Inc., is expecting the following annual cash flows beginning at the end of the year—$113,245, $132,709, $141,554, and $180,760. If their opportunity cost is 9.6 percent, find the future value of these cash flows. (Round to the nearest dollar.)
    a. $644,406
    b. $732,114
    c. $685,312
    d. $900,810

12. Brett Tangley is expecting the following cash flows beginning at the end of the year—$43,245, $32,709, and $41,554. If his opportunity cost is 9 percent, find the future value of these cash flows. (Round to the nearest dollar.)

    a. $128,586

    b. $132,114

    c. $85,312

    d. $90,810

13. Hassan Ali has made an investment that will pay him the annual cash flows $11,455, $16,376, and $19,812 for the next three years. His investment was to fetch him a return of 14 percent. What is the present value of these cash flows? (Round to the nearest dollar.)

    a. $33,124

    b. $36,022

    c. $41,675

    d. $39,208

14. Yuan Li has made an investment that will pay her $944, $776, and $812 at the end of each of the next three years. Her investment will fetch a return of 12 percent. What is the present value of these cash flows? (Round to the nearest dollar.)

    a. $2,124

    b. $2,039

    c. $2,675

    d. $2,208

15. Transit Insurance Company has made an investment in another company's preferred stock that will guarantee it a cash flow of $37,250 each year for the next five years. If the company uses a discount rate of 15 percent on its investments, what is the present value of this investment? (Round to the nearest dollar.)

    a. $101,766

    b. $124,868

    c. $251,154

    d. $186,250

16. Lorraine Jackson won a lottery. She will have a choice of receiving $25,000 at the end of each year for the next 30 years, or a lump sum today. If she can earn a return of 10 percent on any investment she makes, what is the minimum amount she should be willing to accept today as a lump-sum payment? (Round to the nearest hundred dollars.)

    a. $750,000

    b. $334,600

    c. $212,400

    d. $235,700

17. You plan to save $1,250 at the end of each of the next three years to pay for a vacation. If you can invest it at 7 percent, how much will you have at the end of three years? (Round to the nearest dollar.)

    a. $3,750

    b. $3,918

    c. $4,019

    d. $4,589

18. Roger Stamp wants to save $1,450 at the end of each of the next four years to use as a down payment for a car. If he can invest it at 6 percent, how much will he have at the end of four years? (Round to the nearest dollar.)

a. $6,343

b. $5,918

c. $6,019

d. $6,589

19. Maricela Sanchez needs to have $25,000 in five years. If she can earn 8 percent on any investment, what is the amount that she will have to invest every year for the next five years? (Round to the nearest dollar.)

a. $5,000

b. $4,261

c. $4,640

d. $4,445

20. Jackson Electricals has borrowed $27,850 from its bank at an annual rate of 8.5 percent. It plans to repay the loan in eight equal installments, beginning at the end of next year. What is its annual loan payment? (Round to the nearest dollar.)

a. $4,708

b. $5,134

c. $4,939

d. $4,748

21. Your father is 60 years old and wants to set up a cash flow stream that would be forever. He would like to receive $20,000 every year, beginning at the end of this year. If he could invest in an account earning 9 percent, how much would he have to invest today to receive his perpetual cash flow? (Round to the nearest dollar.)

a. $222,222

b. $200,000

c. $189,000

d. $235,200

22. Roger Barkley wants to set up a scholarship at his alma mater. He is willing to invest $500,000 in an account earning 10 percent. What will be the annual scholarship that can be given from this investment? (Round to the nearest dollar.)

a. $5,000

b. $500,000

c. $50,000

d. None of the above

23. Mark Holcomb has a five-year loan on which he will make annual payments of $2,235 beginning now. If the interest rate on the loan is 8.3 percent, what is the present value of this annuity? Round to the nearest dollar.

a. $9,588

b. $8,854

c. $8,612

d. $9,122

24. Jack Benny is planning to invest in an insurance company product. The product will pay $10,000 at the end of this year. Thereafter, the payments will grow annually at a 3 percent rate forever. Jack will be able to invest his cash flows at a rate of 6.5 percent. What is the present value of this investment cash flow stream? (Round to the nearest dollar.)

a. $326,908

b. $312,766

c. $285,714

d. $258,133

25. Desire Cosmetics borrowed $152,300 from a bank for three years. If the quoted rate (APR) is 11.75 percent, and the compounding is daily, what is the effective annual rate (EAR)? (Round to one decimal place.)

a. 11.8%

b. 14.3%

c. 12.5%

d. 11.6%

VI. Answers to True or False Questions

1. a　**2.** a　**3.** a　**4.** b　**5.** a

6. a　**7.** b　**8.** b　**9.** a　**10.** b

11. b　**12.** b

VII. Answers to Multiple-Choice Questions

1. d　**2.** c　**3.** b　**4.** b　**5.** b

6. d　**7.** c　**8.** b　**9.** b　**10.** d

11. a　**12.** a　**13.** b　**14.** b　**15.** b

16. d　**17.** c　**18.** a　**19.** b　**20.** c

21. a　**22.** c　**23.** a　**24.** c　**25.** c

VIII. Solutions to Multiple-Choice Questions

11. **Solution:**

0	1	2	3	4
	\$113,245	\$132,709	\$141,554	\$180,760

$n = 4$;　$i = 9.6\%$

$$\begin{aligned} FV_4 &= \$113{,}245(1.096)^3 + \$132{,}709(1.096)^2 + \$141{,}554(1.096)^1 + \$180{,}760 \\ &= \$149{,}090.75 + \$159{,}412.17 + \$155{,}143.18 + \$180{,}760 \\ &= \mathbf{\$644{,}406.11} \end{aligned}$$

12. **Solution:**

0	1	2	3
	\$43,245	\$32,709	\$41,554

$n = 3$;　$i = 9\%$

$$\begin{aligned} FV_4 &= \$43{,}245(1.09)^2 + \$32{,}709(1.09) + \$41{,}554 \\ &= \$51{,}379.38 + \$35{,}652.81 + \$41{,}554 \\ &= \mathbf{\$128{,}586.19} \end{aligned}$$

13. **Solution:**

0	1	2	3
	\$11,455	\$16,376	\$19,812

$n = 3$;　$i = 14\%$

$$PV = \frac{\$11,455}{(1.14)} + \frac{\$16,376}{(1.14)^2} + \frac{\$19,812}{(1.14)^3}$$

$$= \$10,048.25 + \$12,600.80 + \$13,372.54$$

$$= \mathbf{\$36,021.58}$$

14. Solution:

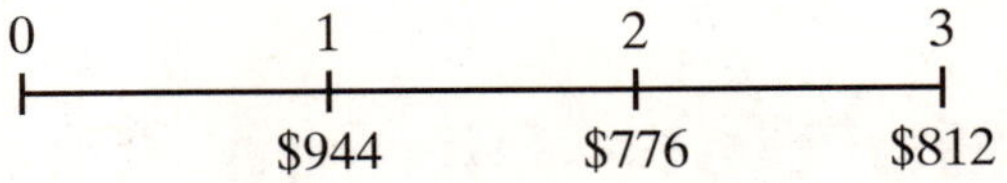

$n = 3$; $i = 12\%$

$$PV = \frac{\$944}{(1.12)} + \frac{\$776}{(1.12)^2} + \frac{\$812}{(1.12)^3}$$

$$= \$842.86 + \$618.62 + \$577.97$$

$$= \mathbf{\$2,039.45}$$

15. Solution:

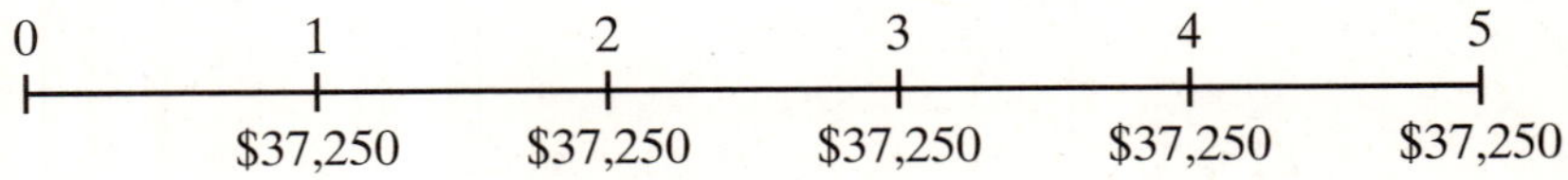

$n = 5$; $i = 15\%$

Annual payment = PMT = $37,250
No. of payments = n = 5
Required rate of return = 15%
Present value of investment = PVA_5

$$PVA_n = PMT \times \left[\frac{1 - \frac{1}{(1+i)^n}}{i}\right]$$

$$= \$37,250 \times \left[\frac{1 - \frac{1}{(1.15)^5}}{0.15}\right] = \$37,250 \times 3.3522$$

$$= \mathbf{\$124,867.78}$$

16. Solution:

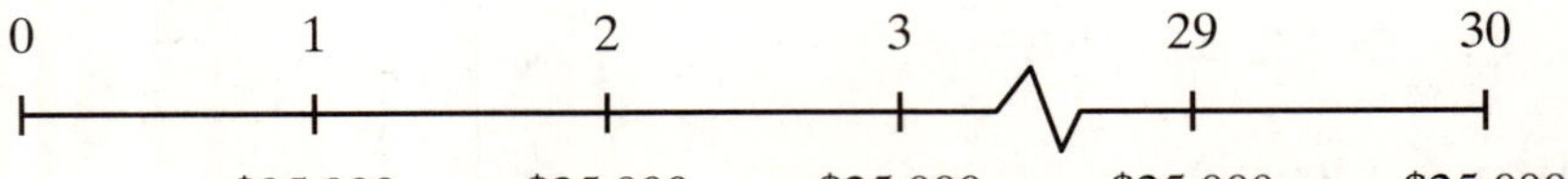

$n = 30$; $i = 10\%$

$$PVA_n = PMT \times \left[\frac{1 - \frac{1}{(1+i)^n}}{i}\right]$$

$$= \$25,000 \times \left[\frac{1 - \frac{1}{(1.10)^{30}}}{0.10}\right] = \$25,000 \times 9.4269$$

$$= \mathbf{\$235,672.86}$$

17. Solution:

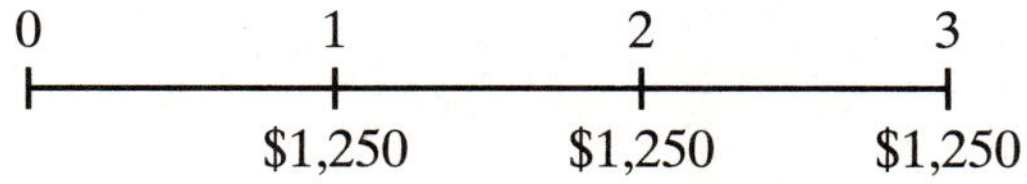

$n = 3;$ $i = 7\%$

$$\begin{aligned} FVA_n &= PMT \times \left[\frac{(1+i)^n - 1}{i}\right] \\ &= \$1{,}250 \times \frac{(1.07)^3 - 1}{0.07} = \$1{,}250 \times 3.2149 \\ &= \mathbf{\$4{,}018.63} \end{aligned}$$

18. Solution:

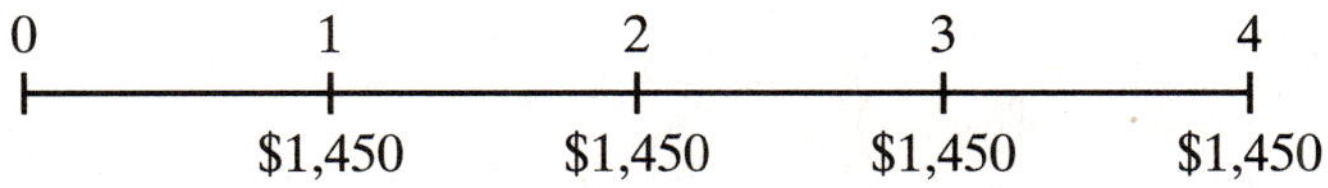

$n = 4;$ $i = 6\%$

$$\begin{aligned} FVA_n &= PMT \times \left[\frac{(1+i)^n - 1}{i}\right] \\ &= \$1{,}450 \times \frac{(1.06)^4 - 1}{0.06} = \$1{,}450 \times 4.3746 \\ &= \mathbf{\$6{,}343.19} \end{aligned}$$

19. Solution:

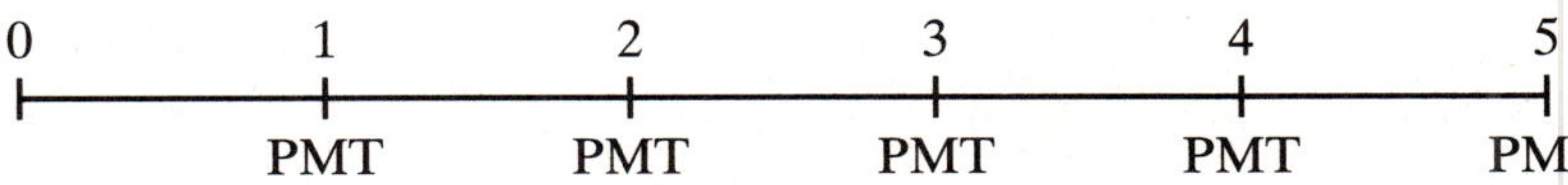

$n = 5;$ $i = 8\%$ **FVA = $25,000**

$$\begin{aligned} FVA_n &= PMT \times \left[\frac{(1+i)^n - 1}{i}\right] \\ \$25{,}000 &= PMT \times \frac{(1.08)^5 - 1}{0.08} \\ PMT &= \frac{\$25{,}000}{\left[\frac{(1.08)^5 - 1}{0.08}\right]} = \frac{\$25{,}000}{5.8666} \\ &= \mathbf{\$4{,}261.41} \end{aligned}$$

20. Solution:

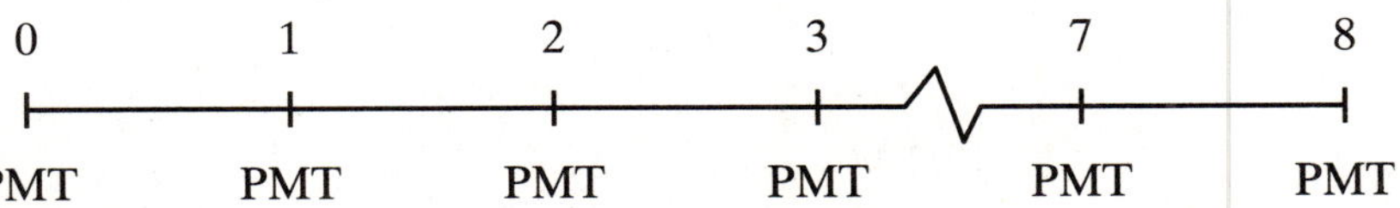

$\mathbf{PVA_n = \$27{,}850}$ $n = 8;$ $i = 8.5\%$

Present value of annuity = PVA = $27,850

Return on investment = i = 8.5%

Payment required to meet target = PMT

Using the PVA equation:

$$PVA_n = PMT \times \left[\frac{1 - \dfrac{1}{(1+i)^n}}{i}\right](1+i)$$

$$PMT = \frac{\$27{,}850}{\left[\dfrac{1 - \dfrac{1}{(1.085)^8}}{0.085}\right]} = \frac{\$27{,}850}{5.6392}$$

$$= \mathbf{\$4{,}938.66}$$

Each payment made by Jackson Electricals will be $4,938.66, starting at the end of next year.

21. Solution:

Annual payment needed = PMT = $20,000

Investment rate of return = i = 9%

Term of payment = Perpetuity.

Present value of investment needed = PV

$$\text{PV of Perpetuity} = \frac{PMT}{i} = \frac{\$20{,}000}{0.09}$$

$$= \mathbf{\$222{,}222.22}$$

22. Solution:

Annual payment needed = PMT

Present value of investment = PVA = $500,000

Investment rate of return = i = 10%

Term of payment = Perpetuity.

$$\text{PV of Perpetuity} = \frac{PMT}{i}$$

$$\boldsymbol{PMT} = \text{PV of Perpetuity} \times i$$

$$= \$500{,}000 \times 0.10$$

$$= \mathbf{\$50{,}000}$$

23. Solution:

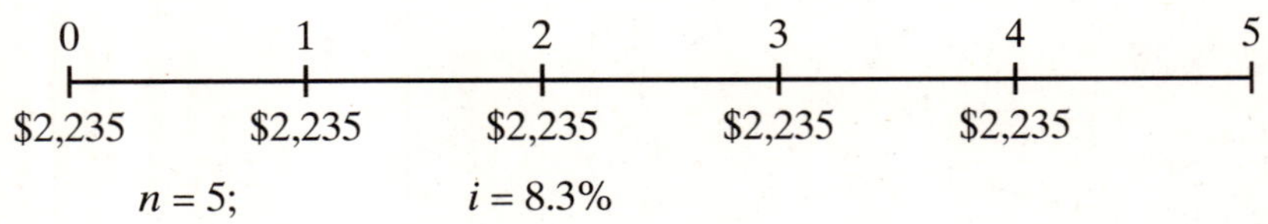

Annual payment = PMT = $2,235

No. of payments = n = 5

Required rate of return = 8.3%

Present value of investment = PVA_5

$$PVA = PMT \times \left[\frac{1 - \dfrac{1}{(1+i)^n}}{i}\right] \times (1+i)$$

$$= \$2{,}235 \times \left[\frac{1 - \dfrac{1}{(1.083)^5}}{0.083}\right] \times (1.083)$$

$$= \$2{,}235 \times 3.9613 \times 1.083$$

$$= \mathbf{\$9{,}588.44}$$

24. Solution:

Cash flow at $t = 1 = CF_1 = \$10{,}000$

Annual growth rate $= g = 3\%$

Discount rate $= i = 6.5\%$

Present value of growing perpetuity $= PVA_\infty$

$$PVA_\infty = \frac{CF_1}{(i - g)} = \frac{\$10{,}000}{(0.065 - 0.03)}$$

$= \mathbf{\$285{,}714.29}$

25. Solution:

Loan amount $= PV = \$152{,}300$

Interest rate on loan $= i = 11.75\%$

Frequency of compounding $= m = 365$

Effective annual rate $= EAR$

$$EAR = \left[1 + \frac{i}{m}\right]^{m \times 1} - 1 = \left[1 + \frac{0.1175}{365}\right]^{365} - 1$$

$= 1.12455 - 1 = \mathbf{12.46}\%$

CHAPTER 7

Risk and Return

LEARNING OBJECTIVES

1. Explain the relation between risk and return.
2. Describe the two components of a total holding period return, and calculate this return for an asset.
3. Explain what an expected return is, and calculate the expected return for an asset.
4. Explain what the standard deviation of returns is, explain why it is especially useful in finance, and be able to calculate it.
5. Explain the concept of diversification.
6. Discuss which type of risk matters to investors and why.
7. Describe what the Capital Asset Pricing Model (CAPM) tells us and how to use it to evaluate whether the expected return of an asset is sufficient to compensate an investor for the risks associated with that asset.

I. Chapter Outline

7.1 Risk and Return

- The greater the risk, the larger the return investors require as compensation for bearing that risk.
- Higher risk means you are less certain.

7.2 Quantitative Measures Return

A. *Holding Period Returns*

- The total holding period return consists of two components: (1) capital appreciation and (2) income. The capital appreciation component of a return, R_{CA}:

$$R_{CA} = \frac{\text{Capital Appreciation}}{\text{Initial Price}} = \frac{P_1 - P_0}{P_0} = \frac{\Delta P}{P_0},$$

where P_0 is the price paid for the asset at time zero, and P_1 is the price at a later point in time.

- The income component of a return R_I:

$$R_I = \frac{\text{Cash Flow}}{\text{Initial Price}} = \frac{CF_1}{P_0},$$

where CF_1 is the cash flow from the dividend.

- The total holding period return is simply

$$R_T = R_{CA} + R_I = \frac{\Delta P}{P_0} + \frac{CF_1}{P_0} = \frac{\Delta P + CF_1}{P_0}.$$

B. *Expected Returns*

- Expected value represents the sum of the products of the possible outcomes and the probabilities that those outcomes will be realized.
- The expected return, $E(R_{Asset})$, is an average of the possible returns from an investment, where each of these returns is weighted by the probability that it will occur:

$$E(R_{Asset}) = \sum_{i=1}^{n}(p_i \times R_i) = (p_1 \times R_1) + (p_2 \times R_2) + \ldots. + (p_n \times R_n).$$

When setting up the problem, make sure that the sum of the p_i's is equal to one, which means you have considered every possible result that can happen.

- If each of the possible outcomes is equally likely (that is, $p_1 = p_2 = p_3 = \ldots = p_n = p = 1/n$), this formula reduces to:

$$E(R_{Asset}) = \frac{\sum_{i=1}^{n}(R_i)}{n} = \frac{R_1 + R_2 + \ldots + R_n}{n}.$$

Many times we call that the simple average.

7.3 The Variance and Standard Deviation as Measures of Risk

A. *Calculating the Variance and Standard Deviation*

- The **variance** $(\sigma)^2$ squares the difference between each possible occurrence and the mean (squaring the differences makes all the numbers positive) and multiplies each difference by its associated probability before summing them up:

$$\text{Var}(R) = \sigma_R^2 = \sum_{i=1}^{n}(p_i \times [R_i - E(R)]^2)$$

- If all of the possible outcomes are equally likely, then the formula becomes:

$$\sigma_R^2 = \frac{\sum_{i=1}^{n}[R_i - E(R)]^2}{n}.$$

Note that we are not dividing by $n - 1$, which is what we would do if the data that we were using was an historical sampling of the data. We divide by $n - 1$ in that case to correct for bias.

- Take the square root of the variance to get the **standard deviation (σ)**.

B. *Interpreting the Variance and Standard Deviation*

- The **normal distribution** is a symmetric frequency distribution that is completely described by its mean (average) and standard deviation.
- The normal distribution is symmetric in that the left and right sides are mirror images of each other. The mean falls directly in the center of the distribution, and the probability that an outcome is a particular distance from the mean is the same whether the outcome is on the left or the right side of the distribution.
  - o The standard deviation tells us the probability that an outcome will fall a particular distance from the mean or within a particular range:

Number of Standard Deviations from the Mean	Fraction of Total Observations Within the Indicated Number of Standard Deviations of the Mean
1.000	68.26%
1.645	90%
1.960	95%
2.575	99%

  - o Example: if the expected return for an asset is 30 percent and the standard deviation is 5 percent, then 90 percent of the observations should be between $(0.3 - (1.645 \times 0.05))$ and $(0.3 + (1.645 \times 0.05))$

C. *Historical Market Performance*

- The key point is that, on average, annual returns have been higher for riskier securities. For instance, Exhibit 8.4 shows that small stocks, which have the largest standard deviation of total returns, also have the largest average return. On the other end of the spectrum, Treasury bills have the smallest standard deviation and the smallest average annual return.

7.4 Risk and Diversification

- By investing in two or more assets whose values do not always move in the same direction at the same time, an investor can reduce the risk of his or her investments, or portfolio.
  - This is the idea behind the concept of diversification.

A. *Single-Asset Portfolios*

- Returns for individual stocks from one day to the next have been found to be largely independent of each other and approximately normally distributed.
- A first pass at comparing risk and return for individual stocks is the coefficient of variation, CV, $CV_i = \frac{\sigma_{R_i}}{E(R_i)}$. A lower value for the CV is what we are looking for in a stock.

B. *Portfolios with More Than One Asset*

- The coefficient of variation has a critical shortcoming that is not quite evident when we are only considering a single asset.
- The expected return of a portfolio is made up of two assets: $E(R_{Portfolio}) = x_1E(R_1) + x_2E(R_2)$, where x_i = the proportion of the portfolio that is invested in asset i.
- The expected return of a portfolio is made up of multiple assets:

$$E(R_{Portfolio}) = \sum_{i=1}^{n}(x_i \times E(R_i))$$
$$= (x_1 \times E(R_1)) + (x_2 \times E(R_2)) + ... + (x_n \times E(R_n)).$$

- The expected return of each asset must be found before applying either of these two formulas. The fraction of the portfolio invested in each asset must also be known.
- The prices of two stocks in a portfolio will rarely, if ever, change by the same amount or proportion and in the same direction at the same time.
- When the stock prices move in opposite directions, the change in the price of one stock offsets at least some of the change in the price of the other stock.
- As a result, the level of risk for a portfolio of the two stocks is less than the average of the risks associated with the individual shares.
- $\sigma^2_{R_{2\ \text{Asset Portfolio}}} = x_1^2\sigma^2_{R_1} + x_2^2\sigma^2_{R_2} + 2x_1x_2\sigma_{R_{12}}$
- $\sigma_{R1,2}$ is the **covariance** between stocks 1 and 2. The covariance is a measure of how the returns on two assets covary, or move together:

$$\text{Cov}(R_1, R_2) = \sigma_{R_{12}} = \sum_{i=1}^{n}(p_i \times [(R_{1,i} - E(R_1)] \times [(R_{2,i} - E(R_2)])$$

- The covariance calculation is very similar to the variance calculation. The difference is that, instead of squaring the difference between the value from each outcome and the expected value for an individual asset, we calculate the product of this difference for two different assets.
- In order to ease the interpretation of the covariance, we divide the covariance by the product of the standard deviations of the returns for the two assets. This gives us the correlation coefficient between the returns on the two assets, $\rho = \frac{\sigma_{R_{12}}}{\sigma_{R_1}\sigma_{R_2}}$.
- The value of the correlation between the returns on two assets will always have a value between −1 and +1.
  - A *negative correlation* means that the returns tend to have opposite signs.
  - A *positive correlation* means that when the return on one asset is positive, the return on the other asset also tends to be positive.
  - A *correlation of 0* means that the returns on the assets are not correlated.
- If we have imperfect correlation between assets, or a correlation coefficient less than +1, then we have a benefit from diversification by holding more than one asset with different risk characteristics.
- As we add more and more stocks to a portfolio, calculating the variance becomes increasingly complex because we have to account for the covariance between each pair of assets.

C. *The Limits of Diversification*

- If the returns on the individual stocks added to our portfolio do not all change in the same way, then increasing the number of stocks in the portfolio will reduce the standard deviation of the portfolio returns even further.
- However, the decrease in the standard deviation for the portfolio gets smaller and smaller as more assets are added.

- As the number of assets becomes very large, the portfolio standard deviation does not approach zero. It only decreases so far.
- That is because investors can diversify away risk that is unique to the individual assets, but they cannot diversify away risk that is common to all assets.
- The risk that can be diversified away is called **diversifiable, unsystematic, or unique risk** and the risk that cannot be diversified away is called **nondiversifiable, or systematic risk**.
- Most of the risk-reduction benefits from diversification can be achieved in a portfolio with 15 to 20 assets.

7.5 Systematic Risk

- With complete diversification, all of the unique risk is eliminated from the portfolio but the investor still faces systematic risk.

A. *Why Systematic Risk Is All That Matters*

- Diversified investors face only systematic risk, whereas investors whose portfolios are not well diversified face systematic risk plus unsystematic risk.
- Because diversified investors face less risk, they will be willing to pay higher prices (and accept lower expected returns) for individual assets than the other investors.
- Therefore, expected returns on individual assets will be lower than the total risk (systematic plus unsystematic risk) of those assets suggests they should be.
- Only systematic risk is rewarded in asset markets and this is why we are only concerned about systematic risk when we think about the relation between risk and return in finance.

B. *Measuring Systematic Risk*

- If systematic risk is all that matters when we think about expected returns, then we cannot use the standard deviation as a measure of risk since the standard deviation is a measure of total risk.
- Since systematic risk is, by definition, risk that cannot be diversified away, the systematic risk (or **market risk**) of an individual asset is really just a measure of the relation between the returns on the individual asset and the returns on the market, which is the ultimate diversified portfolio.
- We quantify the relation between the returns on a stock and the general market by finding the slope of the *line of best fit* between the returns of the stock and the general market.
- We call the slope of the line of best fit **beta**.
- If the beta of an asset is:
  - o equal to one, then the asset has the same systematic risk as the market.
  - o greater than one, then the asset has more systematic risk than the market.
  - o less than one, then the asset has less systematic risk than the market.
  - o equal to zero, then the asset has the no systematic risk.

7.6 Compensation for Bearing Systematic Risk

- The difference between required returns on government securities and required returns for risky investments represents the compensation investors require for taking risk: $E(R_i) = R_{rf} + \text{Compensation for taking risk}_i$.
- If we recognize that the compensation for taking risk varies with asset risk and that systematic risk is what matters, we find:

  $E(R_i) = R_{rf} + (\text{Units of systematic risk}_i \times \text{Compensation per unit of systemic risk})$
- If beta, β, is the appropriate measure for the number of units of systematic risk, we find:

  Compensation for taking risk $= \beta \times$ Compensation per unit of systemic risk
- The required rate of return on the market, over and above that of the risk-free return, represents compensation required by investors for bearing a market (systematic) risk:

  Compensation per unit of risk $= E(R_m) - R_{rf}$
- Which brings us to the equation for expected return:

  $E(R_i) = R_{rf} + \beta_i(E(R_m) - R_{rf})$

7.7 The Capital Asset Pricing Model

- The **Capital Asset Pricing Model (CAPM)** is a model that describes the relation between risk and expected return. The equation that relates risk and return is $E(R_i) = R_{rf} + \beta_i(E(R_m) - R_{rf})$.

A. *The Security Market Line*

- **The Security Market Line (SML)** is the line described by:

$$E(R_i) = R_{rf} + \beta_i(E(R_m) - R_{rf})$$

- The SML illustrates what the CAPM predicts the expected total return should be for various values of beta. The actual expected total return depends on the price of the asset:

$$R_T + \frac{\Delta P + CF_1}{P_0}.$$

If an asset's price implies that the expected return is greater than that predicted by the CAPM, that asset will plot above the SML.

B. *The Capital Asset Pricing Model and Portfolio Returns*

- The expected return for a portfolio:

$$E(R_{n\text{ Asset portfolio}}) = R_{rf} + \beta_{n\text{ Asset portfolio}}(E[R_m] - R_{rf})$$

- The expected return of a portfolio:

$$E(R_{\text{Portfolio}}) = \sum_{i=1}^{n}(x_i \times E(R_i))$$

$$= (x_1 \times E(R_1)) + (x_2 \times E(R_2)) + \ldots. + (x_n \times E(R_n)).$$

- $\beta_{n\ Asset\ Portfolio} = \sum_{i=1}^{n} x_i\beta_i = x_1\beta_1 + x_2\beta_2 + x_3\beta_3 + \ldots + x_n\beta_n.$

II. Suggested Approach to Material

This is a key chapter in that it addresses the measurable aspect of the risk and return relationship for assets. The chapter begins with simple statistical concepts of expected return and variance/standard deviation. The chapter quickly points out that these simple statistical tools do not properly capture the correct measure of risk for an asset. Covariance and correlation coefficients are then introduced for their impact on the variance of a multiasset portfolio where the benefits of diversification can be easily seen. The difference between systematic and nonsystematic risk is then discussed as well as the need for a new measure of the systematic risk component, separate from the nonsystematic risk component. Beta is then introduced as well as the intuitional arguments for the CAPM and the SML and the SML equation. Applications for all of the concepts are spread throughout the chapter.

The basis for how a student should approach this chapter depends on the statistical background of that student. Less prepared students may need to take time to review statistical concepts before proceeding. Regardless of the level of student preparedness, this chapter holds important intuitional arguments that will be required for future material such as the cost of capital, capital budgeting, and dividends.

III. Chapter Glossary

Total holding period return	The total return on an asset over a specific period of time or holding period.
Expected return	An average of the possible returns from an investment, where each return is weighted by the probability that it will occur.
Variance (σ^2)	A measure of the uncertainty surrounding an outcome.
Standard deviation (σ)	The square root of the variance.
Normal distributions	A symmetric frequency distribution that is completely described by its mean and standard deviation. Also known as a bell curve due to its shape.
Portfolio	The collection of assets an investor owns.
Diversification	A strategy of reducing risk by investing in two or more assets whose values do not always move in the same direction at the same time.

Coefficient of variation (CV)	A measure of the risk associated with an investment for each 1 percent of expected return.
Covariance	A measure of how the returns on two assets covary, or move together.
Diversifiable, unsystematic, or unique risk	Risk that can be eliminated through diversification.
Nondiversifiable or systematic risk	Risk that cannot be eliminated through diversification.
Market portfolio	The portfolio of all assets.
Market risk	A term commonly used to refer to nondiversifiable, or systematic, risk.
Beta (β)	A measure of nondiversifiable, systematic, or market risk.
Capital Asset Pricing Model (CAPM)	A model that describes the relation between risk and expected return.
Security Market Line (SML)	A plot of the relation between expected return and systematic risk.

IV. Summary of Key Equations

Equation	Description	Formula
7.1	Total holding period return	$R_T = R_{CA} + R_I = \frac{P_1 - P_0}{P_0} + \frac{CF_1}{P_0}$
7.2	Expected return on an asset	$E(R_{Asset}) = \sum_{i=1}^{n}(p_i \times R_i)$
7.3	Variance of return on an asset	$Var(R) = \sigma_R^2 = \sum_{i=1}^{n}\left(p_i \times [R_i - E(R)]^2\right)$
7.4	Coefficient of variation	$CV_i = \frac{\sigma_{R_i}}{E(R_i)}$
7.5	Expected return for a portfolio	$E(R_{Portfolio}) = \sum_{i=1}^{n}\left(x_i \times E(R_i)\right)$
7.6	Variance for a two-asset portfolio	$\sigma^2_{R_{2\,AssetPortfolio}} = x_1^2\sigma^2_{R_1} + x_2^2\sigma^2_{R_2} + 2x_1x_2\sigma_{R_{12}}$
7.7	Covariance between two assets	$\sigma_{R_{12}} = \sum_{i=1}^{n}\left(p_i \times [(R_{1,i} - E(R_1)] \times [(R_{2,i} - E(R_2)]\right)$
7.8	Correlation between two assets	$\rho = \frac{\sigma_{R_{12}}}{\sigma_{R_1}\sigma_{R_2}}$
7.9	Expected return and systematic risk	$E(R_i) = R_{rf} + \beta_i(E(R_m) - R_{rf})$
7.10	Portfolio beta	$\beta_{nAssetPortfolio} = \sum_{i=1}^{n} x_i\beta_i$

V. True or False Questions

1. Expected return is the average of the possible returns from an investment, where each return is weighted by the probability that it will occur.

   a. True

   b. False

2. The normal distribution is completely described by its mean and standard deviation where 40 percent of the distribution's probability is less than the mean and 60 percent is greater than the mean.
   a. True
   b. False

3. An assets return from capital appreciation is comprised of the total holding period return and the return from income.
   a. True
   b. False

4. The appropriate measure of risk for a one-stock portfolio is a measure of total risk.
   a. True
   b. False

5. The appropriate measure of risk for a diversified portfolio is a measure of total risk.
   a. True
   b. False

6. The coefficient of variation tells us the level of systematic risk per unit of return that an asset is currently priced to provide.
   a. True
   b. False

7. The coefficient of variation is useful if you are interested in the risk/return relationship in stocks that will be held in a portfolio that is not diversified (assume that it is completely undiversified).
   a. True
   b. False

8. If the assets in a portfolio have a correlation coefficient less than one with each other, then the variance of the portfolio will be less than the value-weighted average of the variance of the individual stocks in that portfolio.
   a. True
   b. False

9. The expected return of the market portfolio is equal to that of the risk-free risk security.
   a. True
   b. False

10. Complete diversification implies that the beta of the portfolio is equal to one.
   a. True
   b. False

VI. Multiple-Choice Questions

1. Expected returns will always be which of the following?
   a. Less than the probabilistically weighted average of the returns in a portfolio.
   b. Less than the probabilistically weighted average of squared returns in a portfolio.
   c. Equal to the probabilistically weighted average of the returns in a portfolio.
   d. Equal to the probabilistically weighted average of the squared returns in a portfolio.

2. In a drawing for a prize, the probability of drawing a $10 prize is 30 percent and the probability of drawing a $20 prize is 70 percent. What is the expected value of a prize in this drawing?

a. $10
b. $15
c. $17
d. $20

3. Which of the following tools would be most appropriate for understanding which of two stocks to invest in a single-holding portfolio?

a. the coefficient of variation for each of the two stocks
b. the correlation coefficient between the two stocks
c. the covariance between the two stocks
d. the beta of the two stocks

4. The CAPM could be used to price which of the following assets?

a. commons stocks
b. bonds
c. preferred stocks
d. all of the above

5. Two stocks are combined in equal dollar amounts in a portfolio. If the standard deviation of the returns of Stock 1 is 0.2 and the standard deviation of the returns of Stock 2 is 0.4, then what is the standard deviation of the portfolio if the correlation coefficient between the returns of the two stocks is exactly 1.0?

a. 0.09
b. 0.20
c. 0.30
d. 0.40

6. Two stocks are combined in a portfolio where 20 percent is invested in Stock 1 and 80 percent is invested in Stock 2. If the standard deviation of the returns of Stock 1 is 0.2 and the standard deviation of the returns of Stock 2 is 0.4, then what is the standard deviation of the portfolio if the correlation coefficient between the returns of the two stocks is exactly 1.0?

a. 0.1296
b. 0.3000
c. 0.3600
d. 0.4000

7. Two stocks are combined in equal dollar amounts in a portfolio. If the standard deviation of the returns of Stock 1 is 0.2 and the standard deviation of the returns of Stock 2 is 0.4, then what is the standard deviation of the portfolio if the correlation coefficient between the returns of the two stocks is 0.5? Choose the closest answer.

a. 0.0700
b. 0.2646
c. 0.3000
d. 0.4000

8. Stock A, with an expected return of 8 percent, Stock B, with an expected return of 12 percent, and Stock C, with an expected return of 15 percent are invested in a portfolio. Half of the portfolio will be invested in A, while 30 percent will be invested in B, with the remainder in C. What is the expected return of the portfolio?

a. 0.080
b. 0.106
c. 0.116
d. 0.120

9. If you are an investor who is not diversified, then you should expect to be compensated for

a. taking on the systematic risk associated with each particular investment.
b. taking on only the unique risk associated with each particular investment.
c. taking on only the nonsystematic risk associated with each particular investment.
d. taking on all risks associated with each particular investment.

10. One premise of the Capital Asset Pricing Model is that

a. diversified investors will not need to be compensated for taking on risk that they do not incur.

b. diversified investors are concerned about unique risk, but they cannot be compensated for taking on such risk.

c. nondiversified investors do not concern themselves with unique risk.

d. nondiversified investors do not incur unique risk on their investments.

11. Which of the following is not included in the Security Market Line equation?

a. the expected return on the market

b. the market risk premium

c. the beta of the asset being priced

d. the beta of the market portfolio

12. A beta of 2.0 for a stock suggests that

a. the market portfolio return is twice as risky as that of the stock in question.

b. the market portfolio return is twice as much as that of the stock in question.

c. the return of the stock in question is twice as risky as that of the market portfolio return.

d. the return of the stock in question is twice as much as that of the market portfolio return.

13. The best measure for the amount of systematic risk in the return of an asset is

a. the standard deviation of the asset's return.

b. the beta of the asset's return.

c. the covariance between the asset and the market return.

d. the correlation coefficient between the asset and the market return.

14. You are going to invest 10 percent of your portfolio in the risk-free asset and 90 percent of the portfolio in a stock mutual fund with a beta of 1.5. What will be the beta of your new portfolio?

a. 0.750

b. 0.900

c. 0.135

d. 0.150

15. You are going to invest 10 percent of your portfolio in the market portfolio and 90 percent of the portfolio in a stock mutual fund with a beta of 1.5. What will be the beta of your new portfolio?

a. 0.125

b. 0.145

c. 0.148

d. 0.150

16. The beta for a mystery stock is 1.25, while the expected return on the market is 15 percent. If the risk-free rate is currently 10 percent, then what is the expected return on the mystery stock?

a. 0.1500

b. 0.1625

c. 0.2250

d. 0.2875

17. The expected return for Velma Stock is 25 percent. If the risk-free rate is currently 10 percent while the expected return on the market is 20 percent, then what is Velma's beta?

a. 1.25

b. 1.50

c. 1.75

d. 2.00

18. The expected return for Shaggy Stock is 25 percent. If the risk-free rate is currently 10 percent while the expected return on the market is 25 percent, then what is Shaggy's beta?

a. 0.75

b. 1.00

c. 1.25

d. 2.00

19. When looking at the graph of the Security Market Line, what is the interpretation of where the line crosses the return axis (y-axis)?

a. The Security Market Line crosses the return axis at the expected rate of return for the market.

b. The Security Market Line crosses the return axis at the risk-free rate of return.

c. The Security Market Line crosses the return axis at the expected rate of return for the stock in question.

d. The Security Market Line crosses the return axis at the market risk premium.

20. Which of the following is true?

a. As you add more and more stocks to your portfolio, the beta of your portfolio will decrease.

b. As you add more and more stocks to your portfolio, the beta of your portfolio will move closer to one since your portfolio is behaving more like the market portfolio.

c. As you add more and more stocks to your portfolio, the beta of your portfolio decreases because you are eliminating the unique risk from your portfolio.

d. All of the above are true.

Answers to True or False Questions

1. a	**2.** b	**3.** b	**4.** a	**5.** b
6. b	**7.** a	**8.** a	**9.** b	**10.** a

Answers to Multiple-Choice Questions

1. c	**2.** c	**3.** a	**4.** d	**5.** c
6. c	**7.** b	**8.** b	**9.** a	**10.** a
11. d	**12.** c	**13.** b	**14.** c	**15.** b
16. b	**17.** b	**18.** b	**19.** b	**20.** b

Solutions to Multiple-Choice Questions

2. (0.3)($10) + (0.7)($20) = $17

5. We know that the variance of a two-stock portfolio is given by

$$\sigma^2_{R_{2\ \text{Asset Portfolio}}} = x_1^2\sigma^2_{R_1} + x_2^2\sigma^2_{R_2} + 2x_1x_2\sigma_{R_{12}}$$

We can use the fact that the correlation coefficient between two stocks can be written in terms of the variance of the portfolio below:

$$\rho = \frac{\sigma_{R_{12}}}{\sigma_{R_1}\sigma_{R_2}}.$$

Now, the variance between the two stocks can be written in terms of the correlation coefficient and the standard deviation of the returns of the individual stocks. We also know that 50 percent of the portfolio was invested in each of the two stocks.

Variance of Portfolio = $(0.5)^2(0.2)^2 + (0.5)^2(0.4)^2 + 2(0.5)(0.5)(0.2)(0.4)(1) = 0.09$

The standard deviation of the portfolio is the square root of the variance, which is $(0.09)^{0.5} = 0.03$

6. Using the same logic as with Problem 5, we find:
Variance of Portfolio = $(0.2)^2(0.2)^2 + (0.8)^2(0.4)^2 + 2(0.2)(0.8)(0.2)(0.4)(1) = 0.1296$
The standard deviation of the portfolio is the square root of the variance, which is $(0.1296)^{0.5} = 0.36$

7. Using the same logic as used with Problem 5, we find:
Variance of Portfolio = $(0.5)^2(0.2)^2 + (0.5)^2(0.4)^2 + 2(0.5)(0.5)(0.2)(0.4)(0.5) = 0.07$
The standard deviation of the portfolio is the square root of the variance, which is $(0.07)^{0.5} = 0.264575$

8. $(0.08)(0.5) + (0.12)(0.3) + (0.15)(0.2) = 0.106$ (Note that 20 percent must be invested in Stock C since the other 80 percent of the portfolio is invested in the other two stocks.)

14. Since the beta of the risk-free asset is zero, then $(0.1)(0) + (0.9)(0.15) = 0.135$.

15. Since the beta of the market portfolio is one, then $(0.1)(1) + (0.9)(0.15) = 0.145$.

16. Using $E(R_i) = R_{rf} + \beta_i(E(R_m) - R_{rf})$, we have $E(R_i) = 0.1 + 1.25(0.15 - 0.1) = 0.1625$.

17. Using $E(R_i) = R_{rf} + \beta_i(E(R_m) - R_{rf})$, we have $0.25 = 0.1 + \beta\,(0.2 - 0.1) \longrightarrow \beta = 1.5$.

18. Using $E(R_i) = R_{rf} + \beta_i(E(R_m) - R_{rf})$, we have $0.25 = 0.1 + \beta\,(0.25 - 0.1) \longrightarrow \beta = 1.0$.

CHAPTER 8

Bond Valuation and the Structure of Interest Rates

LEARNING OBJECTIVES

1. Explain what an efficient capital market is and why "market efficiency" is important to financial managers.
2. Describe the market for corporate bonds and three types of corporate bonds.
3. Explain how to calculate the price of a bond and why bond prices vary negatively with interest rate movements.
4. Distinguish between a bond's coupon rate, yield to maturity, and effective annual yield, and be able to calculate their values.
5. Explain why investors in bonds are subject to interest rate risk and why it is important to understand the bond theorems.
6. Discuss the concept of default risk and know how to compute a default risk premium.
7. Describe the factors that determine the level and shape of the yield curve.

I. Chapter Outline

8.1 Capital Market Efficiency

A. ***Overview***

- A **security's true value** is the price that reflects investors' estimates of the value of the cash flows they expect to receive in the future.
- In an **efficient capital market,** security prices fully reflect the knowledge and expectations of all investors at a particular point in time.
    - o The overall efficiency of a capital market depends on its ***operational efficiency*** and its ***informational efficiency***.
    - o Markets exhibit **informational efficiency** if market prices reflect all relevant information about securities at a particular point in time.

B. ***Efficient Market Hypotheses***

- Prices of securities adjust as the buying and selling from investors lead to the price that truly reflects the market's consensus. This reflects the market's efficiency.
- Market efficiency can be explained at three levels—strong form, semistrong form, and weak form.
    - o **Strong-form** market efficiency states that the price of a security in the market reflects all information—public as well as private or inside information.

- o **Semistrong** market efficiency implies that only public information that is available to all investors is reflected in a security's market price.
- o In **weak-form** market efficiency, all information contained in past prices of a security is reflected in current prices.

8.2 Corporate Bonds

A. ***Market for Corporate Bonds***

- The largest investors in corporate bonds are life insurance companies and pension funds, with trades in this market tending to be in very large blocks of securities.
- Less than 1 percent of all corporate bonds are traded on exchanges.
- The market for corporate bonds is *thin* compared to the market for money market securities or corporate stocks. A thin market implies that trading for bonds is not as frequent as that for other securities.
- Corporate bonds are less marketable than the securities that have higher daily trading volumes.

B. ***Bond Price Information***

- The corporate bond market is not considered to be very transparent because it trades predominantly over the counter and investors do not find it easy to view prices and trading volume.
- In addition, many corporate bond transactions are negotiated between the buyer and the seller, and there is little centralized reporting of these deals.

C. ***Types of Corporate Bonds***

- There are three types of corporate bonds—vanilla bonds, zero coupon bonds, and convertible bonds.

1. Vanilla Bonds

- These bonds have coupon payments that are fixed for the life of the bond, and at maturity, the principal is paid and the bonds are retired.
- Vanilla bonds have no special provisions, and the provisions they do have are conventional and common to most bonds, such as a call provision.
- Payments are usually made annually or semiannually.
- The **face value,** or **par value,** for most corporate bonds is $1,000.

2. Zero Coupon Bonds

- Corporations sometimes issue bonds that have no coupon payments over their life and only offer a single payment at maturity.
- Zero coupon bonds sell well below their face value (at a deep discount) because they offer no coupons.

3. Convertible Bonds

- These are bonds that can be converted into shares of common stock at some predetermined ratio at the discretion of the bondholder.
- The convertible feature allows the bondholders to share in the good fortunes of the firm if the firm's stock rises above a certain level.

8.3 Bond Valuation

- The value, or price, of any asset is the present value of its future cash flows.
- The general equation for the price of a bond can be written as follows in Equation 8.1:

$$P_B = \frac{C_1}{1+i} + \frac{C_2}{(1+i)^2} + \ldots + \frac{C_n + F_n}{(1+i)^n}$$

Alternatively, we can use the present value annuity factor from chapter 6 and the present value equation from chapter 5 to solve for the price of the bond.

$$P_B = \frac{C_1}{(1+i)^1} + \frac{C_2}{(1+i)^2} + \frac{C_3}{(1+i)^3} + \ldots\ldots + \frac{C_n + F}{(1+i)^n}$$

$$= C \times \left[\frac{1 - \frac{1}{(1+i)^n}}{i}\right] + \frac{F}{(1+i)^n}$$

A. *Par, Premium, and Discount Bonds*

- If a bond's coupon rate is equal to the market rate, then the bond will sell at a price equal to its face value. Such bonds are called **par** bonds.
- If a bond's coupon rate is less than the market rate, then the bond will sell at a price that is less than its face value. Such bonds are called **discount** bonds.
- If a bond's coupon rate is greater than the market rate, then the bond will sell at a price that is more than its face value. Such bonds are called **premium** bonds.

B. *Semiannual Compounding*

- While bonds in Europe pay annual coupons, bonds in the United States pay coupons semiannually.
- In calculating the current price of a bond paying semiannual coupons, one needs to modify Equation 8.1.

$$P_B = \frac{\$C_1/m}{(1+i/m)} + \frac{\$C_2/m}{(1+i/m)^2} + \frac{\$C_3/m}{(1+i/m)^3} + \ldots\ldots + \frac{(\$C_{mn}/m) + F_{mn}}{(1+i/m)^{mn}} \quad \textbf{(8.2)}$$

C. *Zero Coupon Bonds*

- Zero coupon bonds have no coupon payments but promise a single payment at maturity.
- Zero coupon bonds, for which all the cash payments are made at maturity, must sell for less than similar bonds that make periodic coupon payments.

8.4 Bond Yields

A. *Yield to Maturity*

- The **yield to maturity** of a bond is the discount rate that makes the present value of the coupon and principal payments equal to the price of the bond.
- We can compute a bond's yield to maturity using a trial-and-error approach.

B. *Effective Annual Yield*

- The correct way to annualize the yield on a bond is as follows:

  EAY = $(1 + \text{Quoted interest rate}/m)^m - 1$

- The simple annual yield is the yield per period multiplied by the number of compounding periods. For bonds with annual compounding, the simple annual yield = semiannual yield × 2.

C. *Realized Yield*

- The **realized yield** is the return earned on a bond given the cash flows *actually* received by the investor.

8.5 Interest Rate Risk

- The prices of bonds fluctuate with changes in interest rates, giving rise to **interest rate risk**.

A. *Bond Theorems*

1. Bond prices are negatively related to interest rate movements.
2. For a given change in interest rates, the prices of long-term bonds will change more than the prices of short-term bonds.
3. For a given change in interest rates, the prices of lower-coupon bonds change more than the prices of higher-coupon bonds.

B. *Bond Theorem Applications*

- If rates are expected to increase, a portfolio manager should avoid investing in long-term securities. The portfolio could see a significant decline in value.
- Similarly, if interest rates are expected to decrease, a portfolio manager should invest in long-term securities. This will lead to the portfolio increasing substantially.

8.6 The Structure of Interest Rates

- Market analysts have identified four risk characteristics of debt instruments that are responsible for most of the differences in corporate borrowing costs: the security's **marketability, call feature, default risk,** and **term to maturity**.

A. *Marketability*

- **Marketability** refers to the ability of an investor to sell a security quickly, at a low transaction cost, and at its fair market value.
- The lower these costs are, the greater a security's marketability.
- U.S. Treasury bills have the largest and most active secondary market and are considered to be the most marketable of all securities.

B. *Call Provision*

- A call provision gives the firm issuing the bonds the option to purchase the bond from an investor at a predetermined price (the call price); the investor must sell the bond at that price.
- When bonds are called, investors suffer a financial loss because they are forced to surrender their high-yielding bonds and reinvest their funds at the lower prevailing market rate of interest.
- Bonds with a call provision sell at higher market yields than comparable noncallable bonds.

C. *Default Risk*

- The risk that the lender may not receive payments as promised is called default risk.
- Investors must be paid a premium to purchase a security that exposes them to default risk.
- U.S. Treasury securities do not have any default risk and are the best proxy measure for the risk-free rate.

D. *Bond Ratings*

- Individuals and small business have to rely on outside agencies to provide them information on the default potential of bonds.
- The two most prominent credit rating agencies are Moody's Investors Service (Moody's) and Standard and Poor's (S&P). Both credit rating services rank bonds in order of their expected probability of default and publish the ratings as letter grades.
- The rating schemes used are shown in **Exhibit 8.5**.
- Bonds in the top four rating categories are called **investment-grade bonds**—AAA to Baa.

E. *The Term Structure of Interest Rates*

- The relationship between yield and term to maturity is known as the **term structure of interest rates**.
- Yield curves show graphically how market yields vary as term to maturity changes.
- The shape of the yield curve is not constant over time.
- There are three basic shapes (slopes) of yield curves in the marketplace.
  - Ascending or **normal** yield curves are upward-sloping yield curves that occur when an economy is growing.
  - Descending or **inverted** yield curves are downward-sloping yield curves that occur when an economy is declining or heading into a recession.
  - Flat yield curves imply that interest rates are unlikely to change in the near future.

F. *The Shape of the Yield Curve*

- Three economic factors determine the shape of the yield curve: (1) the real rate of interest, (2) the expected rate of inflation, and (3) interest rate risk.
  - **The Real Rate of Interest**
    - Changes in the expected future real rate of interest can affect the slope of the yield curve.
  - **The Expected Rate of Inflation**
    - If investors believe that inflation will be increasing in the future, the yield curve will be upward sloping because long-term interest rates will contain a larger inflation premium than short-term interest rates.
    - If investors believe inflation will be subsiding in the future, the prevailing yield will be downward sloping.
  - **Interest Rate Risk**
    - The interest risk premium always adds an upward bias to the slope of the yield curve.

G. *The Cumulative Effect*

- Exhibit 8.6 shows the cumulative effect of the three economic factors that influence the shape of the yield curve: the real rate of interest, the inflation premium, and the interest rate risk premium.
- In a period of economic expansion, both the real rate of interest and the inflation premium increase monotonically over time.
- In a period of contraction, both the real rate of interest and the inflation premium decrease monotonically over time.

II. Suggested Approach to Material

This chapter is all about bonds and how they are valued or priced in the marketplace. The bond valuation models presented in this chapter are derived from the present value materials discussed in Chapters 5 and 6. In the first part of the chapter, the authors discuss the concept of *efficient capital markets*. Next, the discussion centers on the corporate bond market, bond price information that is available, and the types of bonds found in the market. The development of the basic equation used to calculate bond prices follows and leads to the steps required to compute a bond's (1) yield to maturity, (2) realized yield, and (3) effective annual yield. This is followed by a discussion on interest rate risk, and the three bond theorems that describe how bond prices respond to changes in interest rates are identified. The chapter concludes with a discussion on the term structure of interest rates and yield curves.

III. Chapter Glossary

True (intrinsic) value	For a security, price that reflects investors' estimates of the present value of the cash flows they expect to receive in the future.
Efficient capital market	Market where prices reflect the knowledge and expectations of all investors.
Operational efficiency	The degree to which the transactions costs of bringing buyers and sellers together are minimized.
Market informational efficiency	The degree to which current market prices reflect relevant information and therefore the true value of the security.
Efficient market hypothesis	A theory concerning the extent to which information is incorporated in security prices and how information is incorporated into security prices.
Strong-form (of the efficient market hypothesis)	The theory that security prices reflect all available information.
Private information	Information that is not available to all investors.
Semistrong-form (of the efficient market hypothesis)	The theory that security prices reflect all public information but not all private information.
Public information	Information that is available to all investors.
Weak-form (of the efficient market hypothesis)	The theory that security prices reflect all information in past prices but do not reflect all private or all public information.
Fixed-income securities	Debt instruments that pay interest income in amounts fixed for the life of the contract.
Principal	The outstanding balance on a loan.
Coupon payments	The interest payments made to bondholders.
Face value, or **par value**	The amount on which interest is calculated and that is owed to the bondholder when the bond reaches maturity.
Coupon rate	The annual coupon payment of a bond divided by the bond's face value.
Opportunity cost	The alternative return with a similar risk that an investor gives up when he or she makes a certain investment.
Par-value bonds	Bonds that sell at par value, or face value. Whenever a bond's coupon rate is equal to the market rate of interest on similar bonds, the bond will *always* sell at par.
Discount bonds	Bonds that sell at below par value.
Premium bonds	Bonds that sell at above par value.
Yield to maturity	For a bond, the discount rate that makes the present value of the coupon and principal payments equal to the price of the bond.

(Continued)

Effective annual yield (EAY)	The annual yield that takes compounding into account; another name for the *effective annual interest rate (EAR)*.
Realized yield	For a bond, the interest rate at which the present value of the actual cash flows generated by the bond equals the bond's price.
Interest rate risk	Uncertainty caused by the unpredictability of interest rates in the economy.
Default risk	The risk that a bondholder or other lender may not receive payments as promised.
Investment-grade bonds	Bonds placed in the top four rating categories by rating agencies.
Noninvestment-grade bonds	Bonds rated below Baa (or BBB) by rating agencies; often called *speculative grade bonds, high-yield bonds,* or *junk bonds.*
Term structure of interest rates	The relationship between yield and term to maturity.
Yield curve	A graph representing the term structure of interest rates, with the term to maturity on the horizontal axis and the yield on the vertical axis.

IV. Summary of Key Equations

Equation	Description	Formula
8.1	Price of a bond	$P_B = \frac{C_1}{(1+i)^1} + \frac{C_2}{(1+i)^2} + \ldots + \frac{C_n + F_n}{(1+i)^n}$
8.2	Price of a bond semiannual compounding	$P_B = \frac{C_1/m}{(1+i/m)^1} + \frac{C_2/m}{(1+i/m)^2} + \frac{C_3/m}{(1+i/m)^3} + \ldots + \frac{C_{mn}/m + F_{mn}}{(1+i/m)^{mn}}$
8.3	Price of zero coupon bond	$P_B = \frac{F_{mn}}{(1+i/m)^{mn}}$

V. True or False Questions

1. In an efficient capital market, security prices fully reflect only the historical information of a firm at a particular point in time

a. True

b. False

2. Operational efficiency relates to bringing buyers and sellers together at the lowest possible cost.

a. True

b. False

3. In an informationally efficient market, market prices adjust quickly to new information about a security as it becomes available.

a. True

b. False

4. Strong-form market efficiency states that the price of a security in the market reflects both public and private or inside information.

a. True

b. False

5. If a market is semistrong-form market efficient, one will not be able to beat the market with inside information.
   a. True
   b. False

6. Vanilla bonds have special provisions that are not common to most bonds.
   a. True
   b. False

7. The face or par value for most bonds is $100.
   a. True
   b. False

8. Zero coupon bonds have no coupon payments over their life and only offer a single payment at maturity.
   a. True
   b. False

9. The realized yield is the return earned on a bond given the cash flows that are *expected* by the investor.
   a. True
   b. False

10. Short-term bonds have greater price volatility than long-term bonds.
    a. True
    b. False

11. Marketability refers to the ability of an investor to sell a security quickly, at a low transaction cost, and at a price close to its fair market value.
    a. True
    b. False

12. The relationship between yield and term to maturity is known as the term structure of interest rates.
    a. True
    b. False

13. The longer the maturity of a security, the greater its interest rate risk.
    a. True
    b. False

14. As interest rates fall, the prices of bonds decline.
    a. True
    b. False

15. Bonds with a call provision sell at lower market yields than comparable noncallable bonds.
    a. True
    b. False

VI. Multiple-Choice Questions and Problems

1. A security's true price is
   a. the price that reflects investors' estimates of the value of the cash flows they expect to receive in the future.
   b. the price that reflects all the cash flows that investors have received until the present time.
   c. the price arrived at when supply for the security equals the demand for it.
   d. None of the above.

2. Which **ONE** of the following statements is true?
   a. Markets exhibit operational efficiency if market prices reflect all relevant information about securities at a particular point in time.
   b. Operational efficiency focuses on bringing buyers and sellers together at the lowest possible cost.
   c. In an informationally efficient market, market prices take time to adjust to new information about a security as it becomes available.
   d. None of the above are true.

3. Weak-form market efficiency implies that
   a. the price of a security in the market reflects all public information only.
   b. it would be possible to earn abnormally high returns by trading on public information.
   c. investors who have access to inside or private information will be unable to earn abnormal returns.
   d. None of the above.

4. Which **ONE** of the following statements best describes the bond market?
   a. It is the largest market for capital market securities.
   b. Bonds are predominantly traded on exchanges.
   c. The largest investors in corporate bonds are U.S. government agencies.
   d. Corporate bonds have high daily trading volumes.

5. Which **ONE** of the following statements is true?
   a. Corporate bonds are long-term IOUs that represent claims against a firm's assets.
   b. Corporate bonds are fixed-income securities.
   c. Three types of corporate bonds that are traded are vanilla bonds, zero coupon bonds, and convertible bonds.
   d. All of the above are true.

6. Vanilla bonds are bonds
   a. with special provisions.
   b. that make annual or semiannual coupon payments to investors.
   c. with a face value of $10,000
   d. with a variable-rate coupon.

7. Zero coupon bonds
   a. make annual or semiannual coupon payments to investors.
   b. sell well below their face value because they offer no coupons.
   c. are issued only by corporations.
   d. None of the above.

8. To calculate the price of the bond, one must
   a. estimate the expected future cash flows.
   b. determine the required rate of return.
   c. calculate the present value of the bond's expected cash flows.
   d. All of the above steps are required to compute the current price of a bond.

9. Bonds that sell at a price greater than its par value are called
   a. par bonds.
   b. discount bonds.
   c. premium bonds.
   d. convertible bonds.

10. Which **ONE** of the following statements is true?

a. The lower a bond's coupon rate, the greater its price volatility.

b. The lower the bond's coupon rate, the greater the proportion of the bond's cash flow investors will receive at maturity.

c. All other things being equal, a given change in the interest rates will have a greater impact on the price of a low-coupon bond than a higher-coupon bond with the same maturity.

d. All of the above are true.

11. Which **ONE** of the following statements is true?

a. A call provision gives the firm issuing the bonds the option to purchase the bond from an investor.

b. When bonds are called, investors suffer a financial loss because they are forced to surrender their high-yielding bonds and reinvest their funds at the lower prevailing market rate of interest.

c. Bonds with a call provision sell at higher market yields than comparable noncallable bonds.

d. All of the above are true.

12. Normal yield curves are observed when

a. the economy is growing.

b. the economy is stagnant.

c. the economy is in recession.

d. None of the above.

13. Which one of the following statements is **NOT** true?

a. The longer the maturity of a security, the greater its interest rate risk.

b. If investors believe inflation will be subsiding in the future, the prevailing yield will be downward sloping.

c. The real rate of interest varies with the business cycle, with the highest rates seen at the end of a period of business expansion and the lowest at the bottom of a recession.

d. The interest risk premium always adds a downward bias to the slope of the yield curve.

14. Bonds that sell at a price less than its par value are called

a. par bonds.

b. discount bonds.

c. premium bonds.

d. convertible bonds.

15. The yield to maturity of a bond is the discount rate that makes the present value of the coupon and principal payments

a. exceed the price of the bond.

b. equal to zero.

c. equal to the price of the bond.

d. less than the price of the bond.

16. Jack Korner is looking into buying a 15-year bond issued by Jurgen Corp. The bond pays a coupon of 7.5 percent annually. Similar bonds will yield 7 percent in the market now. (Round to the nearest dollar.)

a. $1,046

b. $1,112

c. $910

d. $878

17. Your friend recommends that you invest in a three-year bond issued by Trimer, Inc., that will pay annual coupons of 10 percent. Similar investments today will yield 6 percent. How much should you pay for the bond? (Round to the nearest dollar.)

a. $1,024

b. $979

c. $886

d. $1,107

18. Giant Electronics is issuing 20-year bonds that will pay coupons semiannually. The coupon rate on this bond is 7.8 percent. If the market rate for such bonds is 7 percent, what will the bonds sell for today? (Round to the nearest dollar.)

a. $1,037

b. $1,085

c. $861

d. $923

19. Kevin Oh is planning to sell a bond that he owns. This bond has four years to maturity and pays a coupon of 10 percent on a semiannual basis. Similar bonds in the current market will yield 12 percent. What price will he get for his bond? (Round to the nearest dollar.)

a. $1,044

b. $938

c. $970

d. $1,102

20. Twenty-year zero coupon bonds issued by the James Corp. have a face value of $1,000. Assume annual compounding. If the opportunity cost in the market is 12 percent, what is the market value for these bonds? (Round to the nearest dollar.)

a. $104

b. $1,104

c. $612

d. $893

21. Jarmine Corp. is planning to fund a project by issuing 10-year zero coupon bonds with a face value of $1,000. Assuming semiannual coupons to be the norm, what will be the price of these bonds if the appropriate discount rate is 14 percent?

a. $852

b. $258

c. $419

d. $841

22. Nathan Akpan is planning to invest in a seven-year bond that pays annual coupons at a rate of 7 percent. It is currently selling at $927.23. What is the current market yield on such bonds?

a. 10.4%

b. 9.5%

c. 8.4%

d. 7.5%

23. Jose Rodriguez wants to buy five-year bonds that pay semiannual coupons at a rate of 7.25 percent. They are currently selling at $1,023.90. What is the yield to maturity on these bonds?

a. 6.7%

b. 7.5%

c. 7.9%

d. 6.1%

24. Four years ago you bought a 15-year bond for $812.44. The bond pays a coupon of 12.5 percent semiannually. Today, the bond is priced at $945.90. If you sold the bond today, what would your realized yield be? (Round to the nearest percent.)

a. 17%

b. 18%

c. 12%

d. 15%

25. Shirley invested in a U.S. government bond and earned a semiannual yield of 3.8 percent. The bond pays coupons twice a year. What is the effective annual yield (EAY) on this investment?

a. 7.74%

b. 7.60%

c. 3.80%

d. None of the above

VI. Answers to True or False Questions

1. b	**2.** a	**3.** a	**4.** a	**5.** b
6. b	**7.** b	**8.** a	**9.** b	**10.** b
11. a	**12.** a	**13.** a	**14.** b	**15.** b

VII. Answers to Multiple-Choice Questions

1. a.	**2.** b	**3.** b	**4.** a	**5.** d
6. b	**7.** b	**8.** d	**9.** c	**10.** d
11. d	**12.** a	**13.** d	**14.** b	**15.** c
16. a	**17.** d	**18.** b	**19.** b	**20.** a
21. b	**22.** c	**23.** a	**24.** b	**25.** a

VIII. Solutions to Multiple-Choice Problems

16. Solution:

Years to maturity = n = 15

Coupon rate = C = 7%

Annual coupon = \$1,000 × 0.075 = \$75.00

Current market rate = i = 7%

$$P_B = \frac{C_1}{(1+i)} + \frac{C_2}{(1+i)^2} + \dots\dots\dots + \frac{C_n}{(1+i)^n}$$

$$= C \times \left[\frac{1 - \dfrac{1}{(1+i)^n}}{i}\right] + \frac{F}{(1+i)^n} = \$75 \times \left[\frac{1 - \dfrac{1}{(1.07)^{15}}}{0.07}\right] + \frac{\$1{,}000}{*(1.07)^{15}}$$

$$= \$683.09 + \$362.45 = \mathbf{\$1{,}045.54}$$

17. Solution:

Years to maturity = n = 3

Coupon rate = C = 10%

Annual coupon = $1,000 × 0.10 = $100

Current market rate = i = 6%

$$P_B = \frac{C_1}{(1+i)} + \frac{C_2}{(1+i)^2} + \text{.........} + \frac{C_n}{(1+i)^n}$$

$$= C \times \left[\frac{1 - \frac{1}{(1+i)^n}}{i}\right] + \frac{F}{(1+i)^n} = \$100 \times \left[\frac{1 - \frac{1}{(1.06)^3}}{0.06}\right] + \frac{\$1{,}000}{*(1.06)^3}$$

= $267.30 + $839.62 = **$1,106.92**

18. Solution:

Years to maturity = n = 20

Coupon rate = C = 7.8%

Frequency of payment = m = 2

Semiannual coupon = $1,000 × (0.078/2) = $39.00

Current market rate = i = 7%

Present value of bond = P_B

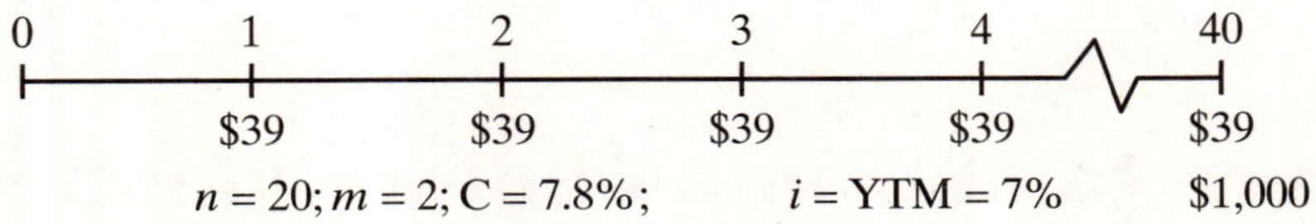

$$P_B = C/2 \times \left[\frac{1 - \frac{1}{(1+i/2)^{2n}}}{i/2}\right] + \frac{F}{(1+i/2)^{2n}} = \$39 \times \left[\frac{1 - \frac{1}{(1.035)^{40}}}{0.035}\right] + \frac{\$1{,}000}{(1.035)^{40}}$$

= $832.85 + $252.57 = **$1,085.42**

19. Solution:

Years to maturity = n = 4

Coupon rate = C = 10%

Frequency of payment = m = 2

Semiannual coupon = $1,000 × (0.10/2) = $50.00

Current market rate = i = 12%

Present value of bond = P_B

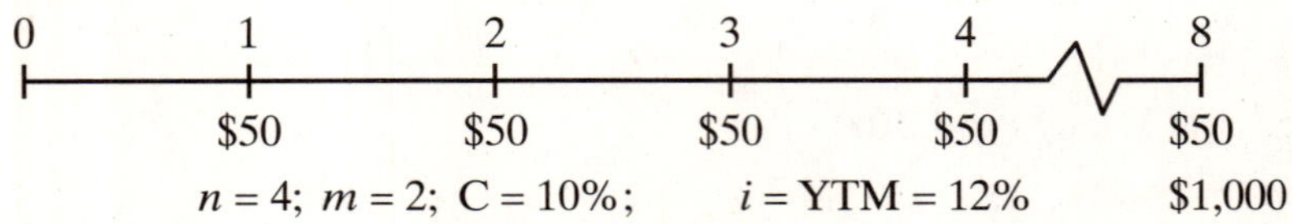

$$P_B = C/2 \times \left[\frac{1 - \frac{1}{(1+i/2)^{2n}}}{i/2}\right] + \frac{F}{(1+i/2)^{2n}} = \$50 \times \left[\frac{1 - \frac{1}{(1.06)^8}}{0.06}\right] + \frac{\$1{,}000}{(1.06)^8}$$

= $310.49 + $627.41 = **$937.90**

20. Solution:

Years to maturity = n = 20

Coupon rate = C = 0%

Current market rate = i = 12%

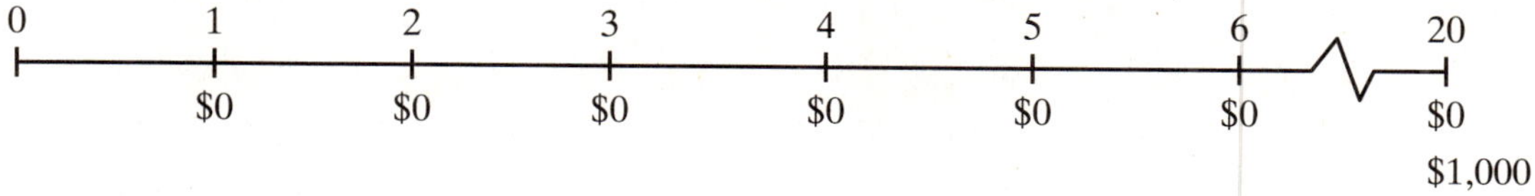

$$P_B = \frac{F_{mn}}{(1 + i/m)^{mn}} = \frac{\$1,000}{(1.12)^{20}} = \mathbf{\$103.67}$$

21. **<u>Solution:</u>**

Years to maturity = n = 10

Coupon rate = C = 0%

Current market rate = i = 14%

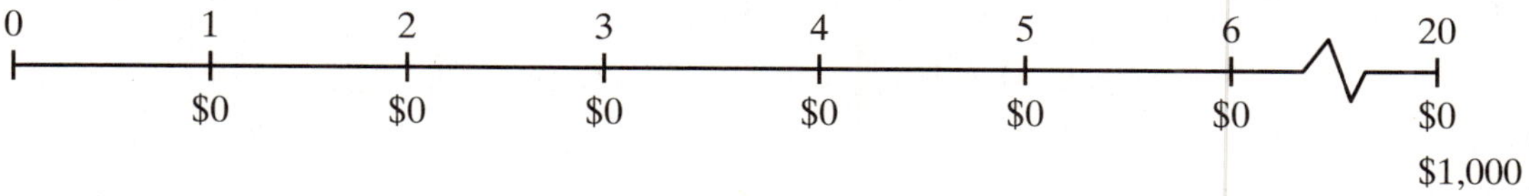

$$P_B = \frac{F_{mn}}{(1 + i/m)^{mn}} = \frac{\$1,000}{(1 + 0.14/2)^{20}} = \mathbf{\$258.42}$$

22. **<u>Solution:</u>**

Years to maturity = n = 7

Coupon rate = C = 7%

Annual coupon = $1,000 × (0.07) = $70

Yield to maturity = i

Present value of bond = P_B = $927.23

Use the trial-and-error approach to solve for YTM: Since the bond is selling at a discount, we know that the yield to maturity is higher than the coupon rate. Try, YTM = 8%:

$$P_B = C(PVIFA_{i,\,n}) + F(PVIF_{i,\,n})$$

$$\$927.23 \neq \$70 * \left[\frac{1 - \dfrac{1}{(1 + 0.08)^7}}{0.08}\right] + \frac{\$1,000}{(1.08)^7}$$

$$\neq \$364.45 + 583.49 = \$947.94$$

Next, try a higher rate, say YTM = 8.5%:

$$P_B = C(PVIFA_{i,\,n}) + F(PVIF_{i,\,n})$$

$$\$927.23 \neq \$70 * \left[\frac{1 - \dfrac{1}{(1 + 0.085)^7}}{0.085}\right] + \frac{\$1,000}{(1.85)^7}$$

$$\neq \$358.30 + 564.93 = \$923.22$$

Try a lower rate, say YTM = 8.4%:

$$P_B = C(PVIFA_{i,\,n}) + F(PVIF_{i,\,n})$$

$$\$927.23 \neq \$70 * \left[\frac{1 - \dfrac{1}{(1 + 0.084)^7}}{0.084}\right] + \frac{\$1,000}{(1.84)^7}$$

$$\neq \$359.51 + 568.59 \cong \$928.10$$

The YTM is approximately **8.4 percent**. Using a financial calculator provided an exact YTM of **8.42 percent**.

	N	i%	PMT	PV	FV
Enter	7		\$70	−\$927.23	\$1,000
Answer		**8.42%**			

23. <u>Solution:</u>

Years to maturity = n = 5

Coupon rate = C = 7.25%

Semiannual coupon = \$1,000 × (0.0725/2) = \$36.25

Yield to maturity = i

Present value of bond = P_B = \$1,023.90

Use the trial-and-error approach to solve for YTM. Since the bond is selling at a premium, we know that the yield to maturity is lower than the coupon rate. First, try YTM = 6.5%:

$$\$1{,}023.90 = C/2 \times \left[\frac{1 - \dfrac{1}{(1+i/2)^{2n}}}{i/2}\right] + \frac{F}{(1+i/2)^{2n}} = \$36.25 \times \left[\frac{1 - \dfrac{1}{(1.0325)^{10}}}{0.0325}\right] + \frac{\$1{,}000}{(1.0325)^{10}}$$

$$= \$305.31 + \$726.27 \neq \mathbf{\$1{,}031.58}$$

Now try a higher rate, say YTM = 6.7%:

$$\$1{,}023.90 = C/2 \times \left[\frac{1 - \dfrac{1}{(1+i/2)^{2n}}}{i/2}\right] + \frac{F}{(1+i/2)^{2n}} = \$36.25 \times \left[\frac{1 - \dfrac{1}{(1.0335)^{10}}}{0.0335}\right] + \frac{\$1{,}000}{(1.0335)^{10}}$$

$$= \$303.77 + \$719.28 \cong \mathbf{\$1{,}023.04}$$

The YTM is approximately **6.7 percent**. Using a financial calculator provided an exact YTM of **6.68 percent (2 × 3.34%)**.

	N	i%	PMT	PV	FV
Enter	10		\$36.25	−\$1,023.90	\$1,000
Answer		**3.34%**			

24. <u>Solution:</u>

Purchase price of bond = \$812.44

Years investment held = n = 4

Coupon rate = C = 12.5%

Frequency of payment = m = 2

Annual coupon = \$1,000 × (0.0125/2) = \$62.50

Realized Yield = i

Selling price of bond = P_B = \$945.90

To compute the realized return, either the trial-and-error approach or the financial calculator can be used. Since the price has increased, market rates must have decreased. So, the realized return is going to be greater than the bond's coupon. Try rates higher than the coupon rate. Try i = 16%, or $i/2$ = 8%:

$$P_B = \frac{C}{2} \times \left[\frac{1 - \dfrac{1}{(1+i/2)^{m\times n}}}{i/2}\right] + \frac{FV}{(1+i/2)^{m\times n}}$$

$$\$812.44 = \$62.50 \times \left[\frac{1 - \dfrac{1}{(1.08)^8}}{0.08}\right] + \frac{\$945.90}{(1.08)^8}$$

$$= \$359.17 + \$511.04 \neq \$870.21$$

Next, try a higher rate, i = 18% or $i/2$ = 9%:

$$P_B = \frac{C}{2} \times \left[\frac{1 - \frac{1}{(1 + i/2)^{m \times n}}}{i/2}\right] + \frac{FV}{(1 + i/2)^{m \times n}}$$

$$\$812.44 = \$62.50 \times \left[\frac{1 - \frac{1}{(1.09)^8}}{0.09}\right] + \frac{\$945.90}{(1.09)^8}$$

$$= \$345.93 + \$501.87 \neq \$847.79$$

Now try a higher rate, i = 18.3% or $i/2$ = 9.15%:

$$P_B = \frac{C}{2} \times \left[\frac{1 - \frac{1}{(1 + i/2)^{m \times n}}}{i/2}\right] + \frac{FV}{(1 + i/2)^{m \times n}}$$

$$\$812.44 = \$62.50 \times \left[\frac{1 - \frac{1}{(1.0915)^8}}{0.0915}\right] + \frac{\$945.90}{(1.0915)^8}$$

$$= \$344.01 + \$469.52 \cong \$813.53$$

The realized rate of return is approximately **18.3 percent**. Using a financial calculator provided an exact yield of **18.34 percent**.

25. Solution:

Semiannual yield = 3.8%

The effective annual yield can be computed as:

$$EAY = 1 - \left(\frac{\text{Quoted rate}}{m}\right)^m - 1$$

$$= \left(1 - \frac{0.038}{2}\right)^2 - 1$$

$$= 0.0774 = \mathbf{7.74}\%$$

CHAPTER 9

Stock Valuation

LEARNING OBJECTIVES

1 List and describe the four types of secondary markets.
2. Explain why many financial analysts treat preferred stock as a special type of bond rather than as a true equity security.
3. Describe how the general dividend-valuation model values a share of stock.
4. Discuss the assumptions that are necessary to make the general dividend-valuation model easier to use, and be able to use the model to compute the value of a firm's stock.
5. Explain why g must be less than R in the constant-growth dividend model.
6. Explain how valuing a preferred stock with a stated maturity differs from valuing a preferred stock with no maturity date, and be able to calculate the price of a share of preferred stock under both conditions.

I. Chapter Outline

9.1 The Market for Stocks

- Equity securities are certificates of ownership of a corporation.
- While households dominate the holdings of equity securities, owning more than 36 percent of outstanding corporate equities, pension funds are the largest institutional investors in equities, holding 21 percent, followed by mutual funds (20 percent), and foreign investors (10 percent).

A. *Secondary Markets*

- In secondary markets, outstanding shares of stock are bought and sold among investors.
- From an investor's perspective, the function of secondary markets is to provide marketability for the shares of securities they own at a fair price.
- An active secondary market enables firms to sell their new debt or equity issues at a lower funding cost than firms selling similar securities that have no secondary market.

B. *Secondary Markets and Their Efficiency*

- In the United States, most secondary market transactions are conducted on one of the many stock exchanges.
  - o In terms of total volume of activity and total capitalization of the firms listed, the NYSE is the largest in the world and NASDAQ is the second largest.
  - o In terms of the number of companies listed and shares traded on a daily basis, NASDAQ is larger than the NYSE.
  - o Firms listed on the NYSE tend to be, on average, larger in size and their shares trade more frequently than firms whose securities trade on NASDAQ.

- There are four types of secondary markets, and each type differs according to the amount of price information available to investors, which in turn, affects the efficiency of the market.

1. Direct Search
- The secondary markets farthest from our ideal of complete price information are those in which buyer and seller must seek each other out directly.
- Securities that sell in direct search markets are usually bought and sold so infrequently that no third party, such as a broker or dealer, has an incentive to serve the market.
- The sale of common stock of small private companies and private placement transactions are good examples of direct search markets.
- Direct search is the least efficient type of secondary market.

2. Broker
- Brokers bring buyers and sellers together to earn a fee, called a commission.
- Brokers' extensive contacts provide them with a pool of price information that individual investors could not economically duplicate themselves.
- By charging a commission fee less than the cost of direct search, they give investors an incentive to make use of the information by hiring them as brokers.

3. Dealer
- Market efficiency is improved by dealers providing continuous bidding (selling or buying) for the security.
- Dealers provide this service by holding inventories of securities, which they own, then buying and selling from the inventory to earn a profit.
- The advantage of a dealer over a brokered market is that brokers cannot guarantee that an order will be executed promptly, while dealers can because they have an inventory of securities.
- NASDAQ is the best-known example of a dealer market.

4. Auction
- In an auction market, buyers and sellers confront each other directly and bargain over price as at the NYSE.
- In the NYSE, the auction for a security takes place at a specific location on the floor of the exchange, called a **post**.
- The auctioneer in this case is the **specialist**, who is designated by the exchange to represent orders placed by public customers and is allowed by the exchange to act as dealer.
- The NYSE is the most efficient equity market in the United States.

C. *Reading the Stock Market Listings*
- The *Wall Street Journal,* the *New York Times,* and other newspapers in large metropolitan areas provide stock listings for the major stock exchanges, such as the NYSE and the relevant regional exchanges.
- **Exhibit 9.1** shows a section of the listing in the *Wall Street Journal* for the NYSE.

D. *Types of Equity Securities*
- The two types of equity securities are common stock and preferred stock.
- **Common stock** represents the basic ownership claim in a corporation.
  - o One of the rights of the owners is to vote on all important matters that affect the life of the company, such as to elect the board of directors, approve the capital budget, or vote on a proposed merger or acquisition.
  - o Owners of common stock are not guaranteed any dividend payments and have the lowest-priority claim on the firm's assets in the event of bankruptcy.
  - o Legally, common stockholders enjoy limited liability.
  - o Common stocks are perpetuities in the sense that they have no maturity.
- **Preferred stock** also represents ownership interest in the corporation, but preferred stock receives preferential treatment over common stock in certain matters.
  - o Preferred dividend payments are fixed obligations of the firm, similar to the interest payments on corporate bonds.
  - o Preferred stock owners are given priority treatment over common stock with respect to dividends payments and the claims against the firm's assets in the event of bankruptcy or liquidation.
  - o Dividends payments are paid with after-tax dollars subject to taxation.
  - o Even though preferred stock is equity, the owners have no voting privileges.
  - o Preferred stocks are legally classified as perpetuities because they have no maturity.

E. *Preferred Stock: Debt or Equity?*
- Legally, preferred stock is equity.
- Like the dividends on common stock, preferred stock dividends are taxable.

- A strong case can be made that preferred stock is really a special type of bond.
  - First, regular preferred stock confers no voting powers.
  - Second, preferred stockholders receive a fixed dividend, regardless of the firm's earnings, and if the firm is liquidated, they receive a stated value (usually par) and not the residual value.
  - Third, preferred stocks often have "credit" ratings that are similar in nature to those issued to bonds.
  - Fourth, preferred stock is sometimes convertible into common stock.
  - Finally, most preferred stock issues today are not true perpetuities. Increasingly, preferred stock issues have the sinking fund feature, which require *mandatory* annual retirement schedules.

9.2 Common Stock Valuation

- Valuation of common and preferred stock is done by using the same basic methodology that was discussed for bond valuations (Chapter 8).
- Applying the valuation procedure to common stocks is more difficult than applying it to bonds for various reasons.
  - First, in contrast to coupon payments on bonds, the size and timing of the dividend cash flows are less certain.
  - Second, common stocks are true perpetuities in that they have no final maturity date.
  - Finally, unlike the rate of return, or yield, on bonds, the rate of return on common stock is not directly observable.

A. *A One-Period Model*

- A one-period model provides an estimate of the market price.
- The value of an asset is the present value of its future cash flows—the future dividend and the end-of-period stock price.

B. *A Two-Period Model*

- This can be viewed as two one-period models strung together.

C. *A Perpetuity Model*

- A series of one-period stock pricing models is strung together to arrive at a stock perpetuity model.
- Though theoretically sound, this model is not practical to apply because the number of dividends could be infinite.

D. *The General Dividend Valuation Model*

- Equation 9.1 is a general expression for the value of a share of stock. It says that the price of a share of stock is the present value of *all* expected future dividends.
  - The formula does not assume any specific pattern for future cash dividends, such as a constant-growth rate.
  - It does not make any assumption about when the share of stock is going to be sold in the future.
  - Finally, the model says that to compute a stock's current value, we need to forecast an infinite number of dividends.

E. *The Growth Stock Pricing Paradox*

- *Growth stocks* are typically defined as the stocks of companies whose earnings are growing at above-average rates and are expected to continue to do so for some time.
- Fast growing companies typically pay no dividends on their stock during their growth phase because management believes that the companies have a number of high-return investment opportunities and that both the companies and their investors will be better off if earnings are reinvested.
- If the internal investments succeed, the stock's price should go up significantly, and investors can sell their stock at a price much higher than what they paid.

9.3 Stock Valuation: Some Simplifying Assumptions

- To make Equation 9.1 more applicable, some simplifying assumptions about the pattern of dividends are necessary.
- Three different assumptions can cover most growth patterns.
  - Dividend payments remain constant over time; that is, they have a growth rate of zero.

- o Dividends have a constant-growth rate.
- o Dividends have a mixed growth rate pattern; that is, dividends have one payment pattern and then switch to another.

A. *Zero-Growth Dividend Model*

- The dividend payment pattern remains constant over time:

$D_1 = D_2 = D_3 = \quad = D_\infty$

- In this case, the dividend-discount model (Equation 9.1) becomes:

$$P_0 = \frac{D}{(1+R)} + \frac{D}{(1+R)^2} + \frac{D}{(1+R)^2} + \frac{D}{(1+R)^3} + \ldots..$$

- This cash flow pattern essentially describes a perpetuity with a constant cash flow. In Chapter 6 we developed the present value of a perpetuity with a constant cash flow of CF/i, where CF is the constant cash flow and i is the interest rate. Similarly, Equation 9.2 gives the valuation model for a zero-growth stock.

$$P_0 = \frac{D}{R}$$

B. *Constant-Growth Dividend Model*

- Cash dividends do not remain constant but instead grow at some average rate g from one period to the next forever.
- Constant dividend growth is an appropriate assumption for mature companies with a history of stable growth.
- While an infinite horizon is still hard to comprehend, far-distant dividends have a small present value and contribute very little to the price of the stock.
- Deriving the constant-growth dividend model is fairly straightforward. First, we need to build a model to compute the value of dividend payments for any time period.
- The constant-growth dividend model is easy to do because it is just an application of Equation 6.6 from Chapter 6.
- Equation 9.4 shows how to value a constant-growth stock:

$$P_0 = \frac{D_1}{(R - g)}$$

C. *Computing Future Stock Prices*

- The constant-growth dividend model (Equation 9.4) can be modified to determine the value, or price, of a share of stock at any point in time.
- This results in Equation 9.5, which shows that the price of a share of stock at time t is as follows:

$$P_t = \frac{D_{t+1}}{(R - g)}$$

D. *The Relationship between R and g*

- The constant-growth dividend model yields solutions that are invalid anytime the dividend growth rate equals or exceeds the discount rate ($g \geq R$).
- If $g = R$, the value of the denominator is zero and the value of the stock is infinite, which makes no sense.
- If $g > R$, the present value of the dividend gets bigger and bigger rather than smaller and smaller as it should. This implies that a firm that is growing at a very fast rate does so forever.

E. *Mixed (Supernormal) Growth Dividend Model*

- During the early part of their lives, very successful firms experience a supernormal rate of growth in earnings.
- To value a share of stock for a firm with supernormal dividend growth patterns, we can apply Equation 9.1, our general dividend model, and Equation 9.5, which gives us the price of a share of stock with constant dividend growth at any point in time.
- Thus, our valuation model is (Equation 9.6):

P_0 = PV (Mixed dividend growth) + PV (Constant dividend growth)

$$P_0 = \frac{D_1}{(1+R)} + \frac{D_2}{(1+R)^2} + \ldots + \frac{D_t}{(1+R)^t} + \frac{P_t}{(1+R)^t}$$

9.4 Valuing Preferred Stock

- In computing the value of preferred stock, one needs to know whether the preferred stock has an effective "maturity" because of a sinking fund option or call option.

- The most significant difference between preferred stock with a fixed maturity and a bond is the risk of default.
- Since preferred stock dividends are declared by the board of directors, failure to pay dividends does not result in default.
- The failure to pay a preferred stock dividend as promised is a serious financial breach and signals to the market that the firm is in serious financial difficulty.

A. *Preferred Stock with a Fixed Maturity*

- We can use the bond valuation model developed in Chapter 8 to determine its price, or value.
- Equation 8.2 can be restated as the price of a share of preferred stock (PS_0):

  Preferred stock price = PV (Dividend payments) + PV (Par value)

$$PS_0 = \frac{D_1/m}{1 + i/m} + \frac{D_2/m}{(1 + i/m)^2} + \frac{D_3/m}{(1 + i/m)^3} + \ldots + \frac{D_{mn}/m + P_{mn}}{(1 + i/m)^{mn}} \quad \textbf{(9.7)}$$

- Since most preferred stocks make quarterly dividend payments, m equals 4.

B. *Perpetuity Preferred Stock*

- Some preferred stock issues have no maturity.
  - o Dividends are constant over time ($g = 0$).
  - o Fixed dividend payments go on forever.
  - o We can use Equation 9.2 to value such preferred stock issues.

$$P_0 = \frac{D}{R}$$

II. Suggested Approach to Material

This chapter begins with a discussion of the secondary markets for equity securities and their market efficiency. Next, the authors explain how to read stock market price listings in the newspaper, and introduce the types of equity securities that firms typically issue. Then they develop a general valuation model and conclude that the value of a share of stock is the present value of *all* expected future cash dividends. Some simplifying assumptions about dividend payments are used to implement this valuation model. These assumptions correspond to actual practice and allow for the development of several valuation models that are theoretically sound and easy to apply.

The concept of discounting that was introduced in Chapter 5 is utilized for the purpose of valuing stocks. As in the previous chapter on bonds, we recognize the value of stocks to be the present value of all future cash flows from the investment—the future cash flows being the dividends expected.

III. Chapter Glossary

Bid price	The price a securities dealer will pay for a given stock.
Offer (cash) price	The price at which a securities dealer seeks to sell a given stock.
Post	Specific location on the floor of a stock exchange at which auctions for a particular security take place.
Specialist	The trader designated by an exchange to represent orders placed by public customers at auctions of securities; specialists handle a small set of securities and are also allowed to act as dealers.
Dividend yield	A stock's dividend payout divided by its current price.
Common stock	An equity share that represents the basic ownership claim in a corporation; the most common type of equity security.
Preferred stock	An equity share in a corporation that entitles the owner to preferred treatment over owners of common stock with respect to dividend payments and claims against the firm's assets in the event of bankruptcy or liquidation but that typically have no voting rights.

IV. Summary of Key Equations

Euation	Description	Formula
9.1	The general maturity dividend-valuation model	$P_0 = \frac{D_1}{1+R} + \frac{D_2}{(1+R)^2} + \frac{D_3}{(1+R)^3} + \frac{D_4}{(1+R)^4} + \frac{D_5}{(1+R)^5} + \ldots + \frac{D_\infty}{(1+R)^\infty} = \sum_{t=1}^{\infty} \frac{D_t}{(1+R)^t}$
9.2	Zero-growth dividend model	$P_0 = \frac{D}{R}$
9.3	Value of a dividend at time *t* in a constant-growth scenario	$D_t = D_0 \times (1+g)^t$
9.4	Constant-growth dividend model	$P_0 = \frac{D_1}{(R-g)}$
9.5	Value of a stock at time *t* when dividends grow at a constant rate	$P_t = \frac{D_{t+1}}{(R-g)}$
9.6	Supernormal growth stock-valuation model	$P_0 = \frac{D_1}{(1+R)} + \frac{D_2}{(1+R)^2} + \ldots + \frac{D_t}{(1+R)^t} + \frac{P_t}{(1+R)^t}$
9.7	Value of preferred stock with a fixed maturity	$PS_0 = \frac{D_1/m}{(1+i/m)} + \frac{D_2/m}{(1+i/m)^2} + \frac{D_3/m}{(1+i/m)^3} + L + \frac{D_{mn}/m + P_{mn}}{(1+i/m)^{mn}}$

V. True or False Questions

1. Equity securities are real assets.

a. True

b. False

2. The largest investor in equity securities are pension funds.

a. True

b. False

3. In secondary markets, outstanding shares of stock are bought and sold among investors.

a. True

b. False

4. The majority of secondary market transactions in the United States take place in one of the many exchanges.

a. True

b. False

5. NASDAQ is larger than the NYSE in terms of the number of companies listed and shares traded on a daily basis.

a. True

b. False

6. When buyers and sellers seek each other out to make trades, it is known as a direct market.
   a. True
   b. False

7. The sale of common stock of small private companies and private placement transactions are good examples of brokered markets.
   a. True
   b. False

8. The advantage of a dealer over a brokered market is that brokers cannot guarantee that an order will be executed promptly, while dealers can because they have an inventory of securities.
   a. True
   b. False

9. Owners of common stock are not guaranteed any dividend payments and have the lowest-priority claim on the firm's assets in the event of bankruptcy.
   a. True
   b. False

10. Preferred stock owners are given priority treatment over common stock with respect to dividend payments and the claims against the firm's assets in the event of bankruptcy or liquidation.
    a. True
    b. False

11. Legally, preferred stock is equity.
    a. True
    b. False

12. The value of a common stock is the present value of future dividends and end-of-period stock price.
    a. True
    b. False

13. Growth stocks are stocks of companies whose earnings are growing at above-average rates and are expected to continue to do so for some time.
    a. True
    b. False

14. Zero-growth stocks are valued as perpetuities.
    a. True
    b. False

15. For preferred stocks, failure to pay the dividend results in default.
    a. True
    b. False

VI. Multiple-Choice Questions and Problems

1. The largest holder of equity securities are
   a. mutual funds.
   b. pension funds.
   c. foreign investors.
   d. households.

2. Which one of the following statements is **NOT** true about secondary markets?
   - **a.** In secondary markets, outstanding shares of stock are bought and sold among investors.
   - **b.** For an investor, the function of secondary markets is to provide marketability for the shares of securities they own at a fair price.
   - **c.** Firms sell new securities to investors in the secondary markets.
   - **d.** An active secondary market allows firms to sell their new debt or equity issues at a lower cost of funds.

3. Which **ONE** of the following statements is true about secondary markets in the United States?
   - **a.** In terms of total volume of activity and total capitalization of the firms listed, the NASDAQ is the largest in the world and NYSE is the second largest.
   - **b.** In terms of the number of companies listed and shares traded on a daily basis, NASDAQ is larger than the NYSE.
   - **c.** Firms listed on the NASDAQ tend to be, on average, larger in size and their shares trade more frequently than firms whose securities trade on the NYSE.
   - **d.** In the United States, most secondary market transactions are conducted over the counter.

4. The four types of secondary markets are
   - **a.** direct search, broker, dealer, and online.
   - **b.** broker, dealer, direct search, and dealer-broker.
   - **c.** indirect search, direct search, broker, and dealer.
   - **d.** direct search, broker, dealer, and auction.

5. Direct search markets are characterized by
   - **a.** a lack of broker and dealer participation.
   - **b.** a lack of efficiency.
   - **c.** sale of common stock of small private companies.
   - **d.** All of the above.

6. Which one of the following statements is **NOT** true about dealer markets?
   - **a.** Dealers improve market efficiency by providing continuous bid and ask prices for securities.
   - **b.** Dealers hold an inventory of securities that is used to generate profits.
   - **c.** Dealers cannot guarantee an order will be filled, whereas brokers can.
   - **d.** NASDAQ is the best-known example of a dealer market.

7. Which **ONE** of the following statements is true about auction markets?
   - **a.** In an auction market, buyers and sellers face each other directly and bargain over price.
   - **b.** The NASDAQ is the most efficient equity market in the United States.
   - **c.** The NASDAQ is the best-known example of an auction market.
   - **d.** The auctioneer in this case is the **specialist** who is designated by brokerage houses to represent orders placed by public customers.

8. Owners of common stock
   - **a.** have limited liability.
   - **b.** are not guaranteed dividend payments.
   - **c.** have the lowest-priority claim on the firm's assets in the event of bankruptcy.
   - **d.** All of the above are true.

9. Which one of the following statements is **NOT** true about preferred stock?
   - **a.** Preferred stock has credit ratings just like bonds.
   - **b.** More and more preferred stock issues have fixed maturities like bonds.
   - **c.** Preferred stockholders receive a residual value and not a stated value.
   - **d.** Regular preferred stock has no voting powers.

10. Which **ONE** of the following statements is true about the general dividend valuation model?

a. The model assumes a specific pattern for dividend growth.

b. It makes a specific assumption about when the stock is going to be sold in the future.

c. The model calls for forecasting an infinite number of dividends for a stock.

d. All of the above are true.

11. Gemstone, Inc., paid a dividend of $2.00 last year. It expects to increase its dividend by $0.40 in each of their next four years. If its required rate of return is 15 percent, what is the present value of its dividends over the next four years?

a. $12.00

b. $8.37

c. $12.50

d. $10.40

12. Freedom Corp is a fast growing communications company that paid a $1.50 dividend last week. The company's expected growth rates over the next four years are as follows—45 percent, 35 percent 30 percent, and 20 percent. The company then expects to settle down to a constant growth rate of 9 percent annually. If the required rate of return is 24 percent, what is the present value of the dividends over the fast growth phase?

a. $3.25

b. $6.46

c. $7.60

d. $7.24

13. Stover Electricals is a company with no growth potential. Its last dividend was $3.75, and it expects no change in future dividends. What is the current price of the company's stock given a discount rate of 12 percent?

a. $40.50

b. $31.25

c. $37.50

d. $45.00

14. Horatio Corp. sells consumer products generating a revenue stream that has remained unchanged in the last few years. The firm does not expect any change in its sales or earnings in the next several years. The stock is currently selling at $27.33. If the required rate of return is 14 percent, what is the dividend paid by this company?

a. $2.73

b. $4.65

c. $6.89

d. $3.83

15. Mike Jones is interested in buying the stock of a company that expects to grow steadily at an annual rate of 8 percent for the foreseeable future. The firm paid a dividend of $2.50 last year. If your required rate of return is 15 percent, what is the most Jones should be willing to pay for this stock? Round to the nearest dollar.

a. $58

b. $61

c. $39

d. $25

16. Santiago Manufacturing Company is growing at a constant rate of 10 percent. Recently, it paid a dividend of $3.25. If the required rate of return is 18 percent, what is the price of the stock five years from now?

a. $71.97

b. $64.29

c. $58.50

d. $42.83

17. Century Corp. has issued perpetual preferred stock with a $100 par value. The firm pays a quarterly dividend of $2.60 on this stock. What is the current price of this preferred stock given a required rate of return of 7.25 percent?

a. $123.06

b. $167.88

c. $137.57

d. $143.45

18. Arjay Company has issued perpetual preferred stock with a par of $100 and a dividend of 6.5 percent. If the required rate of return is 8.75 percent, what is the stock's current market price?

a. $12.90

b. $74.29

c. $53.27

d. $62.14

19. Zolac, Inc., is a fast growing technology company. The firm projects a rapid growth of 30 percent for each of the next two years and then an annual growth rate of 25 percent for the following two years. After that, the firm expects a constant-growth rate of 7 percent. The firm expects to pay its first dividend of $2.25 a year from now. If your required rate of return on such stocks is 20 percent, what is the current price of the stock?

a. $15.63

b. $14.70

c. $37.62

d. $26.38

20. Sankey, Inc., is a fast growth stock and expects to grow at an annual rate of 35 percent for the next three years. It then will settle to a constant-growth rate of 10 percent. The first dividend will be paid out in year 2 and be equal to $3.00. If the required rate of return is 18 percent, what is the current price of the stock?

a. $38.51

b. $47.19

c. $51.56

d. $65.68

VI. Answers to True or False Questions

1. b	**2.** b	**3.** a	**4.** a	**5.** a
6. a	**7.** b	**8.** a	**9.** a	**10.** a
11. a	**12.** a	**13.** a	**14.** a	**15.** b

VII. Answers to Multiple-Choice Questions

1. d	**2.** c	**3.** b	**4.** d	**5.** d
6. c	**7.** a	**8.** d	**9.** c	**10.** c
11. b	**12.** c	**13.** b	**14.** d	**15.** c
16. a	**17.** d	**18.** b	**19.** d	**20.** a

VIII. Solutions to Multiple-Choice Problems

11. Solution:

Expected dividends for Gemstone and their present value:

$D_1 = \$2.40;\ D_2 = \$2.80;\ D_3 = \$3.20;\ D_4 = \$3.60$

$$\text{Present value of the dividends} = PV(D_1) + PV(D_2) + PV(D_3) + PV(D_4)$$
$$= \frac{\$2.40}{(1.15)} + \frac{\$2.80}{(1.15)^2} + \frac{\$3.20}{(1.15)^3} + \frac{\$3.60}{(1.15)^4}$$
$$= \$2.09 + \$2.12 + \$2.10 + \$2.06$$
$$= \mathbf{\$8.37}$$

12. Solution:

Expected dividends for Freedom Corp. and their present value:

$D_0 = \$1.50$

$D_1 = D_0(1 + g) = \$1.50(1.45) = \$2.175$

$D_2 = D_1(1 + g) = \$2.175(1.35) = \$2.936$

$D_3 = D_2(1 + g) = \$2.9361(1.30) = \$3.817$

$D_4 = D_3(1 + g) = \$3.817(1.20) = \$4.581$

$$\text{Present value of the dividends} = PV(D_1) + PV(D_2) + PV(D_3) + PV(D_4)$$
$$= \frac{\$2.175}{(1.24)} + \frac{\$2.936}{(1.24)^2} + \frac{\$3.817}{(1.24)^3} + \frac{\$4.581}{(1.24)^4}$$
$$= \$1.75 + \$1.91 + \$2.00 + \$1.94$$
$$= \mathbf{\$7.60}$$

13. Solution:

$D_0 = \$3.75;\quad g = 0;\quad R = 12\%$

$$P_0 = \frac{D}{R} = \frac{\$3.75}{0.12} = \mathbf{\$31.25}$$

14. Solution:

$P_0 = \$27.33;\quad g = 0;\quad R = 14\%$

$$P_0 = \frac{D}{R} = \frac{D_0}{0.14} = \mathbf{\$27.33}$$

$\mathbf{D_0} = \$27.33 \times 0.14 = \mathbf{\$3.83}$

15. Solution:

$D_0 = \$2.50;\quad g = 8\%;\quad R = 15\%$

$$P_0 = \frac{D_1}{R - g} = \frac{D_0(1 + g)}{R - g}$$
$$= \frac{\$2.50(1.08)}{0.15 - 0.08} = \frac{\$2.70}{0.07} = \mathbf{\$38.57}$$

16. Solution:

$R = 13\%;\quad D_0 = \$3.25;\quad g = 10\%$

$$P_5 = \frac{D_6}{R - g} = \frac{D_0(1 + g)^6}{R - g}$$
$$= \frac{3.25(1.10)^6}{0.18 - 0.10} = \mathbf{\$71.97}$$

17. Solution:

Quarterly dividend = \$2.60

Required rate of return = R = 7.25%

$$P_0 = \frac{D}{R} = \frac{(2.60 \times 4)}{0.0725} = \mathbf{\$143.45}$$

18. Solution:

Dividend = 6.5% of \$100 = \$6.50

Required rate of return = R = 8.75%

$$P_0 = \frac{D}{R} = \frac{\$6.50}{0.0875} = \mathbf{\$74.29}$$

19. Solution:

$g_1 = g_2 = 30\%, \quad g_3 = g_4 = 25\%, \quad g = 7\%, \quad D_1 = \$2.25, \quad R = 20\%$

$D_1 = \$2.25, \quad D_2 = \$2.25(1.30) = \$2.925, \quad D_3 = \$2.925(1.25) = \$3.656$

$D_4 = \$3.656(1.25) = \$4.570, \quad D_5 = 4.57(1.07) = \$4.89$

$$P_4 = \frac{D_5}{R - g} = \frac{\$4.89}{0.20 - 0.07} = \$37.62$$

$$P_0 = \frac{D_1}{(1 + R)^1} + \frac{D_2}{(1 + R)^2} + \frac{D_3}{(1 + R)^3} + \frac{D_4}{(1 + R)^4} + \frac{P_4}{(1 + R)^4}$$

$$P_0 = \frac{\$2.25}{1.20} + \frac{\$2.925}{(1.20)^2} + \frac{\$3.656}{(1.20)^3} + \frac{(\$4.57 + 37.62)}{(1.20)^4}$$

$P_0 = \$1.88 + \$2.03 + \$2.12 + 20.35$

$P_0 = \mathbf{\$26.38}$

20. Solution:

$g_{1\text{-}3} = 35\%; \quad g = 10\%; \quad D_1 = S0; \quad D_2 = \$3.00; \quad R = 18\%;$

$D_3 = D_2\,(1.35) = \$3.00(1.35) = \$4.05; \quad D_4 = \$4.05(1.10) = \$4.455$

$$P_3 = \frac{D_4}{R - g} = \frac{\$4.455}{0.18 - 0.10} = \$55.69$$

$$P_0 = \frac{D_1}{(1 + R)} + \frac{D_2}{(1 + R)^2} + \frac{D_3 + P_3}{(1 + R)^3}$$

$$P_0 = 0 + \frac{\$3.00}{(1.18)^2} + \frac{(\$4.05 + \$55.69)}{(1.18)^3}$$

$P_0 = \$2.15 + \$36.36 = \mathbf{\$38.51}$

CHAPTER 10

The Fundamentals of Capital Budgeting

LEARNING OBJECTIVES

1. Discuss why capital budgeting decisions are the most important decisions made by a firm's management.
2. Explain the benefits of using the net present value (NPV) method to analyze capital expenditure decisions, and be able to calculate the NPV for a capital project.
3. Describe the strengths and weaknesses of the payback period as a capital expenditure decision-making tool, and be able to compute the payback period for a capital project.
4. Explain why the accounting rate of return (ARR) is not recommended for use as a capital expenditure decision-making tool.
5. Be able to compute the internal rate of return (IRR) for a capital project, and discuss the conditions under which the IRR technique and the NPV technique produce different results.
6. Explain the benefits of a postaudit review of a capital project.

I. Chapter Outline

10.1 An Introduction to Capital Budgeting

A. *The Importance of Capital Budgeting*

- Capital budgeting decisions are the most important investment decisions made by management.
- The goal of these decisions is to select capital projects that will increase the value of the firm.
- Capital investments are important because they involve substantial cash outlays and, once made, are not easily reversed.

B. *The Capital Budgeting Process*

- Capital budgeting starts with a firm's strategic plan, which spells out its strategy for the next three to five years.
- The firm's strategic objectives are then converted into business plans by division managers. These business plans have a one- to two-year time horizon and provide a detailed description of what each division should accomplish over the year.
- Behind each division's business plan is a capital budget that details the resources management believes it needs to get the job done.
- The capital budget is prepared jointly by the CFO's staff and financial staffs at the divisional and plant levels and reflects, in large part, the activities outlined in the divisional business plans.

C. *Sources of Information*

- Most of the information needed to make capital budgeting decisions is generated internally, beginning likely with the sales force.
- Then the production team is involved, followed by the accountants.
- All this information is then reviewed by the financial managers, who evaluate the feasibility of the project.

D. *Classification of Investment Projects*

- Capital budgeting projects can be broadly classified into three types: (1) independent projects; (2) mutually exclusive projects; and (3) contingent projects.

  1. Independent Projects
  - If two projects are independent, accepting or rejecting one project has no bearing on the decision on the other.

  2. Mutually Exclusive Projects
  - When two projects are mutually exclusive, accepting one automatically precludes the other.

  3. Contingent Projects
  - Contingent projects are those in which the acceptance of one project is dependent on another project.

E. *Basic Capital Budgeting Terms*

- The **cost of capital** is the minimum return that a capital budgeting project must earn for it to be accepted.
- **Capital rationing** implies that a firm does not have the resources necessary to fund all of the available projects.

10.2 Net Present Value (NPV)

- The NPV is a capital budgeting technique that is consistent with the goal of maximizing shareholder wealth.
- The method estimates the amount by which the benefits or cash flows from a project exceed the cost of the project in present value terms.

A. *Valuation of Real Assets*

- Valuing real assets calls for the same steps as valuing financial assets—estimate future cash flows, determine the investor's cost of capital or required rate of return, and calculate the present value of the future cash flows.
- However, there are some practical difficulties in following the process for real assets—first, cash flow estimates are not readily available as they are for financial assets in legal contracts; and second, estimates of required rates of return are more difficult than they are for financial assets because no market data is available for real assets.

B. *NPV—The Basic Concept*

- The present value of a project is the difference between the present value of the expected future cash flows and the present value of the project's cost.
- Accepting a positive NPV project leads to an increase in shareholder wealth, while accepting a negative NPV project leads to a decline in shareholder wealth.

C. *Framework for Calculating NPV*

- The NPV technique uses the discounted cash flow technique.
- Our goal is to compute the **net cash flow (NCF)** for each time period t.
- A five-step approach can be utilized to compute the NPV.
  - o Determine the cost of the project.
  - o Estimate the project's future cash flows over its forecasted life.
  - o Determine the riskiness of the project and estimate the appropriate cost of capital.
  - o Compute the project's NPV.
  - o Make a decision.

D. *Concluding Comments on NPV*

- Beware of optimistic estimates of future cash flows.
- Recognize that the estimates going into calculating NPV are estimates and not market data.
- The NPV method of determining project viability is the recommended approach for making capital investment decisions.
- The NPV decision criteria can be summed up as follows:

Summary of Net Present Value (NPV) Method

Decision Rule: NPV > 0: Accept the project.
NPV < 0: Reject the project.

Key Advantages	Key Disadvantages
1. Uses the discounted cash flow valuation technique. 2. Provides a direct measure of how much a capital project will increase the value of the firm. 3. Consistent with the goal of maximizing shareholder wealth.	1. Difficult to understand without an accounting and finance background.

10.3 The Payback Period

- The **payback period** represents the number of years it takes for the cash flows from a project to recover the project's initial investment.
- A project is accepted if its payback period is below some pre-specified threshold.

A. *Computing the Payback Period*

- To compute the payback period, we need to know the project's cost and to estimate its future net cash flows.
- There is no economic rationale that links the payback method to shareholder wealth maximization.
- If a firm has a number of projects that are mutually exclusive, the projects are selected in order of their payback rank: projects with the lowest payback period are selected first.

B. *How the Payback Period Performs*

- The payback period analysis can lead to erroneous decisions because the rule does not consider cash flows after the payback period.
- A rapid payback does not necessarily mean a good investment.

C. *The Discounted Payback Period*

- The **discounted payback period** calculation calls for future cash flows to be discounted by the firm's cost of capital.
- The major advantage of the discounted payback is that it tells management how long it takes a project to reach a positive NPV.
- However, this method still ignores all cash flows after the arbitrary cutoff period, which is a major flaw.

D. *Evaluating the Payback Rule*

- The following table summarizes this capital budgeting technique.

Summary of Payback Method

Decision Rule: Payback period ≤ Payback cutoff point ⟶ Accept the project.
Payback period > Payback cutoff point ⟶ Reject the project.

Key Advantages	Key Disadvantages
1. Easy to calculate and understand for people without strong finance backgrounds. 2. A simple measure of a project's liquidity.	1. Most common version does not account for time value of money. 2. Does not consider cash flows past the payback period. 3. Arbitrary cutoff point. 4. Bias against long-term projects such as research and development and new product launches.

10.4 The Accounting Rate of Return (ARR)

- The ARR is sometimes called the *book rate of return*.
- This method computes the return on a capital project using accounting numbers—the project's net income (NI) and book value (BV) rather than cash flow data.
- It has a number of major flaws as a tool for evaluating capital expenditure decisions.

10.5 Internal Rate of Return (IRR)

- The **IRR** is an important and legitimate alternative to the NPV method.
- The NPV and IRR techniques are similar in that both depend on discounting the cash flows from a project.
- The IRR is the discount rate that equates the NPV to zero.

A. *Calculating the IRR*

- The IRR is an expected rate of return, much like the yield to maturity calculation that was made on bonds.
- We will need to apply the same trial-and-error method to compute the IRR.

B. *When the IRR and NPV Methods Agree*

- The two methods will *always* agree when the projects are *independent* and the projects' cash flows are *conventional.*
- An additional requirement is that if, after the initial investment is made (cash outflow), all the cash flows in each future year are positive (inflows).

C. *When the IRR and NPV Methods Disagree*

- The IRR and NPV methods can produce different accept/reject decisions if a project either has unconventional cash flows or the projects are mutually exclusive.
- A conventional project is one in which the initial cash flow is positive and all the subsequent cash flows are negative.

D. *Modified Internal Rate of Return (MIRR)*

- A major weakness of the IRR compared to the NPV method is the reinvestment rate assumption.
  - o IRR assumes that the cash flows from the project are reinvested at the IRR, while the NPV assumes that they are invested at the firm's cost of capital.
  - o This optimistic assumption in the IRR method leads to some projects being accepted when they should not be.
- An alternative technique is the **modified internal rate of return (MIRR)**. Here, each operating cash flow is reinvested at the firm's cost of capital.
- The compounded values are summed up to get the project's ***terminal value***.
- The MIRR is the interest rate that equates the project's cost to the terminal value at the end of the project.
- Equation 10.5 shows how to calculate the MIRR.

E. *IRR versus NPV: A Final Comment*

- While the IRR has an intuitive appeal to managers because the output is in the form of a return, the technique has some critical problems.
- On the other hand, decisions made based on the project's NPV are consistent with the goal of shareholder wealth maximization. In addition, the result shows management the dollar amount by which each project is expected to increase the value of the firm.
- For these reasons, the NPV method should be used to make capital budgeting decisions.
- The following table summarizes the IRR decision-making criteria.

Review of Internal Rate of Return (IRR)

Decision Rule: IRR $>$ Cost of capital ⟶ Accept the project.
IRR $<$ Cost of capital ⟶ Reject the project.

Key Advantages	Key Disadvantages
1. Intuitively easy to understand.	1. With nonconventional cash flows, IRR approach can yield no or multiple answers.
2. Based on the discounted cash flow technique.	2. A lower IRR can be better if a cash inflow is followed by cash outflows.
	3. With mutually exclusive projects, IRR can lead to incorrect investment decisions.

10.6 Capital Budgeting in Practice

A. ***Practitioners' Methods of Choice***

- Exhibit 10.12 summarizes surveys of practitioners on the capital budgeting methods of choice.
- In a recent study of Fortune 1000 managers showed 85 percent of managers used the NPV while 77 percent used the IRR. Surprisingly, over 50 percent of managers used the payback method.

B. ***Ongoing and Postaudit Reviews***

- Management should systematically review the status of all ongoing capital projects and perform postaudits on all completed capital projects.
- In a **postaudit review**, management compares the actual results of a project with what was projected in the capital budgeting proposal.
- Managers should also conduct **ongoing reviews** of capital projects in progress.
- Management must also evaluate people responsible for implementing a capital project.

II. Suggested Approach to Material

The chapter starts with a discussion of the types of capital projects that firms undertake and how the capital budgeting process is managed within the firm. Next, some of the techniques used by financial managers to evaluate capital budgeting decisions are examined. The net present value (NPV) method, the capital budgeting approach recommended in this book, is the first technique to be discussed. Two other capital budgeting techniques that have some serious deficiencies with regard to selecting capital projects—the payback period and the accounting rate of return—are discussed. These techniques do not consider the time value of money and can lead to decisions that decrease stockholders' wealth. The fourth and last capital budgeting technique discussed in this chapter is the internal rate of return (IRR), which is the expected rate of return for a capital project. The chapter wraps up by looking at survey data that provide information on which capital budgeting techniques financial managers actually use when making capital decisions.

The techniques discussed in the chapter are straightforward and apply the methodology that you are already familiar with—discounting cash flows. There are a variety of conceptual questions and problems in this chapter as well as in this Study Guide to help you master these concepts. This material forms the foundation for the discussion in the following chapter.

III. Chapter Glossary

Capital budgeting	The process of choosing the productive assets in which the firm will invest.
Independent projects	Projects whose cash flows are unrelated.
Mutually exclusive projects	Projects for which acceptance of one precludes acceptance of the other.
Contingent project	A project whose acceptance depends on the acceptance of another project.
Cost of capital	The required rate of return for a capital budgeting project.
Opportunity cost of capital	The return an investor gives up when his or her money is invested in one asset rather than the best alternative asset.
Capital rationing	A situation where a firm does not have enough capital to invest in all attractive projects and must therefore ration capital.
Net present value (NPV) method	A method of evaluating a capital investment project which measures the difference between its cost and the present value of its expected cash flows.
Net cash flow (NCF)	Cash inflows minus cash outflows in a particular time period.
Payback period	The length of time required for the cash flows from a project to recover the project's initial cost.
Discounted payback period	The length of time required to recover a project's initial cost from its discounted future cash flows.

Accounting rate of return (ARR)	A rate of return on a capital project based on average net income divided by average assets over the project's life; also called the *book value rate of return.*
Internal rate of return (IRR)	The discount rate at which the present value of a project's expected cash inflows equal the present value of the project's outflows.
Conventional cash flow	A cash flow pattern made up of an initial cash outflow that is followed by one or more cash inflows.
NPV profile	A graph showing NPV as a function of the discount rate.
Crossover point	The discount rate at which the NPV profiles of two projects cross and, thus, at which the NPVs of the projects are equal.
Modified internal rate of return (MIRR)	An internal rate of return (IRR) measure which assumes that cash inflows are reinvested at the opportunity cost of capital until the end of the project.
Postaudit review	An audit to compare actual project results with the results projected in the capital budgeting proposal.

IV. Summary of Key Equations

Equation	Description	Formula
10.1	Net present value	$NPV = NCF_0 + \frac{NCF_1}{1 + k} + \frac{NCF_2}{(1 + k)^2} + \cdots + \frac{NCF_n}{(1 + k)^n} = \sum_{t=0}^{n} \frac{NCF_t}{(1 + k)^t}$
10.2	Payback period	$PB = \text{Years to recover cost} + \frac{\text{Remaining cost to recover}}{\text{Cash flow during year}}$
10.3	Average rate of return	$ARR = \frac{\text{Average net income}}{\text{Average book value}}$
10.4	Internal rate of return	$NPV = \sum_{t=0}^{n} \frac{CF_t}{(1 + IRR)^t} = 0$
10.5	Modified internal rate of return	$PV_{Cost} = \frac{TV}{(1 + MIRR)^n}$

V. True or False Questions

1. Capital budgeting decisions are the most important investment decisions made by management.

a. True

b. False

2. A firm's capital budgeting plan is developed by the firm's CEO and the board of directors.

a. True

b. False

3. All the information needed to make capital budgeting decisions is generated from external sources.

a. True

b. False

4. Capital budgeting projects may be classified as independent, mutually exclusive, or contingent.
   a. True
   b. False

5. When two projects are independent, accepting or rejecting one project has no bearing on the decision on the other.
   a. True
   b. False

6. Projects are considered to be contingent projects if the decision on one is tied to the decision on the other.
   a. True
   b. False

7. All contingent projects are optional projects..
   a. True
   b. False

8. The cost of capital is the minimum return a project has to earn in order for it to be accepted.
   a. True
   b. False

9. Capital rationing refers to the allocation of available capital to the set of projects that will add the most to the firm's value.
   a. True
   b. False

10. The present value of a project is the difference between the present value of the expected future cash inflows and the present value of the outflows of the project.
    a. True
    b. False

11. Accepting a negative NPV project decreases shareholder wealth.
    a. True
    b. False

12. The NPV method is called a discounted cash flow technique.
    a. True
    b. False

13. The payback period represents the number of years it takes for the cash flows from a project to recover the project's initial investment.
    a. True
    b. False

14. The payback method can lead to incorrect capital budgeting decisions because cash flows after the payback period are not considered.
    a. True
    b. False

15. The major advantage of the discounted payback is that it tells management how long it takes a project to reach a positive NPV.
    a. True
    b. False

16. The accounting rate of return method ignores the time value of money.

a. True

b. False

17. The internal rate of return is a discounted cash flow technique.

a. True

b. False

18. The IRR is the discount rate that makes the NPV of a project equal to zero.

a. True

b. False

19. The IRR and NPV decisions are consistent with each other when the projects under consideration are independent and the cash flows are conventional.

a. True

b. False

20. When future cash flows from a project include both positive and negative cash flows, the cash flow pattern is said to be conventional.

a. True

b. False

VI. Multiple-Choice Questions and Problems

1. Capital budgeting is important because

a. the goal of these decisions is to identify projects that will add to the firm's value.

b. it involves substantial capital outlays that once made cannot be easily reversed.

c. this allows the firm's management to analyze potential business opportunities and decide on which ones to undertake.

d. All of the above are true.

2. Capital budgeting projects can be classified into

a. independent, mutually exclusive, and continuous projects.

b. independent, mutually exclusive, and contingent projects.

c. dependent, mutually exclusive, and contingent projects.

d. None of the above.

3. Two projects are considered to be mutually exclusive if

a. the projects perform completely different function.

b. their cash flows are unrelated.

c. selecting one would automatically eliminate accepting the other.

d. None of the above.

4. Contingent projects would imply that

a. the acceptance of one project is dependent on the acceptance of the other.

b. the projects can be either mandatory or optional.

c. Both a and b.

d. None of the above.

5. The cost of capital is
   a. the minimum return that a capital budgeting project must earn for it to be accepted.
   b. the opportunity cost that represents the return that would be earned on projects of similar risk.
   c. Both a and b.
   d. None of the above.

6. Practical difficulties involving valuing real assets include:
   a. estimating future cash flows in-house.
   b. identifying an appropriate discount rate for cash flows associated with real assets because no market data is available.
   c. Both a and b.
   d. None of the above.

7. Which one of the following statements is **NOT** true?
   a. Accepting a positive NPV project increases shareholder wealth.
   b. Accepting a negative NPV project decreases shareholder wealth.
   c. Accepting a zero NPV project has a negative impact on shareholder wealth.
   d. Managers are indifferent about accepting or rejecting a zero NPV project.

8. Which one of the following statements about the payback method is **NOT** true?
   a. The payback method is consistent with the goal of shareholder wealth maximization
   b. The payback method represents the number of years it takes a project to recover its initial investment.
   c. The payback method calls for the project to be accepted if the payback period is less than a target period.
   d. The payback method is a risk indicator.

9. For a capital budgeting project to be accepted
   a. the IRR should be equal to the cost of capital.
   b. the IRR should exceed the cost of capital.
   c. the IRR should be less than the cost of capital.
   d. None of the above.

10. When evaluating capital projects, the decisions using the NPV method and the IRR method will agree if
    a. the projects are independent.
    b. the cash flow pattern is conventional.
    c. the projects are mutually exclusive.
    d. Both a and b.

11. Stembridge Company is setting up to manufacture a new line of products. The cost of the manufacturing equipment is $750,000. Expected cash flows over the next four years are $125,000, $250,000, $400,000 and $500,000. Given the company's required rate of return of 15 percent, what is the NPV of this project?
    a. $96,615
    b. $119,806
    c. $69,806
    d. $22,607

12. Gao Enterprises have just planned to build a new plant at a cost of $3,250,000. The plant is expected to generate annual cash flows of $1,225,000 for the next five years. If the firm's required rate of return is 18 percent, what is the NPV of this project?
    a. $2,875,000
    b. $3,830,785

c. $580,785

d. $2,1225,875

13. Sao Paulo Sporting Goods is getting ready to produce a new line of soccer equipment by investing $1.5 million. The investment will result in additional cash flows of $435,000, $782,500, and 1,000,000 over the next three years. What is the payback period for this project?

a. 3 years

b. 2.3 years

c. 1.6 years

d. more than 3 years

14. Kathleen Dancewear Co. purchased some new machinery at a cost of $1,250,000. The impact of the new machinery will be felt in the additional annual cash flows of $375,000 over the next five years. What is the payback period for this project? If their acceptance period is three years, will this project be accepted?

a. 2.67 years; yes

b. 2.67 years; no

c. 3.33 years; yes

d. 3.33 years; no

15. Stockman Plumbing bought new machinery for $4 million. This is expected to result in additional annual cash flows of $930,000 for the next eight years. The firm's cost of capital is 15 percent. What is the discounted payback period for this project? If their acceptance period is five years, will this project be accepted?

a. 5.4 years; no

b. 7.4 years; no

c. 4.6 years; yes

d. 4.2 years; yes

16. Stain Corp. has forecasted that over the next four years the average annual after-tax income will be $500,731. The average book value of the manufacturing equipment that is used is $737,095. What is the accounting rate of return?

a. 53.3%

b. 71.4%

c. 67.9%

d. 42.3%

17. Quick Sale Real Estate Company is planning to invest in a new development. The cost of the project will be $23 million, and the project is expected to generate cash flows of $14,000,000, $11,750,000, and $6,350,000 over the next three years. The company's cost of capital is 20 percent. What is the internal rate of return on this project? (Round to the nearest percent.)

a. 22%

b. 20%

c. 24%

d. 28%

18. Casa Del Sol Property Development Company is refurbishing a 200-unit condominium complex at a cost of $1,875,000. The firm expects that this will lead to expected annual cash flows of $415,350 for the next seven years. What internal rate of return can the firm earn from this project? (Round to the nearest percent.)

a. 10%

b. 12%

c. 14%

d. 16%

19. Jenkins Corp. is adding a new assembly line at a cost of $18.5 million. The firm expects the project to generate cash flows of $6 million, $5 million, $4 million, and $5 million over the next four years. If its cost of capital is 15 percent, what is the modified IRR? (Round to the nearest percent.)

    a. 8%

    b. 10%

    c. 14%

    d. 16%

20. A firm's cost of capital is 15 percent, and it plans to invest in a project that will generate a modified internal rate of return of 12 percent. What should be the firm's decision regarding its project?

    a. Accept the project because the MIRR exceeds 10 percent.

    b. Reject the project because the MIRR is lower than the cost of capital.

    c. Accept the project because the MIRR is lower than the cost of capital.

    d. Reject the project because we do not know the IRR for the project.

VI. Answers to True or False Questions

1. a	**2.** b	**3.** b	**4.** a	**5.** a
6. a	**7.** b	**8.** a	**9.** a	**10.** a
11. a	**12.** a	**13.** a	**14.** a	**15.** a
16. a	**17.** a	**18.** a	**19.** a	**20.** b

VII. Answers to Multiple-Choice Questions

1. d	**2.** b	**3.** c	**4.** c	**5.** c
6. c	**7.** c	**8.** a	**9.** b	**10.** d
11. a	**12.** c	**13.** b	**14.** d	**15.** b
16. c	**17.** a	**18.** b	**19.** a	**20.** b

VIII. Solutions to Multiple-Choice Problems

11. <u>Solution:</u>

Initial investment = 750,000

Length of project = n = 4 years

Required rate of return = k = *15%*

Net present value = NPV

$$\text{NPV} = \sum_{t=0}^{n} \frac{\text{NCF}_t}{(1+k)^t} = -\$750{,}000 + \frac{\$125{,}000}{(1.15)^1} + \frac{\$250{,}000}{(1.15)^2} + \frac{\$400{,}000}{(1.15)^3} + \frac{\$500{,}000}{(1.15)^4}$$

$$= -\$750{,}000 + \$108{,}696 + \$189{,}036 + \$263{,}006 + \$285{,}877$$

= **$96,615**

12. <u>Solution:</u>

Initial investment = $3,250,000

Annual cash flows = $1,225,000

Length of project = n = 5 years

Required rate of return = k = 18%

Net present value = NPV

$$\text{NPV} = \sum_{t=0}^{n} \frac{\text{NCF}_t}{(1+k)^t} = -\$3{,}250{,}000 + \$1{,}225{,}000 \times \left[\frac{1 - \dfrac{1}{(1.18)^5}}{0.18} \right]$$
$$= -\$3{,}250{,}000 + \$3{,}830{,}785$$
$$= \mathbf{\$580{,}785}$$

13. Solution:

Elmer Sporting Goods

Year	Cash flow	Cumulative CF
0	$(1,500,000)	$(1,500,000)
1	435,000	(1,065,000)
2	782,500	(282,500)
3	1,000,000	717,500

PB = Years before cost recovery + (Remaining cost to recover/Cash flow during the year
= 2 + ($282,500 / $1,000,000)
= **2.28 years**

14. Solution:

Kathleen Dancewear Inc.

Year	Cash flow	Cumulative CF
0	$(1,250,000)	$(1,250,000)
1	375,000	(875,000)
2	375,000	(500,000)
3	375,000	(125,000)
4	375,000	250,000
5	375,000	625,000

PB = Years before cost recovery + (Remaining cost to recover/Cash flow during the year
= 3 + ($125,000 / $375,000)
= **3.33 years**

Since the payback period of 3.33 years exceeds the decision criteria of 3 years, this project should be rejected.

15. Solution:

Year	Cash flow	PVCF	Cumulative PVCF
0	$(4,000,000)	$(4,000,000)	$(4,000,000)
1	930,000	808,696	(3,191,304)
2	930,000	703,214	(2,488,091)
3	930,000	611,490	(1,876,601)
4	930,000	531,731	(1,344,870)
5	930,000	462,374	(882,496)
6	930,000	402,065	(480,431)
7	930,000	349,621	(130,810)
8	930,000	304,019	173,209

PB = Years before cost recovery + (Remaining cost to recover/Cash flow during the year)
= 7 + ($130,810 / $304,019)
= **7.43 years**

Since the payback period of 7.43 years exceeds the decision criteria of 5 years, this project should be rejected.

16. Solution:

Annual after-tax income = \$500,731

Average after-tax income = (\$500,731 + \$500,731 + \$500,731 + \$500,731) / 4 − \$500,731

Average book value of equipment = \$737,095

$$\text{Accounting rate of return} = \frac{\text{Average net income}}{\text{Average book value}}$$

$$= \frac{\$500{,}731}{\$737{,}095} = \mathbf{67.9}\%$$

17. Solution:

Initial investment = \$23,000,000

Length of project = n = 3 years

Required rate of return = k = 20%

To determine the IRR, the trial-and-error approach can be used. Set NPV = 0.

Try IRR = 20%.

$$\text{NPV} = 0 = \sum_{t=0}^{n} \frac{\text{NCF}_t}{(1 + \text{IRR})^t}$$

$$0 = -\ \$23{,}000{,}000 + \frac{\$14{,}000{,}000}{(1.20)^1} + \frac{\$11{,}750{,}000}{(1.20)^2} + \frac{\$6{,}350{,}000}{(1.20)^3}$$

$$= -\ \$23{,}000{,}000 + \$11{,}666{,}667 + \$8{,}159{,}722 + \$3{,}674{,}769$$

$$= \$501{,}157 \neq 0$$

Since NPV is still positive, try IRR = 22%.

$$\text{NPV} = 0 = \sum_{t=0}^{n} \frac{\text{NCF}_t}{(1 + \text{IRR})^t}$$

$$0 = -\ \$23{,}000{,}000 + \frac{\$14{,}000{,}000}{(1.22)^1} + \frac{\$11{,}750{,}000}{(1.22)^2} + \frac{\$6{,}350{,}000}{(1.22)^3}$$

$$= -\ \$23{,}000{,}000 + \$11{,}475{,}410 + \$7{,}894{,}383 + \$3{,}496{,}989$$

$$= -\ \$133{,}218 \neq 0$$

This NPV is negative. Hence IRR is between 20 and 22 percent.

Try IRR = 21.6%.

$$\text{NPV} = 0 = \sum_{t=0}^{n} \frac{\text{NCF}_t}{(1 + \text{IRR})^t}$$

$$0 = -\ \$23{,}000{,}000 + \frac{\$14{,}000{,}000}{(1.216)^1} + \frac{\$11{,}750{,}000}{(1.216)^2} + \frac{\$6{,}350{,}000}{(1.216)^3}$$

$$= -\ \$23{,}000{,}000 + \$11{,}513{,}158 + \$7{,}946{,}405 + \$3{,}531{,}612$$

$$= -\ \$8{,}825 \cong 0$$

The IRR of the project is **21.6 percent**. Using a financial calculator, we find that the IRR is **21.572 percent**.

18. Solution:

Initial investment = \$1,875,000

Annual cash flows = \$415,350

Length of investment = n = 7 years

To determine the IRR, the trial-and-error approach can be used. Set NPV = 0

Try IRR =12%.

$$\text{NPV} = 0 = \sum_{t=0}^{n} \frac{\text{NCF}_t}{(1 + \text{IRR})^t} = -\ \$1{,}875{,}000 + \$415{,}350 \times \left[\frac{1 - \frac{1}{(1.12)^7}}{0.12}\right]$$

$$0 = -\ \$1{,}875{,}000 + \$1{,}895{,}556$$

$$= \mathbf{\$20{,}556 \neq 0}$$

Since NPV is positive, try IRR =12.3%.

$$\text{NPV} = 0 = \sum_{t=0}^{n} \frac{\text{NCF}_t}{(1 + \text{IRR})^t} = -\ \$1{,}875{,}000 + \$415{,}350 \times \left[\frac{1 - \dfrac{1}{(1.123)^7}}{0.123} \right]$$

$$0 = -\ \$1{,}875{,}000 + \$1{,}877{,}660$$

$$= \mathbf{\$2{,}660 \cong 0}$$

The IRR of the project is **12.3 percent**. Using a financial calculator, we find that the IRR is **12.345 percent**.

19. Solution:

Initial investment = \$18,500,000

Length of investment = n = 4 years

Cost of capital = k = 15%

$$\text{TV} = \text{CF}_1(1 + k)^{n-1} + \text{CF}_2(1 + k)^{n-2} + \cdots + \text{CF}_n(1 + k)^{n-n}$$

$$= \$6{,}000{,}000(1.15)^3 + \$5{,}000{,}000(1.15)^2 + \$4{,}000{,}000(1.15)^1 + \$5{,}000{,}000(1.15)^0$$

$$= \$9{,}125{,}250 + \$6{,}612{,}500 + \$4{,}600{,}000 + \$5{,}000{,}000$$

$$= \$25{,}337{,}750$$

$$\text{PV}_{\text{Cost}} = \frac{\text{TV}}{(1 + \text{MIRR})^t}$$

$$\$18{,}500{,}000 = \frac{\$25{,}337{,}750}{(1 + \text{MIRR})^4}$$

$$(1 + \text{MIRR})^4 = \frac{\$16{,}798{,}592}{\$8{,}500{,}000} = 1.3696$$

$$(1 + \text{MIRR}) = (1.3696)^{1/4} = 1.0818$$

$$\text{MIRR} = 0.0818 = \mathbf{8.2}\%$$

20. Solution:

b. Reject the project because the MIRR is lower than the cost of capital.

CHAPTER 11

Cash Flows and Capital Budgeting

LEARNING OBJECTIVES

1. Explain why incremental after-tax free cash flows are relevant in evaluating a project, and be able to calculate them for a project.
2. Discuss the five general rules for incremental after-tax free cash flow calculations, and explain why cash flows stated in nominal (real) dollars should be discounted using a nominal (real) discount rate.
3. Describe how distinguishing between variable and fixed costs can be useful in forecasting operating expenses.
4. Explain the concept of equivalent annual cost, and be able to use it to compare projects with unequal lives, decide when to replace an existing asset, and calculate the opportunity cost of using an existing asset.
5. Determine the appropriate time to harvest an asset.

I. Chapter Outline

11.1 Calculating Project Cash Flows

- In capital budgeting, we estimate the NPV of the cash flows that a project is expected to produce in the future.
- All of the cash flow estimates are forward-looking, which is different from the accounting statement of cash flows.

A. ***Incremental After-Tax Free Cash Flows***

- The cash flows we discount in an NPV analysis are the **incremental after-tax free cash flows**, which refer to the fact that these cash flows reflect the amount by which the firm's total after-tax free cash flows will change if the project is adopted.
- We define FCF as the total cash flows the firm would produce with the project, less the total after-tax free cash flows the firm would produce without the project. See Equation 11.1:

$$FCF_{Project} = FCF_{Firm\ with\ project} - FCF_{Firm\ without\ project}$$

- The term *free cash flows* refers to the fact that the firm is free to distribute these cash flows to creditors and stockholders because these are the cash flows that are left over after a firm has made necessary investments in working capital and long term assets.
- FCF is a measure of a project's impact on the cash flows from *operating* and *investing* decisions at a firm.

B. ***The FCF Calculation***

- Referring to Equation 11.2, which is a more detailed version of Equation 11.1:

$$\text{FCF} = [(\text{Revenue} - \text{Op Exp} - \text{D\&A}) \times (1 - t)] + \text{D\&A} - \text{Cap Ex} - \text{Add WC}$$

- We first compute the incremental cash flow from operations (CF Opns), which is the cash flow that the project is expected to generate after all operating expenses and taxes have been paid.

$$\text{CF Opns} = [(\text{Revenue} - \text{Op Exp} - \text{D\&A}) \times (1 - t)] + \text{D\&A}$$

- We then subtract the incremental capital expenditures (Cap Ex) and incremental additions to working capital (Add WC) required for the project to obtain FCF.
- The FCF is therefore a measure of the after-tax cash flows from operations over and above what is necessary to make any required investments.
- The idea that we can evaluate the cash flows from a project independently of the cash flows for the firm is known as the **stand-alone principle**. It is another way of saying that we can treat the project as if it is a stand-alone firm that has its own revenue, expenses, and investment requirements.

C. ***The Cash Flows from Operations***

- The incremental cash flow from operations, CF Opns, equals the incremental net operating profits after tax (NOPAT) plus the incremental depreciation and amortization (D&A) associated with the project.
- We exclude interest expenses when calculating NOPAT because the cost of financing a project is reflected in the discount rate that is used in the NPV calculation.
- We use the firm's marginal tax rate (t) to calculate NOPAT because the profits from a project are assumed to be incremental to the firm.
- We add incremental depreciation and amortization (D&A) to NOPAT when calculating CF Opns because, as in the accounting statement of cash flows, D&A represents a non-cash charge that reduces the firm's tax obligation.
- Since D&A is a noncash charge, we have to add it back to NOPAT in order to get the cash flow from operations right.

D. ***Cash Flows Associated with Investments***

- Once we have estimated CF Opns, we simply subtract cash flows associated with required investment to obtain FCF for a project in a particular period.
- Investments can be required to purchase long-term tangible assets and intangible assets, or to fund current assets.
- It is, therefore, also necessary to account for incremental additions to working capital (Add WC).

E. ***FCF versus Accounting Earnings***

- The impact of a project on a firm's overall value or on its stock price does not depend on how the project affects the company's accounting earnings. It depends only on how the project affects the company's free cash flows.
- Accounting earnings can differ from cash flows for a number of reasons, making accounting earnings an unreliable measure of the costs and benefits of a project.
- Accounting earnings also reflect non-cash charges, such as depreciation and amortization, which are intended to account for the costs associated with deterioration of the assets in a business as those assets are used.

11.2 Estimating Cash Flows in Practice

A. ***Five General Rules for Incremental After-Tax Cash Flow Calculations***

- **Rule 1:** ***Include cash flows and only cash flows in your calculations.*** Do not include allocated costs or overhead unless they reflect cash flows.
- **Rule 2:** ***Include the impact of the project on cash flows from other product lines.*** If the product associated with a project is expected to cannibalize or boost sales of another product, you must include the expected impact of the new project on the cash flows from the other product in the analysis.
- **Rule 3:** ***Include all opportunity costs.*** By opportunity costs, we mean the cost of giving up another opportunity.
- **Rule 4:** ***Forget sunk costs.*** Sunk costs are costs that have already been incurred, but all that matters when you evaluate a project at a particular point in time is how much you have to invest in the future and what you could expect to receive in return for that investment; this means that past investments are irrelevant.
- **Rule 5:** ***Include only after-tax cash flows in the cash flow calculations.*** The incremental pretax earnings of a project only matter to the extent that they affect the after-tax cash flows that the firm's investors receive. Make sure that you include after-tax cash flows in your final calculations.

B. ***Nominal versus Real Cash Flows***

- Nominal dollars are the dollars that we typically think of. They represent the actual dollar amounts that we expect a project to generate in the future, without any adjustments.
- When prices are going up, a given nominal dollar amount will buy less and less over time.
  - Real dollars represent dollars stated in terms of constant purchasing power.
- We can write the cost of capital, k, as

$$1 + k = (1 + \Delta P_e) \times (1 + r)$$

  - r is the real cost of capital
  - (ΔP_e) is the expected rate of inflation
  - (r) is the real rate of return
- It is important to make sure that all cash flows are stated in *either* nominal dollars or real dollars. It is important not to mix the two different types of cash flows within your calculations.

C. ***Taxes and Depreciation***

- A **progressive tax system,** which we have in the United States, is one in which the marginal tax rate at low levels of income is lower than the marginal tax rate at high levels of income.
- One especially important difference from a capital budgeting perspective is that the depreciation methods allowed by GAAP differ from those allowed by the IRS.
  - The straight-line depreciation method illustrated earlier in this chapter in the NASCAR racetrack example is allowed by GAAP and is often used for financial reporting.
  - An accelerated method of depreciation, called the Modified Accelerated Cost Recovery System (MACRS), has been in use for U.S. federal tax calculations since the Tax Reform Act of 1986 went into effect.
    - MACRS thus enables a firm to deduct depreciation charges sooner, thereby realizing the tax savings sooner and increasing the present value of the tax savings.

D. ***Computing Terminal-Year*** ΔFCF

- The FCF in the last, or terminal, year of a project often includes cash flows that are not typically included in the calculations for other years.
  - For instance, in the final year of a project, the assets acquired during the life of the project may be sold and the working capital that has been invested may be recovered.
    - Add WC = Change in cash and cash equivalents + Change in accounts receivable + Change in inventories − Changes in accounts payable
    - When an asset is expected to have a salvage value, we must include the salvage value realized from the sale (net of any tax consequences) of the asset and the impact of the sale on the firm's taxes in the terminal-year FCF calculations.

11.3 Forecasting Free Cash Flows

A. ***Cash Flows from Operations***

- To forecast the incremental cash flows from operations (CF Opns) for a project, we must forecast the incremental net revenue, operating expenses, and depreciations and amortization associated with the project, as well as the firm's marginal tax rate.
  - When forecasting operating expenses, analysts often distinguish between **variable costs,** which vary directly with unit sales, and **fixed costs,** which do not.
  - Since depreciation and amortization is determined by the amounts invested in depreciable assets and the lives over which these assets can be depreciated, it is based on the incremental capital expenditures associated with the project.
  - The tax rate that should be used when forecasting cash flow from operations is the marginal rate the firm expects to pay on the incremental cash flows generated by the project in the future.

B. ***Investment Cash Flows***

- Capital expenditures and additions to working capital must be considered when calculating free cash flow.
  - **Capital Expenditures**
    - Capital expenditure forecast reflect the expected level of investment during each year of the project's life, including any inflows form salvage values and any tax costs or benefits associated with asset sales.
    - Some projects require substantial periodic investments to replace or refurbish assets on to shut down operations (clean-up costs) at the end of the projects' life.

- **Working Capital**
  - Working capital items include:
    - Cash and cash equivalents
    - Account receivable
    - Inventories, and
    - Accounts payable

11.4 Special Cases (Optional)

A. *Projects with Different Lives*

- A problem that arises quite often in capital budgeting involves choosing between two mutually exclusive investments where the investments have different lives.
  - In a situation like this, we can effectively make the lives of the projects the same by assuming repeated investments over some identical period and then comparing the NPVs of their costs.
  - A less cumbersome and more powerful method to handle the problem is to compute the **equivalent annual cost (EAC)**. The EAC can be calculated as follows:

$$EAC_i = k\,NPV_i\left[\frac{(1+k)^t}{(1+k)^t - 1}\right] \quad \textbf{(11.5)}$$

- k is the opportunity cost of capital
- NPV_i is normal NPV of the investment i
- t is the life of the investment.
- EAC simply reflects the annuity that has the same present value as the FCFs of an investment over the investment period we are considering.
  - An algebraic manipulation of this formula will give you an equivalent formula. That is, divide the NPV by the appropriate annuity factor, with the discount rate k and the t number of periods in the project.

B. *When to Harvest an Asset*

- The optimal time to harvest is the point in time at which the rate of increase is no longer greater than the cost of capital.
- At this point in time, it becomes optimal to harvest the trees and invest the proceeds in alternative investments that yield the opportunity cost of capital.

C. *When to Replace an Existing Asset*

- Two fundamental questions are: Do the benefits of replacing the existing asset exceed the costs, and, if they do not now, when will they?
- Solving this problem is simply a matter of computing the EAC for the new mower and comparing it with the annual cash inflows from the old asset.

D. *The Cost of Using an Existing Asset*

- The third rule of calculating incremental after-tax cash flows is *to include all opportunity costs* that are not always directly observable.
  - Sometimes they have to be computed by first figuring the EAC for a given set of cash flows and then adjusting the EAC by the appropriate discount rate and time, if the EAC is not in present value form.

II. Suggested Approach to Material

This is a very important chapter for all students. Finance majors will need the basic capital budgeting concepts introduced here for their more advanced course work, whereas non-majors will require a basic foundation for the material in their professional lives as they will undoubtedly be involved in project analysis at some point in their careers. The chapter begins with a general framework for capital budgeting, so that the overall approach to capital budgeting can be seen before proceeding to the detailed aspects of the subject matter. Free cash flow (FCF) is then formally introduced along with individual sub-calculations that make it up. The chapter includes a number of examples to accompany the individual aspects of the material and finishes by introducing special cases in which the net present value of the projects FCFs will require further adjustments.

Thorough knowledge of the material is required before proceeding to the next chapter where the tools are then applied further. It may therefore be necessary to allocate additional time for this chapter as the material is central to Finance, while it also incorporates a number of tools learned in earlier chapters.

III. Chapter Glossary

Incremental after-tax free cash flows	The difference between the total after-tax free cash flows at a firm with a project and the total after-tax free cash flows at the same firm without that project. A measure of a project's total impact on the free cash flows at a firm.
Incremental cash flow from operations (CF Opns)	The cash flow that a project generates after all operating expenses and taxes have been paid but before any cash outflows for investments.
Incremental capital expenditures (Cap Exp)	The investments in property, plant, and equipment and other long-term assets that must be made if a project is pursued.
Incremental additions to working capital (Add WC)	The investments in working capital items, such as accounts receivable, inventory, and accounts payable, that must be made if the project is pursued.
Incremental depreciation and amortization (D&A)	The depreciation and amortization charges that are associated with a project.
Firm's marginal tax rate (*t*)	The tax rate that is applied to each additional dollar of earnings at a firm.
Stand-alone principle	The principle that allows us to treat each project as a stand-alone firm when we perform an NPV analysis.
Incremental net operating profits after tax (NOPAT)	A measure of the impact of a project on the firm's cash net income, excluding the effects of any interest expenses associated with financing the project.
Tangible assets	Physical assets such as property, plant, and equipment.
Intangible assets	Nonphysical assets such as patents, mailing lists, or brand names.
Current assets	Assets, such as accounts receivable and inventories, that are expected to be liquidated (collected or sold) within one year.
Nominal dollars	Dollar amounts that are not adjusted for inflation. The purchasing power of nominal dollar amounts depends on when that amount is received.
Real dollars	Inflation-adjusted dollars. The actual purchasing power of dollars stated in "real" terms is the same regardless of when those dollars are received.
Progressive tax system	A tax system in which the marginal tax rate at low levels of income is lower than the marginal tax rate at high levels of income.
Modified Accelerated Cost Recovery System (MACRS)	The accelerated depreciation method that has been in use for U.S. federal taxes since the Tax Reform Act of 1986 went into effect.
Variable costs	Costs that vary directly with the number of units sold.
Fixed costs	Costs that do not vary directly with the number of units sold.
Equivalent annual cost (EAC)	The annual dollar amount of an annuity that has a life equal to that of a project and that also has a present value equal to the present value of the cash flows from the project. The term comes from the fact that the EAC calculation is often used to calculate a constant annual cost associated with projects in order to make comparisons.

IV. Summary of Key Equations

Equation	Description	Formula
11.1	Incremental free cash flow definition	$FCF_{Project} = FCF_{Firm\ with\ project} - FCF_{Firm\ without\ project}$
11.2	Incremental free cash flow calculation	$FCF = [(Revenue - Op\ Exp - D\&A) \times (1 - t)] + D\&A - Cap\ Ex - Add\ WC$
11.3	Inflation and real components of cost of capital	$1 + k = (1 + \Delta P_e) \times (1 + r)$
11.4	Incremental additions to working capital	Add WC = Change in cash and cash equivalents + Change in accounts receivable + Change in inventories − Changes in accounts payable
11.5	Equivalent annual cost	$EAC_i = k\,NPV_i \left[\frac{(1 + k)^t}{(1 + k)^t - 1}\right]$

V. True or False Questions

1. The term *free cash flows* refers to the fact that the firm is free to distribute these cash flows to stockholders.
   a. True
   b. False

2. The incremental cash flow from operations for a project equals the incremental net operating profits after tax plus the incremental depreciation and amortization associated with the project.
   a. True
   b. False

3. Depreciation and amortization can be completely ignored in the calculation of free cash flows because they are both noncash expenses.
   a. True
   b. False

4. The impact of a project on the value of a firm depends only on how the project affects the company's free cash flows rather than on its accounting earnings.
   a. True
   b. False

5. Overhead or allocated costs that do not reflect cash flows are important in free cash flow calculations.
   a. True
   b. False

6. If expected inflation is positive, then nominal rates of return will be higher than real rates of return.
   a. True
   b. False

7. A progressive tax system is one in which taxpayers will pay higher tax rates on all of their income as they have higher amounts of earnings.
   a. True
   b. False

8. Working capital items include cash and cash equivalents, accounts receivable, inventories, and accounts payable.
   a. True
   b. False

9. The terminal year of a project often includes cash flows that are not typically included in the calculations of FCF for other years.
   a. True
   b. False

10. When comparing projects with different lives, the net present value of each unadjusted project can be used to determine which project is superior.
   a. True
   b. False

VI. Multiple-Choice Questions

1. If we are trying to calculate the FCF for a project and we have subtracted Op Exp from Revenue and multiplied the result by (1 minus the tax rate), then what item remains to be added or subtracted if there are no capital expenditures or changes in working capital for the project?
   a. Add back D&A.
   b. Subtract D&A.
   c. Add back D&A times the tax rate.
   d. Subtract D&A times the tax rate.

2. The FCF is
   a. a measure of cash flows from operations over and above what is necessary to make any required investments.
   b. a measure of after-tax cash flows from operations over and above what is necessary to make any required investments.
   c. a measure of accounting earnings from operations over and above what is necessary to make any required investments.
   d. None of the above.

3. When comparing real interest rates with nominal rates of return,
   a. nominal rates will be higher than real rates if expected inflation is positive.
   b. real rates will be higher than nominal rates if expected inflation is positive.
   c. nominal rates will be higher than real rates if expected inflation is negative.
   d. None of the above.

4. Mikos, Inc., bought a machine at a cost of $50,000 two years ago. The machine has been depreciated toward a salvage value of zero using the straight-line method with an original life of five years. Mikos can sell the machine now at its market price of $40,000. The marginal tax rate is 30 percent. What is Mikos's after-tax cash flow from the sale?
   a. $40,000
   b. $37,000
   c. $33,000
   d. $3,000

5. Gita, Inc., bought a machine at a cost of $100,000 five years ago. The machine has been depreciated using the straight-line method with an original life of five years. Gita can now sell the machine at its market price of $40,000. The marginal tax rate is 30 percent. What is Gita's after-tax cash flow from the sale?
   a. $40,000
   b. $28,000
   c. $12,000
   d. $0

6. Investment cash flows: MuggelSticks is about to begin selling a product in a new line of business that is expected to generate annual revenue is $3 million. To estimate the increase in working capital, it estimates the ratio of cash and cash equivalents to revenue to be 0.08, and the ratio of payables to revenue to be 0.04 in the same industry. What are the incremental cash flows related to working capital when the new line is started?

   a. $240,000

   b. $120,000

   c. −$120,000

   d. −$240,000

7. Cash flows from operations: ElectricEye Technologies is considering introducing a new line of optic devices. The expected annual sales number of the devices is 10,000 per year; the price is $5,000 per device, and the variable costs of production amount to $2,000 per unit. The fixed costs (including depreciation) are $10 million per year. Depreciation costs are $5 million per year. The marginal tax rate is 40 percent. What is the incremental annual cash flow from operations for the new line?

   a. $25 million

   b. $20 million

   c. $17 million

   d. $12 million

8. Oak Hall Ironworks, Inc., has taken a project that has required additional working capital amounts of $10,000 for the last three years. If a similar pattern is expected to hold for the next three years, then what should be the terminal cash flow at the conclusion of the project, with respect to the additional working capital?

   a. $10,000 inflow

   b. $10,000 outflow

   c. $30,000 inflow

   d. $60,000 inflow

9. Ironwood Boats, Inc., has taken a project that has reduced working capital needs of $12,000 last year as well as $23,000 this year. What should be the terminal cash flow at the conclusion of the project, with respect to the additional working capital?

   a. $23,000 inflow

   b. $23,000 outflow

   c. $35,000 inflow

   d. $35,000 outflow

10. Simplified Micro Devices has a contract to sell 10,000 mousetraps to the Department of Defense. The mousetraps will sell for $5.50 apiece. However, there is a 20 percent probability that total expenses will be $40,000 and a 80 percent probability that total expenses will be $50,000. What is the expected pretax income for the firm's Department of Defense sales?

    a. $7,000

    b. $48,000

    c. $55,000

    d. None of the above

11. Mack's Mild Lemonade has taken a five- year project with an NPV of $4,500. If the discount rate on the project is 12 percent, then what is the equivalent annual annuity for the project? (Round to the nearest dollar.)

    a. $4,500

    b. $1,500

    c. $1,248

    d. None of the above

12. Sedimentary Beverages is considering two mutually exclusive projects. The iced tea project has an NPV of $5,000, and it will have a life of four years. The hot coffee project has an NPV of $6,000 and will have a life of seven years. Which project should the firm choose and why? The discount rate for both projects is 12 percent.

 a. the hot coffee project because it has a higher NPV

 b. the iced tea project because it is a shorter project

 c. the iced tea project because it has a higher EAA

 d. Take them both because they both have positive NPVs.

13. You are deciding whether to purchase a six-year life widget machine for $1,000 or a three-year life widget machine for $500. The six-year machine will produce cash flows of $300 per year, while the three-year machine will produce cash flows of $275 per year. Which machine should you choose if your analysis involves rolling over one of the projects, and why?

 a. Choose the six-year machine because it produces more cash flow per year.

 b. Choose the six-year machine because it saves having to expend more cash in year 3.

 c. Choose the three-year machine because it will create a higher NPV over a total six-year period.

 d. Don't choose either because they both have positive costs.

14. LumberCo. has produced a forecast of lumber prices and is deciding when to harvest a small forest that it currently owns. It has determined that the NPVs increase per the following schedule. If the opportunity cost of capital for the firm is 12 percent, then when should LumberCo. harvest the forest?

Year	Increase in NPV over Prior Year
2008	
2009	18.0%
2010	15.0%
2011	14.0%
2012	12.5%
2013	11.5%
2014	11.0%

 a. 2008

 b. 2012

 c. 2013

 d. 2014

15. Prospecter's Mill has calculated the NPV of beginning to mine the gold in a mine at different points in time. If NPV x,y refers to the NPV of mining the gold at time y and calculated in time x dollars, then when should the firm mine the gold if the opportunity cost of capital is 15 percent? See the following schedule for the NPVs.

$NPV_{5,5}$:	$20,000
$NPV_{5,6}$:	$24,000
$NPV_{5,7}$:	$28,320
$NPV_{5,8}$:	$32,284

 a. Year 5

 b. Year 6

 c. Year 7

 d. Year 8

16. You are reviewing a project that has an NPV equal to zero if the project were started today. However, the NPV of the project will increase (if measured in today's dollars) in the forthcoming years if you postpone starting the project. What rule should you use to determine the appropriate year to commence the project?

 a. Start the project as soon as the NPV of the project is positive.

 b. Start the project when the rate of increase in the NPV of the project (based on the commencement date) is equal to the opportunity cost of capital for the firm.

c. Start the project when the rate of increase in the NPV of the project (based on the commencement date) is above the opportunity cost of capital for the firm but will drop below that during the next period.

d. Start the project when the rate of increase in the NPV of the project (based on the commencement date) is below the opportunity cost of capital for the firm.

17. Myron's Metals owns a tungsten machine that is generating cash flows of $6,000 per year and should be able to do so for the remaining four years of life on the machine. If Myron's buys a new machine for $15,000 (and discards the old), it will last five years and would then be able to generate cash flows of $8,000 per year. Which option should the firm take and why? Assume a cost of capital equal to 12 percent

a. Keep the old machine because the EAC of the new is less than that of the old.

b. Keep the old machine because the old machine is fully depreciated.

c. Buy the new machine because the EAC of the new is greater than that of the old.

d. Buy the new machine because the old machine will not last the entire life of the old.

18. PorticosAreUs has an industrial lathe that can generate cash flows of $14,000 per year for three more years. If the firm purchases a new lathe and discards the old, it will have to spend $100,000 and the new lathe will generate cash flows of $50,000 per year for four years. If the cost of capital for the firm is 15 percent, then which option should the firm take?

a. Keep the old machine because the EAC of the new is less than that of the old.

b. Keep the old machine because the old machine is fully depreciated.

c. Buy the new machine because the EAC of the new is greater than that of the old.

d. Buy the new machine because the old machine will not last the entire life of the old.

19. You are thinking about purchasing a special dump truck used for hauling heavy materials out of a deep open-pit mine. The cost of the truck is $5 million, and it will last five years. If there are no maintenance costs associated with the machine, then what is the annual cost to operate the machine if the cost of capital is 12 percent?

a. $1,000,000.00

b. $1,491,577.76

c. $5,000,000.00

d. $6,491,577.76

20. Pettigout's Seafood Supplies is contemplating using its boat for additional duties. If it does so, then the boat will have to be replaced three years earlier than without the additional duties. The current boat will need to be replaced in seven years. If a new boat will cost $350,000, then what is the cost of using the old boat for the additional duties if the cost of capital is 8 percent?

a. $50,000.00

b. $67,225.34

c. $137,528.44

d. $350,000.00

VII. Answers to True or False Questions

1. b **2.** a **3.** b **4.** a **5.** b

6. a **7.** b **8.** a **9.** a **10.** b

VIII. Answers to Multiple-Choice Questions

1. c **2.** b **3.** a **4.** b **5.** b

6. c **7.** c **8.** d **9.** d **10.** a

11. c **12.** c **13.** c **14.** b **15.** c

16. c **17.** a **18.** c **19.** b **20.** c

Solutions to Multiple-Choice Questions

1. FCF = [(Revenue − Op Exp − D&A) × (1 − t)] + D&A − Cap Ex − Add WC
= [(Revenue − Op Exp − D&A) (1 − t)] + D&A
= [(Revenue − Op Exp) × (1 − t)] [D&A × (1 − t)] + D&A
= Starting result + [− D&A + D&A × t + D&A]
= Starting result + **D&A × t**

4. Annual depreciation: $50,000 / 5 = $10,000
Current book value: $50,000 − (2 × $10,000) = $30,000
Taxable gain from the sale: $40,000 − $30,000 = $10,000
Taxes from the sale: $10,000 × 0.3 = $3,000
Total proceeds from sale of machine: $40,000 − $3,000 = **$37,000**

5. Annual depreciation: $100,000 / 5 = $20,000.
Current book value: $100,000 − (5 × $20,000) = $0
Taxable gain from the sale: $40,000 − $0 = $40,000
Taxes from the sale: $40,000 × 0.3 = $12,000
Total proceeds from sale of machine: $40,000 − $12,000 = **$28,000**
Or note in this case an easier calculation of $40,000 × 0.7 = $28,000 could be used.

6. Revenue × (Add WC ratio requirement) =
Revenue (Increase ratio of cash − Increase ratio of payables) =
− $3,000,000 × (0.08 − 0.04) = **−$120,000**

7. {[(Rev/unit − VC/unit) * Sales units] − FC} * (1 − T) + Deprec Expense
{[(($5,000 − $2,000) * 10,000) − $10,000,000)] * (1 − 0.4)} − 5,000,000 = **$17,000,000**

8. 6 years of additional investments in working capital will be recouped, so 6 × $10,000 = $60,000, which is an inflow.

9. $12,000 + $23,000 = **$35,000,** which is an outflow since the originating amounts were inflows.

10. Expected expenses = 0.2 × $40,000 + 0.8 × $50,000 = $48,000;
Expected pretax income = (10,000 × $5.50) − $48,000 = **$7,000**

$$EAC_i = k\,NPV_i\left[\frac{(1+k)^t}{(1+k)^t - 1}\right]$$

11. $0.12 \times \$4{,}500 \times \left[\frac{(1.12)^5}{(1.12)^5 - 1}\right] = \$1{,}248.34$

$$EAC_i = k\,NPV_i\left[\frac{(1+k)^t}{(1+k)^t - 1}\right]$$

12. $EAC_{\text{iced tea}}\ 0.12 \times \$5{,}000 \times \left[\frac{(1.12)^4}{(1.12)^4 - 1}\right] = \$1{,}646.17$

$EAC_{\text{hot coffee}}\ 0.12 \times \$6{,}000 \times \left[\frac{(1.12)^7}{(1.12)^7 - 1}\right] = \$1{,}314.71,$

Choose the iced tea project with the greater EAA.

13. Another three-year machine will need to be replaced at the end of the third year in order to create a six-year option. The present value of the three-year machine (adjusted to six years) then becomes:

$$NPV_{3-\ year\ adj} = -\$500 + \frac{\$275}{(1.1)^1} + \frac{\$275}{(1.1)^2} + \frac{\$275 - \$500}{(1.1)^3} + \frac{\$275}{(1.1)^4} + \frac{\$275}{(1.1)^5} + \frac{\$275}{(1.1)^6} = \$322.04$$

$$NPV_{6-\ year} = -\$1{,}000 + \frac{\$300}{(1.1)^1} + \frac{\$300}{(1.1)^2} + \frac{\$300}{(1.1)^3} + \frac{\$300}{(1.1)^4} + \frac{\$300}{(1.1)^5} + \frac{\$300}{(1.1)^6} = \$306.58$$

The value of the rolled-over three-year project is greater than that of the six-year unadjusted project.

14. Since the increase in NPV is above the opportunity cost of capital (12 percent) only up to 2012, the lumber should be harvested at that time.

15. The NPV increases by:

($24,000 / $20,000) − 1 = 20% from year 5 to year 6
($28,320 / $24,000) − 1 = 18% from year 6 to year 7
($32,284 / $28,320) − 1 = 14% from year 7 to year 8

The rate of increase is greater than the 15 percent opportunity cost of capital up to year 7, so the gold should start to be mined in year 7.

17. The new machine has an NPV:

$$= -\$15{,}000 + \$8{,}000 \times \left[\frac{1}{0.12} - \frac{1}{0.12} \times \frac{1}{(1.12)^5}\right]$$

$$= \$15{,}000 + \$8{,}000 \times 3.604776202 = -\ \$15{,}000 + \$28{,}838.21 = \$13{,}838.21$$

Next, we calculate the EAC for the new machine, which is $13,838.21 / 3.604776202 = $3,838.85. Since the EAC for the new machine is less than the EAC for the old, $6,000, the firm should stick with the old machine.

18. The new machine has an NPV:

$$= -\$10{,}000 + \$50{,}000 \times \left[\frac{1}{0.15} - \frac{1}{0.15} \times \frac{1}{(1.15)^4}\right]$$

$$= -\$100{,}000 + \$50{,}000 \times 2.854978363$$

$$= -\$100{,}000 + \$142{,}748.92 = \$42{,}748.92$$

Next, we calculate the EAC for the new machine, which is $42,748.92/ 2.854978363 = $14,973.46. Since the EAC for the new machine is greater than the EAC for the old, $14,000, the firm should purchase the new machine.

19. The cost is the same as the EAC for the project, which is given by

$$(0.15)(\$5{,}000{,}000)\left[\frac{(1.15)^5}{(1.15)^5 - 1}\right] = \$1{,}491{,}577.76,$$

an alternative calculation is $\$5{,}000{,}000/\left(\frac{1}{0.15} - \frac{1}{0.15} \times \frac{1}{(1.15)^5}\right) = \$1{,}491{,}577.76$

20. The EAC for the new boat is given by

$$(0.08)(\$350{,}000)\left[\frac{(1.08)^7}{(1.08)^5 - 1}\right] = \$67{,}225.34,$$

an alternative calculation is $\$350{,}000/\left(\frac{1}{0.08} - \frac{1}{0.08} \times \frac{1}{(1.08)^7}\right) = \$67{,}225.34$

Since the costs will be incurred in years 4, 5, and 6, then we can take the present value of those costs to be:

$$\frac{\$67{,}225.34}{(1.08)^4} + \frac{\$67{,}225.34}{(1.08)^5} + \frac{\$67{,}225.34}{(1.08)^6} = \$137{,}528.44$$

CHAPTER 12

Evaluating Project Economics and Capital Rationing

LEARNING OBJECTIVES

1. Explain and be able to demonstrate how variable costs and fixed costs affect the volatility of pretax operating cash flows and accounting operating profits.
2. Calculate and distinguish between the degree of pretax cash flow operating leverage and the degree of accounting operating leverage.
3. Define and calculate the pretax operating cash flow and accounting operating profit break-even points and the cross-over levels of unit sales for a project.
4. Define sensitivity analysis, scenario analysis, and simulation analysis, and describe how they are used to evaluate the risks associated with a project.
5. Explain how the profitability index can be used to rank projects when a firm faces capital rationing, and describe the limitations that apply to the profitability index.

I. Chapter Outline

12.1 Variable Costs, Fixed Costs, and Project Risk

- To fully understand risk, a firm must understand how variable and fixed costs affect the risk of a business.
  - **Variable costs** (VC) are costs that vary directly with the number of units sold.
  - **Fixed costs** (FC), in contrast, do not vary with unit sales in the short run.
- The cash flows and accounting profits for a project are sensitive to the proportion of its costs that are variable and the proportion that are fixed.
  - A project with a higher proportion of fixed costs will have cash flows and accounting profits that are more sensitive to changes in revenues than an otherwise identical project with a lower proportion of fixed costs.
    - The reason for this is that fixed costs do not change when revenue changes.
- EBITDA is often called **pretax operating cash flow** because it equals the incremental pretax *cash* operating profits from a project.
  - EBITDA = Revenue − VC − FC, where
  - Op Ex = VC + FC
- By comparing the sensitivity of EBITDA to changes in revenue between two project alternatives, it may help to better understand the risks and returns for each alternative.
  - Distinguishing between fixed and variable costs will then enable us to calculate the sensitivity of EBITDA to changes in revenue.
    - The greater the proportion that total costs are fixed will make it more difficult to adjust costs when revenue changes.
- EBIT is more sensitive to changes in revenue than EBITDA because the EBITDA does not include depreciation and amortization.

- o Depreciation and amortization acts just like a fixed cost because it is based on the amount that was invested in the project.
  - ▪ Also, it is based on the amount that was invested in the project rather than on unit sales.

12.2 Calculating Operating Leverage

- Operating leverage is a measure of the sensitivity of EBITDA or EBIT to changes in revenue.
- Two measures of operating leverage are often used by analysts: the degree of pretax cash flow operating leverage and the degree of accounting operating leverage.

A. *Degree of Pretax Cash Flow Operating Leverage*

- The **degree of pretax cash flow operating leverage (Cash Flow DOL)** provides us with a measure of how sensitive pretax operating cash flows are to changes in revenue.
  - o $\text{Cash Flow DOL} = 1 + \dfrac{\text{Fixed Costs}}{\text{Pretax Operating Cash Flows}} = 1 + \dfrac{\text{FC}}{\text{EBITDA}}.$
  - o Cash Flow DOL changes with the level of revenue; the sensitivity of operating cash flows is not the same for all levels of revenue.
    - ▪ This makes the tool useful for only modest changes in revenue.

B. *Degree of Accounting Operating Leverage*

- The **degree of accounting operating leverage (Accounting DOL)** is a measure of how sensitive accounting operating profits, EBIT, are to changes in revenue.
- $$\begin{aligned}\text{Accounting DOL} &= 1 + \frac{\text{Fixed Charges}}{\text{Accounting Operating Profits}}\\ &= 1 + \frac{\text{FC} + \text{D\&A}}{\text{EBITDA} - \text{D\&A}}\\ &= 1 + \frac{\text{FC} + \text{D\&A}}{\text{EBIT}}.\end{aligned}$$
  - o D &A is treated as a fixed cost and is added to FC to obtain the total of the cash and noncash fixed costs that would be reflected in the income statement if the project were adopted.
  - o Note that Accounting DOL uses EBIT while Cash Flow DOL uses EBITDA.
  - o Accounting DOL will always be larger than Cash Flow DOL if D&A is greater than zero.

12.3 Break-Even Analysis

- **Break-even analysis** tells us how many units must be sold in order for a project to break even on a cash flow or accounting profit basis.

A. *Cash Flow Break-Even*

The **pretax operating cash flow (EBITDA) break-even point** will help a firm determine what level of unit sales is necessary for the project to break even on operations from a pretax operating cash flow perspective and is calculated as follows:

- $\text{EBITDA Break-Even} = \dfrac{\text{FC}}{\text{Price-Unit VC}}$
  - o Simply divide the fixed costs, FC, by the **per-unit contribution** (Price − Unit VC).
  - o The pretax operating cash flow break-even point is important since it describes whether the firm's pretax operating cash flow will be enough to keep the project going without additional investment.
- The **cross-over level of unit sales (CO)** is calculated as follows

$$\text{CO}_{\text{EBITDA}} = \frac{\text{FC}_{\text{Alternative 1}} - \text{FC}_{\text{Alternative 2}}}{\text{Unit Contribution}_{\text{Alternative 1}} - \text{Unit Contribution}_{\text{Alternative 2}}}$$

where Unit contribution stands for the per-unit contribution.

- o The cross-over level of unit sales describes the level above which one project alternative has higher operating cash flows than another project alternative.

- o When using the above formula, make sure that the smaller value of FC is in the second term in the numerator since putting the smaller number first will usually give you a negative answer.
  - ▪ In a realistic example, the VC per unit of the higher FC alternative should be lower than that of the lower FC alternative.

B. *Accounting Break-Even*

- The **accounting operating profit (EBIT) break-even point** is calculated as

$$\text{EBIT Break-Even} = \frac{\text{FC} + \text{D\&A}}{\text{Price} - \text{Unit VC}}.$$

- When we calculate the accounting operating profit break-even point, we are calculating how many units must be sold to avoid an accounting operating loss.
  - o The **cross-over level of unit sales (CO) for EBIT** is calculated as follows

$$CO_{EBIT} = \frac{(FC + D\&A)_{Alt\,1} - (FC + D\&A)_{Alt\,2}}{(Unit\ Contrib_{Alt\,1} - Unit\ Contrib_{Alt\,2})}$$

where Unit contribution stands for the per-unit contribution.

12.4 Risk Analysis

- Financial analysts must often resort to different types of risk analysis to obtain a better understanding of how errors in forecasting these factors affect the attractiveness of a project.
  - o Since unit sales may not be the only factor affecting a firm's cash flow sensitivity, other analysis is needed.

A. ***Sensitivity analysis*** involves examining the sensitivity of the output from an analysis, such as the NPV estimate, to changes in *individual* assumptions.

- In a sensitivity analysis, an analyst might examine how a project's NPV changes if there is a decrease in the value of individual cash inflow assumptions or an increase in the value of individual cash outflow assumptions.

B. ***Scenario analysis*** will be performed if one wants to examine how the results from a financial analysis will change under alternative scenarios.

- A scenario might describe how a set of project inputs might be different under different economic conditions.
- By comparing the range of NPVs provided by the different scenarios, it is possible to understand how much uncertainty is associated with an NPV estimate.

C. ***Simulation analysis*** is like scenario analysis except that in simulation analysis, an analyst typically uses a computer to examine a large number of scenarios in a short period of time.

- Rather than selecting individual values for each of the assumptions—such as unit sales, unit price, and unit variable costs—the analyst assumes that those assumptions can be represented by statistical distributions.
- A computer program then calculates the cash flows associated with a large number of scenarios by repeatedly drawing values from the distributions for various assumptions, plugging them into the cash flow model, and computing the expected annual cash flows and then the expected NPV.
- In addition to providing an estimate of the expected cash flows, simulation analysis provides information on the distribution of the cash flows that the project is likely to produce in each year.

12.5 Investment Decisions with Capital Rationing

- What does a firm do when it does not have enough cash to invest in all available positive-NPV projects?
  - o The process of identifying the bundle of projects that creates the greatest total value and allocating the available capital to these projects is known as **capital rationing**.
  - o In an ideal world, the firm could accept all positive-NPV projects because it would be able to finance them.
    - ▪ However, the world is not ideal, and so the firm must determine the most efficient method of allocating its capital.
      - The world is not ideal because it can be difficult for outside investors to accurately assess the risks and returns associated with the firm's projects without the benefit of knowing the same set of information about those projects that a firm insider would know.

A. ***Capital Rationing in a Single Period*** involves choosing the set of projects that creates the greatest value in a given period is to select the projects that yield the largest value *per dollar invested.*

- The **profitability index (PI)** is computed for each project, and the firm then chooses the projects with the largest profitability indexes until it runs out of money.

$$PI = \frac{\text{Benefits}}{\text{Costs}} = \frac{\text{Present Value of Future Cash Flows}}{\text{Initial Investment}} = \frac{\text{NPV} + \text{Initial Investment}}{\text{Initial Investment}}$$

- The objective is to identify the bundle or combination of positive-NPV projects that creates the greatest total value for stockholders.
- The following steps should be taken in order:
  - Calculate the PI for each project.
  - Rank the projects from highest PI to lowest PI.
  - Starting at the top of the list (the project with the highest PI) and working our way down (to the project with the lowest PI), we select the projects that the firm can afford.
  - Repeat the third step by starting with the second project on the list, the third project on the list, and so on, to make sure that a more valuable bundle cannot be identified.

B. ***Capital Rationing Across Multiple Periods***

- If you are planning to make investments over several years, the investments you choose this year can affect your ability to make investments in future years.
  - This can happen if you plan on reinvesting some or all of the cash flows generated by the projects you invest in this year.
  - PI can only be relied upon to identify the projects that the firm should invest in for this year only.
- A limitation of the profitability index is that it does not tell us enough to make informed decisions over multiple periods.

II. Suggested Approach to Material

The focus of Chapter 12 is on operational risks, or those that are not related to the financial structure of the firm or the degree to which a firm has relied on debt financing. A large portion of the chapter is allocated to understanding the effects of operating leverage, the degree to which the firm's cost structure is based on fixed costs, a firm's break-even as well as the concept of variability within the estimated revenues, costs, and consequently the net cash flows produced by a project or the firm. As such, the chapter begins with a descriptive understanding of variable and fixed costs. A more formal understanding of a firm's cost structure is then discussed within an operating leverage framework, where the impact of revenue changes can be evaluated for EBIT or EBITDA. That understanding is used to calculate a firm's unit break-even from a cash, as well as from an accounting, perspective.

Those ideas are in turn used to forecast the impact of input changes on cash flow by using sensitivity, scenario, and simulation analysis. Sensitivity analysis is interested in the impact of a single input on a firm's NPV. Scenario analysis focuses on the impact of a number of related input changes, described as a scenario, on the NPV of a firm. Finally, simulation analysis is similar to scenario analysis except that a computer analyzes a large number of scenarios in order to analyze the distribution of the NPV of a project where an expected NPV can be found from that distribution. The chapter concludes with a discussion on capital rationing within capital budgeting decisions.

A good portion of the chapter contains material that should be familiar to students who have completed a managerial accounting course. Therefore the chapter may provide a review of material for the broader discussion found in the later chapters.

III. Chapter Glossary

Variable costs	Costs that vary directly with the number of units sold.
Fixed costs	Costs that do not vary directly with the number of units sold.
Pretax operating cash flow	Earnings before interest, taxes, depreciation and amortization, or EBITDA.
Operating leverage	A measure of the relative amounts of fixed and variable costs in a project's cost structure. Operating leverage is higher with more fixed costs.

Degree of pretax cash flow operating leverage (Cash Flow DOL)	A measure of the sensitivity of cash flows from operations (EBITDA) to changes in revenue.
Degree of accounting operating leverage (Accounting DOL)	A measure of the sensitivity of accounting operating profits (EBIT) to changes in revenue.
Break-even analysis	An analysis that tells us how many units must be sold in order for a project to break even on an accounting or cash flow basis.
Pretax operating cash flow (EBITDA) break-even point	The number of units that must be sold for pretax operating cash flow to equal $0.
Per-unit contribution	The amount that is left over from the sale of a single unit after all the variable costs associated with that unit have been paid. This is the amount that is available to help cover FC for the project.
Cross-over level of unit sales (CO)	The level of unit sales at which the cash flows or profitability for one project alternatively switches from being lower than that of another alternative to being higher.
Accounting operating profit (EBIT) break-even point	The number of units that must be sold for accounting operating profit to equal $0.
Sensitivity analysis	Examination of the sensitivity of the results from a financial analysis to changes in individual assumptions.
Scenario analysis	An analytical method concerned with how the results from a financial analysis will change under alternative scenarios.
Simulation analysis	An analytical method that uses a computer to quickly examine a large number of scenarios and obtain probability estimates for various values in a financial analysis.
Capital rationing	The process of identifying the bundle of projects that creates the greatest total value and allocating the available capital to these projects.
Profitability index (PI)	A measure of the value a project generates for each dollar invested in that project.

IV. Summary of Key Equations

Equation	Description	Formula
12.1	Op Ex in terms of incremental variable and fixed costs.	$\text{Op Ex} = \text{VC} + \text{FC}$
12.2	Degree of pretax cash flow operating leverage	$\text{Cash Flow DOL} = 1 + \frac{\text{FC}}{\text{EBITDA}}.$
12.3	Degree of accounting operating leverage	$\text{Accounting DOL} = 1 + \frac{\text{FC} + \text{D\&A}}{\text{EBIT}}.$
12.4	Pretax operating cash flow break-even point	$\text{EBITDA Break-Even} = \frac{\text{FC}}{\text{Price} - \text{Unit VC}}$

12.5	Cross-over level of unit sales for EBITDA	$CO_{EBITDA} = \frac{FC_{Alternative\ 1} - FC_{Alternative\ 2}}{\text{Unit Contribution}_{Alternative\ 1} - \text{Unit Contribution}_{Alternative\ 2}}$
12.6	Accounting operating profit break-even point	$\text{EBIT Break-Even} = \frac{FC + D\&A}{\text{Price} - \text{Unit VC}}$
12.7	Cross-over level of unit sales for EBIT	$CO_{EBIT} = \frac{(FC + D\&A)_{Alternative\ 1} - (FC + D\&A)_{Alternative\ 2}}{(\text{Unit Contribution}_{Alternative\ 1} - \text{Unit Contribution}_{Alternative\ 2})}$
12.8	Profitability index	$PI = \frac{NPV + \text{Initial Investment}}{\text{Initial Investment}}$

V. True or False Questions

1. Earnings before interest and taxes (EBIT) does not include depreciation and amortization expenses.

a. True

b. False

2. One interpretation of depreciation and amortization is that it is a fixed cost of the firm.

a. True

b. False

3. The higher a firm's unit variable costs, the greater the degree of operating leverage that the firm is utilizing.

a. True

b. False

4. Break-even analysis tells us how many sales dollars must occur in order for a project to break even on a cash flow or an accounting basis.

a. True

b. False

5. The pretax operating cash flow (EBITDA) break-even point is determined by how many units will have to be sold in order to cover the firm's fixed cash expenses.

a. True

b. False

6. The cross-over level of unit sales can be calculated for two alternatives utilizing different levels of operating leverage.

a. True

b. False

7. The accounting operating profit (EBIT) break-even point considers depreciation expenses.

a. True

b. False

8. Accounting operating profit break-even points are smaller than the corresponding pretax operating cash flow break-even points because they do not consider depreciation expense.

a. True

b. False

9. Sensitivity analysis could examine the result of a change in the NPV of a project due to changes in sales and expenses at the same time.
   a. True
   b. False

10. Scenario analysis examines the result of a change in the NPV of a project due to a number of related changes at once.
   a. True
   b. False

VI. Multiple-Choice Questions

1. Another name for EBITDA is
   a. pretax operating cash flow.
   b. operating cash flow.
   c. net income before tax.
   d. net income.

2. Understanding the mix of fixed and variable costs within a project
   a. helps to calculate the relationship between depreciation expenses and revenue.
   b. helps to calculate the sensitivity of EBITDA to changes in revenue.
   c. is not necessary since the NPV of a project will be the same for a given level of revenue assumptions.
   d. None of the above.

3. Accounting operating profits are also known as
   a. EBIT.
   b. EBITDA.
   c. net income.
   d. none of the above.

4. EBITDA and EBIT will vary more as revenue varies if
   a. the proportion of fixed to variable costs is small.
   b. the proportion of fixed to variable costs is large.
   c. the proportion of depreciation expenses to variable costs is large.
   d. the proportion of depreciation expenses to variable costs is small.

5. The operating leverage for a firm will be large if
   a. the firm's fixed costs are small relative to the variable costs.
   b. the firm's fixed costs are large relative to the variable costs.
   c. the firm's capital structure is comprised of a large amount of debt.
   d. the firm's capital structure is comprised of a small amount of debt.

6. The cash flow degree of operating leverage
   a. remains the same as long as fixed costs change faster than EBITDA.
   b. remains the same as long as fixed costs and EBITDA change by the same dollar amount.
   c. is not the same for all levels of revenue.
   d. is the same for all levels of revenue.

7. The difference between the degree of pretax cash flow operating leverage and the degree of accounting operating leverage is
   a. that the cash flow version includes interest expense as a fixed charge.
   b. that the cash flow version includes depreciation and amortization as a fixed charge.
   c. that the accounting version includes depreciation and amortization as a fixed charge.
   d. none of the above.

8. The amount that is left from the sale of a single unit after all the variable costs associated with that unit have been paid is
   a. the pretax operating cash flow break-even point.
   b. the accounting operating profit break-even point.
   c. the pretax operating cash flow.
   d. the per-unit contribution.

9. The accounting operating profit break-even point tells us
   a. how many units must be sold to generate enough of an operating profit to meet the firm's debt obligations.
   b. how many units must be sold to avoid an additional cash investment for a project.
   c. how many units must be sold to avoid a net loss.
   d. how many units must be sold to avoid an accounting operating loss.

10. ________________ provides an estimate of the expected cash flows as well as information on the distribution of the cash flows that the project is likely to produce.
    a. Simulation analysis
    b. Sensitivity analysis
    c. Scenario analysis
    d. None of the above.

11. Woodsmount, Technology had sales of $2,000,000 and total operating expenses of $1,200,000 last year. If the firm had fixed costs of $400,000 on sales of 100,000 ocean maps, then what is the firm's per-unit contribution?
    a. $4
    b. $8
    c. $12
    d. $20

12. SparklingSyders had EBITDA of $7,000 and depreciation and amortization of $1,000 with fixed cash expenses of $2,000 last year. What is SparklingSyders Degree of Accounting Operating Leverage.
    a. 0.50
    b. 1.43
    c. 1.5
    d. 2.33

13. Delescio Produce had a degree of accounting operating leverage equal to 1.875 during the most recent period. If the firm's EBITDA was $50,000 and fixed cash expenses equal to $25,000, then what was Delescio's depreciation and amortization during the same period?
    a. $1,000
    b. $3,667
    c. $10,000
    d. $100,000

14. Natural Footware has total fixed costs of $30,000 per month, including $3,000 per month of depreciation expense. It sells natural sole shoes for $29 a pair, and the variable cost of each pair of shoes is $20. What is the pretax operating cash flow break-even point for Natural Footware?
    a. 931 pairs of shoes
    b. 3,000 pairs of shoes
    c. 3,333 pair of shoes
    d. 3,667 pairs of shoes

15. Moonshine Drinks has discovered that the extent of the demand for its high-octane drink is 4 million bottles per year. If the fixed costs for the new product are $8 million and the sales price per bottle is $25, then what is the maximum variable cost per bottle that the firm needs to break even on a pretax operating cash flow basis?

   a. $2

   b. $22

   c. $23

   d. None of the above.

16. Floating Mattresses is about to introduce a new puncture-proof pool float and has determined that it will charge $30 per float. The firm must decide whether to purchase a high-capacity machine for producing the bladders or a low-capacity machine. If the high-capacity machine is selected, then the fixed costs for the firm will be $10,000 per year with variable costs of $10 per float. Otherwise the fixed costs will be $2,000, with variable costs of $20 per clock. Above what level of expected sales should the firm choose the high fixed cost alternative?

   a. 200 mattresses

   b. 400 mattresses

   c. 800 mattresses

   d. 1,000 mattresses

17. RollingWood is about to introduce a skateboard, and the firm must decide whether to purchase a high-capacity machine for producing the platforms or a low-capacity machine. If the high-capacity machine is selected, then the fixed costs for the firm will be $35,000 per year with variable costs of $85 per board. Otherwise the fixed costs will be $12,000 with variable costs of $110 per clock. Above what level of expected sales units should the firm choose the high fixed cost alternative?

   a. 920 boards

   b. 1,400 boards

   c. 2,333 boards

   d. There is not enough information given to solve the problem.

18. WirelessCable Supplies is in the process of determining whether to purchase a high-capacity machine to make local broadcasting boxes for the upcoming year. The high-capacity machine will generate fixed costs of $12,000 per year versus the $1,000 fixed costs of using a low-capacity machine. The variable costs per unit when using the high-capacity machine will be $30. The firm will charge $50 for each broadcasting box and has determined that the high-capacity machine will be more economically beneficial if sales are greater than 1,100 boxes. What is contribution margin under the low-capacity machine scenario?

   a. $5

   b. $10

   c. $20

   d. $40

19. An aluminum-based manufacturer has determined that it is better off buying a large stamping press if it will be able to sell more than 4,000 sheets per month. The price of a sheet is $98, and the variable costs for a large stamping press are $77 per yard. The variable costs for a small stamping press are $82 per sheet, and the fixed costs for the press are $15,000. What are the fixed costs associated with the large stamping press?

   a. 27,000 sheets

   b. 35,000 sheets

   c. 69,000 sheets

   d. None of the above

20. Dashboard Computers has found that it is indifferent between purchasing a high-capacity spot welder or a lower capacity spot welder as long as sales are above 1,000 units per month. The price of each computer is $500. The high-capacity spot welder has fixed cash expenses of $200,000 per month, while the alternative has cash expenses of $120,000 per month and depreciation and amortization expenses of $30,000 per month. Under high capacity, the variable costs per unit are $280; and they are $3,800 for the other alternative. If the firm bases its decisions on

the Accounting Operating Profit Break-even, then what are the depreciation expenses under the high-capacity alternative?

a. $12,500
b. $25,000
c. $50,000
d. $75,000

VII. Answers to True or False Questions

1. b	**2.** a	**3.** b	**4.** a	**5.** b
6. a	**7.** b	**8.** b	**9.** b	**10.** a

VIII. Answers to Multiple-Choice Questions

1. b	**2.** b	**3.** a	**4.** b	**5.** b
6. c	**7.** c	**8.** d	**9.** d	**10.** a
11. c	**12.** c	**13.** c	**14.** b	**15.** c
16. c	**17.** a	**18.** b	**19.** b	**20.** c

Solutions to Multiple-Choice Questions

11. Solution:

Unit sales = 100,000 units

Sales = $2,000,000

Total fixed costs = $400,000 ⇒

Total variable costs = $1,200,000 − $400,000 = $800,000 ⇒

Unit variable costs = $800,000 / 100,000 = $8.00

Sale price/unit = $2,000,000 / 100,000 units = $20.00 ⇒

Unit contribution margin = $20.00 − $8.00 = **$12.00**

12. Solution:

EBITDA = $7,000 and D&A = $1,000 ⇒ EBIT = $6,000

$$\text{Degree of accounting operating leverage} = 1 + \frac{\text{FC} + \text{D\&A}}{\text{EBITDA} - \text{D\&A}} = 1 + \frac{\text{FC} + \text{D\&A}}{\text{EBIT}}$$

$$\text{Degree of accounting operating leverage} = 1 + \frac{\text{FC} + \text{D\&A}}{\text{EBIT}} = 1 + \frac{\$2{,}000 + \$1{,}000}{\$6{,}000} = 1.50$$

13. Solution:

$$\text{Degree of accounting operating leverage} = 1 + \frac{\text{FC} + \text{D\&A}}{\text{EBITDA} - \text{D\&A}} = 1.875$$

Degree of accounting operating leverage =

$$1 + \frac{\text{FC} + \text{D\&A}}{\text{EBITDA} - \text{D\&A}} = 1 + \frac{\$25{,}000 + \text{D\&A}}{\$50{,}000 - \text{D\&A}} = 1.875 \Rightarrow \text{D\&A} = \$10{,}000$$

14. Solution:

$$\text{EBITDA Break-Even} = \frac{\text{FC}}{\text{Price} - \text{Unit VC}} = \frac{\$27{,}000}{\$29 - \$20} = 3{,}000$$

15. Solution:

$$\text{EBITDA Break-Even} = \frac{\text{FC}}{\text{Price} - \text{Unit VC}} = \frac{\$8{,}000{,}000}{\$25 - \text{Unit VC}} = 4{,}000{,}000 \Rightarrow \text{Unit VC} = \$23$$

16. Solution:

$$\text{CO}_{\text{EBITDA}} = \frac{\text{FC}_{\text{Alt1}} - \text{FC}_{\text{Alt2}}}{\text{Unit Contrib}_{\text{Alt1}} - \text{Unit Contrib}_{\text{Alt2}}} = \frac{\$10{,}000 - \$2{,}000}{\$20 - \$10} = 800 \text{ mattresses}$$

17. Solution:

$$\text{CO}_{\text{EBITDA}} = \frac{\text{FC}_{\text{Alt1}} - \text{FC}_{\text{Alt2}}}{\text{Unit Contrib}_{\text{Alt1}} - \text{Unit Contrib}_{\text{Alt2}}} = \frac{\$35{,}000 - \$12{,}000}{(\text{Price} - \$85) - (\text{Price} - \$110)} = \frac{\$35{,}000 - \$12{,}000}{\$110 - \$85} = 920 \text{ boards}$$

Note that the price is the same in both instances; thus, the price variable cancels out when you apply the correct formula.

18. Solution:

$$\text{CO}_{\text{EBITDA}} = \frac{\text{FC}_{\text{Alt1}} - \text{FC}_{\text{Alt2}}}{\text{Unit Contrib}_{\text{Alt1}} - \text{Unit Contrib}_{\text{Alt2}}} = \frac{\$12{,}000 - \$1{,}000}{(\$50 - \$30) - \text{Unit Contrib}_{\text{Alt2}}} = 1{,}100 \text{ units} \Rightarrow$$

$$\text{Unit Contrib}_{\text{Alt2}} = \$10$$

$$\text{EAC}_1 = k\,NPV_i\left[\frac{(1+k)^t}{(1+k)^t - 1}\right]$$

19. Solution:

$$\text{CO}_{\text{EBITDA}} = \frac{\text{FC}_{\text{Alt1}} - \text{FC}_{\text{Alt2}}}{\text{Unit Contrib}_{\text{Alt1}} - \text{Unit Contrib}_{\text{Alt2}}} = \frac{\text{FC}_{\text{Alt1}} - \$15{,}000}{(\$98 - \$77) - (\$98 - \$82)} = 4{,}000 \text{ sheets} \Rightarrow$$

$$\text{FC}_{\text{Alt1}} = \$35{,}000$$

$$\text{EAC}_1 = k\,NPV_i\left[\frac{(1+k)^t}{(1+k)^t - 1}\right]$$

20. Solution:

$$\text{CO}_{\text{EBIT}} = \frac{(\text{FC} + \text{D\&A})_{\text{Alt1}} - (\text{FC} + \text{D\&A})_{\text{Alt2}}}{(\text{Unit Contrib}_{\text{Alt1}} - \text{Unit Contrib}_{\text{Alt2}})} = 1{,}000 \text{ units} = \frac{(\$200{,}000 + \text{D\&A}_{\text{Alt1}}) - (\$120{,}000 + \$30{,}000)}{\$220 - \$210} \Rightarrow$$

$$\text{D\&A}_{\text{Alt1}} = \$50{,}000$$

CHAPTER 13

The Cost of Capital

LEARNING OBJECTIVES

1. Explain what the weighted average cost of capital for a firm is and why it is often used as a discount rate to evaluate projects.
2. Calculate the cost of debt for a firm.
3. Calculate the cost of common stock and the cost of preferred stock for a firm.
4. Calculate the weighted average cost of capital for a firm, explain the limitations of using a firm's weighted average cost of capital as the discount rate when evaluating a project, and discuss the alternatives that are available.

I. Chapter Outline

13.1 The Firm's Overall Cost of Capital

- Since *unique risk* can be eliminated by holding a diversified portfolio, *systematic risk* is the only risk that investors require compensation for bearing.
- It was concluded in Chapter 7 that we could rely on the CAPM to arrive at the expected rate of return for a particular investment: $E(R_i) = R_{rf} + \beta_i[E(R_m) - R_{rf}]$
  - o In this chapter, practical concerns are addressed that can make that concept difficult to implement.
  - o Firms do not issue publicly traded shares for individual projects.
    - ▪ This means that firms do not have to project historical returns to use a regression analysis in calculating the expected return of the project.
  - o As a result, firms have no way to directly estimate the discount rate that reflects the risk of the incremental cash flows from a particular project.
  - o Sometimes financial managers deal with this problem by estimating the cost of capital for the firm as a whole and then requiring analysts within the firm to use this cost of capital to discount the cash flows for all projects.
    - ▪ This approach ignores the fact that a firm is really a collection of projects with varying levels of risk.

A. ***The Finance Balance Sheet***

- The finance balance sheet is based on market values rather than book values.
  - o The total book value of the assets reported on an accounting balance sheet does not necessarily reflect the total market value of those assets since the book value is largely based on historical costs.
  - o The total market value of the assets equals the present value of the total cash flows that those assets are expected to generate in the future.
- The left-hand side of the accounting balance sheet reports the book values of a firm's assets, while the right-hand side reports how those assets were financed.

- The value of the claims that investors hold must equal the value of the cash flows that they have a right to receive.
  - This is because the total market value of the debt and the equity at a firm equals the present value of the cash flows that the debt holders and the stockholders have the right to receive.
    - The people who have lent money to a firm as well as those who have purchased the firm's stock have the right to receive all of the cash flows that the firm is expected to generate in the future.
- MV of assets = MV of liabilities + MV of equity

B. ***How Firms Estimate Their Cost of Capital***

- If analysts at a firm could estimate the betas for each of the firm's individual projects, then they could estimate the beta for the entire firm as a weighted average of the betas for the individual projects.
  - Unfortunately, because analysts are not typically able to estimate betas for individual projects, they generally cannot use this approach.
  - Instead, analysts must use their knowledge of the finance balance sheet, along with the concept of market efficiency, to estimate the cost of capital for the firm.
- Rather than perform the calculations for the *individual projects* represented on the left-hand side of the finance balance sheet, analysts perform a similar set of calculations for the *different types of financing* (debt and equity) on the right-hand side of the finance balance sheet.
  - As long as they can estimate the cost of each type of financing by observing that cost in the capital markets, they can compute the cost of capital for the firm by using the following equation:

$$k_{\text{Firm}} = \sum_{i=1}^{n} x_i k_i = x_1 k_1 + x_2 k_2 + x_3 k_3 + \ldots + x_n k_n$$

  - If we divide the costs of capital into debt and equity portions of the firm, then we can use the above to arrive at the **weighted average cost of capital (WACC)** for the firm:

$$k_{\text{Firm}} = x_{\text{Debt}} k_{\text{Debt}} + x_{\text{Equity}} k_{\text{Equity}}$$

13.2 The Cost of Debt

- Analysts often cannot directly observe the rate of return that investors require for a particular type of financing and instead must rely on the security prices they can observe in the financial markets to then estimate that required rate of return.
  - It makes sense to rely on security prices only if you believe that the financial markets are reasonably efficient at incorporating new information into these prices.
    - If the markets were not efficient, estimates of expected returns that were based on market security prices would be unreliable.

A. ***Key Concepts for Estimating the Cost of Debt***

- With regard to the cost associated with each type of debt that a firm uses when we estimate the cost of capital for a firm, we are particularly interested in the cost of the firm's long-term debt.
  - When we refer to debt we usually mean the debt that, when it was borrowed, was set to mature in more than one year.
- Debt with a maturity of more than one year can typically be viewed as permanent debt because firms often borrow the money to pay off this debt when it matures.
- The cost of a firm's long-term debt is estimated on the date on which the analysis is performed.
  - This is important because the interest rate (or historical interest rate determined at the time of original debt issuance) that the firm is paying on its outstanding debt does not necessarily reflect its current cost of debt.
- The current cost of long-term debt is the appropriate cost of debt for WACC calculations.
  - This is the relevant cost because the WACC is the opportunity cost of capital for the firm's investors as of today.

B. ***Estimating the Current Cost of a Bond or an Outstanding Loan***

- The current cost of debt for a publicly traded bond is the yield-to-maturity calculation.
  - To do this, we first convert the bond data to reflect semiannual compounding.
  - We can also account for the effective annual interest rate (EAR) to account for the actual current annual cost of the debt.
  - We must also account for the cost of issuing the bond—issuance costs using the net proceeds that the company receives for the bond rather than the price that is paid by the investor.
- For the current cost of long-term bank or other private debt, the firm may simply call its banker and ask what rate the bank would charge if they decided to refinance the debt today.

C. ***Taxes and the Cost of Debt***

- Firms can deduct interest payments for tax purposes.
- The after-tax cost of interest payments equals the pretax cost times 1 minus the tax rate: $k_{\text{Debt after-tax}} = k_{\text{Debt pretax}} \times (1 - t)$.

D. ***Estimating the Cost of Debt for a Firm***

- To estimate the firm's overall cost of debt when it has several debt issues outstanding, we must first estimate the costs of the individual debt issues and then calculate a weighted average of these costs.

13.3 The Cost of Equity

- The cost of equity for a firm is a weighted average of the costs of the different types of stock that the firm has outstanding at a particular point in time.

A. ***Common Stock***

- Just as information about market rates of return is used to estimate the cost of debt, market information is also used to estimate the cost of equity.
  - o There are several ways to do this, and the most appropriate approach will depend on what information is available and how reliable the analyst believes it is.
- Three alternative methods for estimating the cost of common stock are discussed.

- **Method 1: Using the Capital Asset Pricing Model (CAPM)**
  - o Using the CAPM equation, $E(R_i) = R_{rf} + \beta_i[E(R_m) - R_{rf}]$, we find that the cost of common stock equals the risk-free rate of return plus compensation for the systematic risk associated with the common stock.
  - o There are some practical considerations involved in choosing the appropriate risk-free rate, beta, and market risk premium for the above calculation.
    - ▪ The recommended risk-free rate to use is the risk-free rate on a long-term Treasury security because the equity claim is a long-term claim on the firm's cash flows.
      - A long-term risk-free rate better reflects long-term inflation expectations and the cost of getting investors to part with their money for a long period of time than a short-term rate.
    - ▪ You can estimate the beta for a stock using a regression analysis.
      - Identifying the appropriate beta is much more complicated if the common stock is not publicly traded.
        - o This problem may be overcome by identifying a "comparable" company with publicly traded stock that is in the same business and that has a similar amount of debt.
        - o When a good comparable company cannot be identified, it is sometimes possible to use an average of the betas for the public firms in the same industry.
  - o It is not possible to directly observe the market risk premium since we don't know what rate of return investors expect for the market portfolio.
    - ▪ For this reason, financial analysts generally use a measure of the average risk premium investors have actually earned in the past as an indication of the risk premium they might require today.
    - ▪ From 1926 through the end of 2006, actual returns on the U.S. stock market exceeded actual returns on long-term U.S. government bonds by an average of 6.57 percent per year.
      - If a financial analyst believes that the market risk premium in the past is a reasonable estimate of the risk premium today, then he or she might use 6.51 percent (or a value close to it) as the market risk premium for the future.

- **Method 2: Using the Constant-Growth Dividend Model**
  - o Using Equation 9.5, $P_0 = \dfrac{D_1}{R - g}$, we can rearrange to solve for R – or k_{cs} as we now prefer to call it:

$$k_{cs} = \frac{D_1}{P_0} + g$$

  - o In order to solve for the cost of common stock, we must estimate the dividend that stockholders will receive next period, D_1, as well as the rate at which the market expects dividends to grow over the long run, g.

- This approach is useful for a firm that pays dividends that will grow at a constant rate.
  - This approach might be consistent for an electric utility but not for a fast growing high-tech firm.

- **Method 3: Using a Multistage-Growth Dividend Model**
  - The multistage-growth dividend model allows for faster dividend growth rates in the near term, followed by a constant long-term growth rate.
    - The approach is based on the supernormal growth dividend model discussed in Chapter 9.
      - The complexity of this approach lies in choosing the correct number of stages of forecasted growth as well as how long each stage will last.
    - Because of the algebraic complexity in solving for the required rate of return, the value is generally solved for using a trial-and-error method or even using some type of spreadsheet software, after forecasting the different stages of dividend growth.

- **Which Method Should We Use?**
  - In practice, most people use the CAPM (Method 1) to estimate the cost of equity if the result is going to be used in the discount rate for evaluating a project.

B. ***Preferred Stock***

- The characteristics of preferred stock allow us to use the perpetuity model, Equation 6.3, to estimate the cost of preferred equity.
  - Just as with common stock, we can find the cost of preferred equity by rearranging the pricing equation for preferred shares: $k_{ps} = \frac{D_{ps}}{P_{ps}}$.
  - Note that the CAPM can be used to estimate the cost of preferred equity, just as it can be used to estimate the cost of common equity.

13.4 Using the WACC in Practice

- The after-tax version of the formula for the weighted-average cost of capital is:
  $\text{WACC} = x_{Debt}k_{Debt\ pretax}(1 - t) + x_{ps}k_{ps} + x_{cs}k_{cs}$.
- It should be noted that the financial analyst should use market values rather than book values for the return inputs needed for the WACC calculation.

A. ***Limitations of WACC as a Discount Rate for Evaluating Projects***

- Financial theory tells us that the rate that should be used to discount these incremental cash flows is the rate that reflects their systematic risk.
- This means that the WACC is going to be the appropriate discount rate for evaluating a project only when the project has cash flows with systematic risks that are exactly the same as those for the firm as a whole.
  - When a single rate, such as the WACC, is used to discount cash flows for projects with varying levels of risk, the discount rate will be too low in some cases and too high in others.
  - When the discount rate is too low, the firm runs the risk of accepting a negative-NPV project.
    - The estimated NPV will be positive even though the true NPV is negative.
  - When the discount rate is too high, the firm runs the risk of rejecting a positive-NPV project.
    - The estimated NPV will be negative even though the true NPV is positive.
- The point is that it is correct to use a firm's WACC to discount the cash flows for a project if the following condition holds.
  - **Condition 1:** A firm's WACC should be used to evaluate the cash flows for a new project only if the level of systematic risk for that project is the same as that for the portfolio of projects that currently comprise the firm.
- In addition, the following must also hold in order to control for the degree of financial risk that will be embedded within a project.
  - **Condition 2:** A firm's WACC should be used to evaluate a project only if that project uses the same financing mix—the same proportions of debt, preferred shares, and common shares—used to finance the firm as a whole.

B. ***Alternatives to WACC for Evaluating Projects***

- If the discount rate for a project cannot be estimated directly, a financial analyst might try to find a public firm that is in a business similar to the project.

   - This public company would be what financial analysts call a **pure-play comparable** because it is exactly like the project.
   - This approach is generally not feasible due to the difficulty of finding a public firm that is only in the business represented by the project.
- Financial managers sometimes classify projects into categories based on their systematic risks.
   - They then specify a discount rate that is to be used to discount the cash flows for all projects within each category.

II. Suggested Approach to Material

Chapter 13 concentrates on the tools needed to understand the firm's cost of capital as well as the complications and problems embedded in finding such a value. Upon first glance, it appears to be a relatively simple concept that is described by the WACC equation. Instead, the chapter describes the weighted-average cost of capital (WACC) as a snapshot that is dependent on the firm-wide systematic risk that is affected by the current portfolio of project risks as well as the firm's or a project's degree of financial leverage.

After introducing the concept of WACC, the text then proceeds to provide an understanding of the subcomponents of WACC: the cost of debt, the cost of common equity, and the cost of preferred equity for the firm. The cost of debt is reviewed as part of the yield-to-maturity calculation form an earlier chapter, and the cost of preferred equity for the firm is also reviewed as part of its valuation equation. The cost of common equity can be somewhat tricky due to the many assumptions required to estimate the future cash flows associated with common shareholder ownership. Dividend discount models are reviewed as well as the CAPM.

This material is required to be able to proceed toward the later capital budgeting chapters in the text. The current chapter also includes material that is commonly misunderstood by finance practitioners, and as such, the conditions required for using WACC for a firm's new projects should be understood before proceeding.

III. Chapter Glossary

Finance balance sheet	A balance sheet that is based on market values of expected cash flows, rather than book values.
Weighted average cost of capital (WACC)	The weighted average of the costs of the different types of capital (debt and equity) that have been used to finance a firm. The cost of each type of capital is weighted by the proportion of the total capital that it represents.
Multistage-growth dividend model	A model that allows for varying dividend growth rates in the near term, followed by a constant long-term growth rate. Another term used to describe the mixed (supernormal) dividend growth model discussed in Chapter 9.
Pure-play comparable	A public firm that is in a business that is similar to the project or business that a firm is analyzing.

IV. Summary of Key Equations

Equation	Description	Formula
13.1	Finance balance sheet identity	MV of assets = MV of liabilities + MV of equity
13.2	General formula for weighted average cost of capital (WACC) for a firm	$k_{\text{Firm}} = \sum_{i=1}^{n} x_i k_i = x_1 k_1 + x_2 k_2 + x_3 k_3 + \ldots + x_n k_n$
13.3	After-tax cost of debt	$k_{\text{Debt after-tax}} = k_{\text{Debt pretax}} \times (1 - t)$
13.4	CAPM formula for the cost of common stock	$k_{cs} = R_{rf} + (\beta_{cs} \times \text{Market risk premium})$

Equation	Description	Formula
13.5	Constant-growth dividend formula for the cost of common stock	$k_{cs} = \frac{D_1}{P_0} + g$
13.6	Perpetuity formula for the cost of preferred stock	$k_{ps} = \frac{D_{ps}}{P_{ps}}$
13.7	Traditional WACC formula	$WACC = x_{Debt}k_{Debt\ pretax}(1 - t) + x_{ps}k_{ps} + x_{cs}k_{cs}$

V. True or False Questions

1. Firms generally issue publicly traded shares for a specific project.

a. True

b. False

2. The overall cost of capital for a firm is not generally the correct discount rate to evaluate a specific project's cash flows.

a. True

b. False

3. The beta for a firm is equal to the weighted average of the project betas of the firm.

a. True

b. False

4. Analysts can directly observe the cost of publicly traded outstanding debt of the firm.

a. True

b. False

5. The yield to maturity of a firm's outstanding long-term debt is less than or equal to the equivalent annual return of the same debt (assumed semiannual coupon payments).

a. True

b. False

6. The appropriate risk-free rate of return to use in the CAPM is the 3-month Treasury rate.

a. True

b. False

7. The market risk premium can be accurately calculated if we know the expected rate of return on the market.

a. True

b. False

8. The constant-growth dividend model cannot be used if the growth in dividends is expected to be zero into the identifiable future.

a. True

b. False

9. In order to use a multistage-growth dividend model to estimate the cost of equity for a firm, the analyst must estimate multiple growth rates in dividends as well as the amount of time that each growth rate will apply.

a. True

b. False

10. The CAPM can be used to estimate the cost of preferred equity for a firm.
   a. True
   b. False

VI. Multiple-Choice Questions and Problems

1. Using the firm's overall cost of capital to evaluate an individual project ignores
   a. the fact that the firm is composed of projects with the same level of risk.
   b. the fact that the firm is a collection of projects with varying levels of risk.
   c. the issue of different tax rates for different projects within the firm.
   d. None of the above.

2. The difference between the value of the firm and the market value of the equity of the firm
   a. is the market value of the liabilities of the firm.
   b. is the book value of the liabilities of the firm.
   c. is never of importance.
   d. is never able to be determined.

3. A firm's cost of capital is primarily concerned with
   a. the cost of the firm's trade credit.
   b. the cost of the firm's preferred shares.
   c. the cost of the firm's long-term debt.
   d. None of the above.

4. If a firm wishes to indirectly find its cost of debt by looking at the market price of its publicly traded debt, then it is relying on
   a. the efficiency of the market.
   b. the rating agencies to correctly price the debt.
   c. the investment bankers to correctly price the debt.
   d. all of the above.

5. Bond issuance costs include
   a. investment banking fees.
   b. legal fees.
   c. accountant fees.
   d. all of the above.

6. When debt matures, most firms
   a. pay off the debt with cash on hand.
   b. pay off the debt with borrowed funds.
   c. pay off the debt with newly issued equity.
   d. none of the above.

7. The cost of debt for a firm is estimated using
   a. the yield to maturity of the debt.
   b. the doubled yield to maturity of the debt.
   c. the coupon rate of the debt.
   d. none of the above.

8. A firm's after-tax cost of debt
   a. is greater than its cost of equity.
   b. greater than its before-tax cost of debt.
   c. less than or equal to its before-tax cost of debt.
   d. none of the above.

9. In practice, which is the most used method of calculating the firm's cost of common equity?
   a. Constant-Growth Dividend Model
   b. Multistage-Growth Dividend Model
   c. CAPM
   d. none of the above.

10. In order to use the WACC to evaluate a future project's cash flows, which of the following must hold?
    a. The project will be financed with the same proportion of debt and equity as the firm.
    b. The systematic risk of the project is the same as the overall systematic risk of the firm.
    c. The project must be viable.
    d. a and b above.

11. Happy Days Manufacturing has invested all of its capital in two projects. The first project has a beta of 1.2, and the second project has a beta of 1.9. What is the firm's beta if 30 percent of the firm's assets are invested in the first project?
    a. 1.41
    b. 1.55
    c. 1.69
    d. none of the above

12. You are analyzing the cost of debt for a firm and you need to calculate the yield to maturity on an issue that has a 9 percent coupon with six years to maturity. If the bonds have a current market price of $893.75, what is the yield to maturity on the issue?
    a. 9.0%
    b. 11.5%
    c. 11.83%
    d. none of the above

13. You are analyzing the cost of debt for a firm, and you need to calculate the after-tax cost to the firm on an issue that has a 14 percent coupon with 13 years to maturity. The firm is subject to a 40 percent marginal tax rate. If the bonds have a current market price of $1,427.80, then what is the after-tax cost of the bonds to the firm? Use the same calculation that is used on Wall Street.
    a. 5.10%
    b. 8.50%
    c. 8.68%
    d. 14.00%

14. You have just calculated the yield to maturity to be 14 percent on a bond issue. What is the equivalent annual return to an investor for purchasing the bond?
    a. 7.00%
    b. 14.00%
    c. 14.49%
    d. 29.96%

15. Zero Chips, Inc., has a beta of .85 and is trying to calculate its cost of common equity. If the risk-free rate of return is 5 percent and the expected return on the market is 11 percent, then what is the firm's after-tax cost of common equity capital if the firm is subject to a 35 percent marginal tax rate?

a. 5.10%

b. 9.35%

c. 10.10%

d. 14.35%

16. Marigold Products is expected to pay a dividend of $1.98 one year from today. If the firm's growth in dividends is expected to remain at a flat 4 percent forever, then what is the cost of equity capital for Marigold if the price of its common shares is currently $33.00?

a. 6.00%

b. 6.24%

c. 10.00%

d. 10.24%

17. Tulip Products Industries was paid a dividend of $2.05 yesterday. If the firm's growth in dividends is expected to remain at a flat 1.5 percent forever, then what is the cost of equity capital for Tulip if the price of its common shares is currently $24.48?

a. 8.37%

b. 8.50%

c. 9.87%

d. 10.00%

18. Secret Energy Supplies has common shares with a price of $15.44 per share. The firm is expected to pay a dividend of $1.25 one year from today, and dividends are expected to grow at 15 percent for two years after that and then at 2 percent thereafter. What is the implied cost of common equity capital for Secret Energy?

a. 11.00%

b. 12.00%

c. 13.00%

d. 14.00%

19. Level Co. has a preferred share issue outstanding with a current price of $52.00. The issue paid a dividend of $4.16 yesterday. What is the firm's cost of preferred equity?

a. 7.00%

b. 7.50%

c. 8.00%

d. 8.50%

20. Life Balance, Inc., has found that its cost of common equity capital is 15 percent and its cost of debt capital is 9 percent. If the firm is financed with $6,000,000 of common shares (market value) and $4,000,000 of debt, then what is the after-tax weighted average cost of capital for Maloney's if it is subject to a 30 percent marginal tax rate?

a. 9.70%

b. 10.65%

c. 11.16%

d. 11.52%

Answers to True or False Questions

1. b	**2.** a	**3.** a	**4.** b	**5.** a
6. b	**7.** a	**8.** b	**9.** a	**10.** a

Answers to Multiple-Choice Questions

1. b	**2.** a	**3.** c	**4.** a	**5.** d
6. b	**7.** a	**8.** c	**9.** c	**10.** d
11. c	**12.** b	**13.** a	**14.** c	**15.** c
16. c	**17.** d	**18.** b	**19.** c	**20.** d

Solutions to Multiple-Choice Problems

11. Solution:

$$\beta_{n\ Asset\ portfolio} = \sum_{i=1}^{2} x_i\beta_i = 0.3(1.2) + 0.7(1.9) = 1.69,$$

because 30% of the firm's investment was in project one then the other 70% must be invested in the other project.

12. Solution:

Using the formula for pricing bonds, we have

$$\$893.75 = \frac{\$45}{\left(1+\frac{YTM}{2}\right)^1} + \frac{\$45}{\left(1+\frac{YTM}{2}\right)^2} + \ldots + \frac{\$45}{\left(1+\frac{YTM}{2}\right)^{12}} + \frac{\$1{,}000}{\left(1+\frac{YTM}{2}\right)^{12}}$$

and after solving for YTM/2 = 5.75%, we find that YTM = 11.5%.

Note that we assume semi–annual coupons for the bond.

13. Solution:

Using the formula for pricing bonds, we have

$$\$1{,}427.80 = \frac{\$70}{\left(1+\frac{YTM}{2}\right)^1} + \frac{\$70}{\left(1+\frac{YTM}{2}\right)^2} + \ldots + \frac{\$70}{\left(1+\frac{YTM}{2}\right)^{26}} + \frac{\$1{,}000}{\left(1+\frac{YTM}{2}\right)^{26}}$$

and after solving for YTM/2 = 4.25%, we find that YTM = 8.50%.

Note that we assume semi–annual coupons for the bond.

Now, we adjust taxes: 8.50% x(1 − 0.4) = 5.1%

14. Solution:

Since it is assumed that a bond makes semiannual coupon payments, the formula for EAR is

$$EAR = \left(1+\frac{YTM}{2}\right)^2 - 1 \Rightarrow EAR = \left(1+\frac{0.14}{2}\right)^2 - 1 = 0.1449 = 14.49\%$$

15. Solution:

The equation for the CAPM is: $E(R_i) = R_{rf} + \beta_i[E(R_m) - R_{rf}]$

If $\beta_i = 0.85$, $R_{rf} = 0.05$, and $E(R_m) = 0.11$, then we have

$E(R_i) = 0.051 + 0.89[0.11 - 0.05] = 0.1010 = 10.10\%$

16. Solution:

Since the price of common shares is given as well as the expected growth in dividends and the next expected dividend, we can use the following:

$$k_{cs} = \frac{D_1}{P_0} + g = \frac{\$1.98}{\$33.00} + 0.04 = 0.10 = 10\%$$

17. Solution:

Since the price of common shares is given as well as the expected growth in dividends and the last paid dividend, we can use the following:

$$k_{cs} = \frac{D_1}{P_0} + g = \frac{D_0 \times (1 + g)}{P_0} + g = \frac{\$2.05 \times 1.015}{\$24.48} + 0.015 = 0.10 = 10\%$$

18. Solution:

We can use the common stock pricing equation to solve for the cost of common equity capital:

$$\$15.44 = \frac{\$1.25}{(1 + k_{cs})} + \frac{\$1.25(1.15)}{(1 + k_{cs})^2} + \frac{\$1.25(1.15)^2}{(1 + k_{cs})^3} + \frac{\$1.25(1.15)^2(1.02)}{(k_{cs} - 0.02)(1 + k_{cs})^3};$$

Trial and error gives us $k_{cs} = 0.12$

$$\text{EAC}_i = k\,\text{NPV}_i\left[\frac{(1 + k)^t}{(1 + k)^t - 1}\right]$$

19. Solution:

We start with the pricing equation for preferred shares and rearrange to solve for the cost of preferred equity:

$$k_{ps} = \frac{D}{P_0} = \frac{\$4.16}{\$52.00} = 0.08$$

20. Solution:

Noting that the proportion of debt and equity is

$x_{Debt} = \$4{,}000{,}000/(\$6{,}000{,}000 + \$4{,}000{,}000) = 0.4$, $x_{cs} = \$6{,}000{,}000/(\$6{,}000{,}000 + \$4{,}000{,}000) = 0.6$

The formula for WACC is:

$WACC = x_{Debt}k_{Debt\ pretax}(1 - t) + x_{ps}k_{cs} = 0.4 \times 0.09 \times (1 - 0.3) + 0.6 \times 0.15 = 0.1152$

CHAPTER 14

Working Capital Management

LEARNING OBJECTIVES

1. Define net working capital, discuss the importance of working capital management, and be able to compute a firm's net working capital.
2. Define the operating and cash cycles, explain how they are used, and be able to compute their values for a firm.
3. Discuss the relative advantages and disadvantages of pursuing (1) flexible and (2) restrictive current asset investment strategies.
4. Explain how accounts receivable are created and managed, and be able to compute the cost of trade credit.
5. Explain the trade-off between carrying costs and reorder costs, and be able to compute the economic order quantity for a firm's inventory orders.
6. Define cash collection time, discuss how a firm can minimize this time, and be able to compute the cash collection costs and benefits of a lockbox.
7. Identify three current asset financing strategies and discuss the main sources of short-term financing.

I. Chapter Outline

14.1 Working Capital Basics

- Working capital management involves two key issues—the appropriate amount and mix of current assets for the firm to hold and the financing of these current assets.
- Let us review some basic definitions related to working capital.
  - **Current assets** are cash and other assets that the firm expects to convert into cash in a year or less.
  - **Current liabilities** (or short-term liabilities) are obligations that the firm expects to pay off in a year or less.
    - **Working capital**, also called ***gross*** working capital, is the funds invested in a company's cash account, account receivables, inventory, and other current assets.
    - **Net working capital (NWC)** refers to the difference between current assets and current liabilities.
      - NWC is important because it is a measure of liquidity and represents the net short-term investment the firm keeps in the business.
- **Working capital management** involves making decisions regarding the use and sources of current assets.
- **Working capital efficiency** refers to the length of time between when a working capital asset is acquired and when it is converted into cash.
- **Liquidity** is the ability of a company to convert assets—real or financial—into cash quickly without suffering a financial loss.

A. ***Working Capital Accounts and Trade-Offs***

- The various working capital accounts are:
  - o **Cash:** This account includes cash and marketable securities like Treasury securities.
  - o **Receivables**: These represent the amount owed by customers who have taken advantage of the firm's trade credit policy.
  - o **Inventory**: Firms maintain inventory of raw materials, work in process, and finished goods.
  - o **Payables**: The payables balance represents the amount owed to the firm's vendors and suppliers on materials purchased on credit.
    - ▪ The accrual accounts are liabilities incurred but not yet paid, such as accrued wages or taxes.

14.2 The Operating and Cash Conversion Cycles

- The cash conversion cycle begins when the firm invests cash to purchase the raw materials that would be used to produce the goods that the firm manufactures. It ends not with the finished goods being sold to customers and the cash collected on the sales; but when you take into account the time taken by the firm to pay for its purchases. See Exhibit 14.2 for a graphical representation of the cash conversion cycle.
- When managing working capital accounts, financial managers want to do the following:
  - o Delay paying accounts payable as long as possible without suffering any penalties.
  - o Maintain minimal raw material inventories without causing manufacturing delays.
  - o Use as little labor as possible to manufacture the product while producing a quality product.
  - o Maintain minimal finished goods inventories without losing sales.
  - o Offer customers the most attractive credit terms possible on trade credit to maximize sales while minimizing the risk of nonpayment.
  - o Collect cash payments on accounts receivable as fast as possible to close the loop.
- Two tools to measure the working capital management efficiency are the ***operating cycle*** and the ***cash conversion cycle***.

A. ***Operating Cycle***

- The **operating cycle** begins when the firm receives the raw materials it purchased and ends when the firm collects cash payments on its credit sales.
- Two measures—days' sales outstanding and days' sales in inventory—help determine the operating cycle.
  - o **Days' sales in inventory (DSI)** shows how long the firm keeps its inventory before selling it.
    - ▪ It is the ratio of the inventory balance to the daily cost of goods sold.
    - ▪ The quicker a firm can move out its raw materials as finished goods, the shorter the duration when the firm holds its inventory, and the more efficient it is in managing its inventory.
  - o **Days' sales outstanding (DSO)** estimates how long it takes on average for the firm to collect its outstanding accounts receivable balance.
    - ▪ This ratio is also called the **Average Collection Period (ACP)**.
    - ▪ An efficient firm with good working capital management should have a low average collection period compared to its industry.
- The operating cycle is calculated by summing the days' sales outstanding and the days' sales in inventory.

B. ***Cash Conversion Cycle***

- The **cash conversion cycle** is related to the operating cycle, but it does not start until the firm actually pays for its inventory.
  - o The cash conversion cycle is the length of time between the cash outflow for materials and the cash inflow from sales.
- To measure the cash conversion cycle, we need another measure called the day's payables outstanding.
- **Days' payable outstanding (DPO)** shows how long a firm takes to pay off its suppliers for the cost of inventory.
- The cash conversion cycle is then calculated by summing the days' sales outstanding and the days' sales in inventory and subtracting the days' payable outstanding.
  - o The formula is shown in Equation 14.2

14.3 Working Capital Investment Strategies

- Financial managers use two types of strategies for current assets investments: *flexible* and *restrictive*.

A. ***Flexible Current Asset Investment Strategy***

- The flexible strategy has a *high* percentage of current assets to sales, whereas a restrictive policy has a *low* percentage of current assets to sales.

- The **flexible strategy** calls for management to invest large amounts in cash, marketable securities, and inventory.
- The strategy also promotes a liberal trade credit policy for customers, which results in high levels of accounts receivable.
- The flexible strategy is perceived be a low-risk and low-return course of action for management to follow.
- The advantage of this policy is the large working capital balances the firm holds.
- The strategy's downside is the high **inventory carrying cost** associated with owning a high level of inventory and providing liberal credit terms for its customers.
- The higher carrying costs result for two reasons
  - o The investment in the low-return current assets deprives the higher returns that management could earn on longer term assets like plant and equipment.
  - o Higher amounts of inventory results in higher warehousing and storage costs.

B. ***Restrictive Current Asset Investment Strategy***

- Current assets are kept to a minimum in the **restrictive strategy**.
- The firm barely invests in cash and inventory, and has tight terms of sale intended to curb credit sales and accounts receivable.
- The restrictive strategy is a high-risk, high-return alternative to the flexible strategy.
- The high risk comes in the form of **shortage costs**, which can be either financial or operating.
  - o ***Financial shortage*** costs arise mainly from illiquidity shortage of cash and a lack of marketable securities to sell for cash.
  - o ***Operating shortage*** costs result from lost production and sales.

C. ***The Working Capital Trade-Off***

- The optimal current asset investment strategy will depend on the relative magnitudes of carrying costs versus shortage costs. This conflict is often referred to as the *working capital trade-off.*
  - o Financial managers need to balance shortage costs against carrying costs to find an optimal strategy.
  - o If carrying costs are larger than shortage costs, then the firm will maximize value by adopting a more restrictive strategy.
  - o On the other hand, if shortage costs dominate carrying costs, the firm will need to move toward a more flexible policy.
  - o Overall, management will try to find the level of current assets that minimizes the sum of the carrying costs and shortage costs.

14.4 Accounts Receivables

A. ***Terms of Sale***

- Whenever a firm sells a product, the seller spells out the terms and conditions of the sale in a document called the *terms of sale.*
- The agreement specifies when the cash payment is due and the amount of any discount if early payment is made.
- Trade credit, which is short-term financing, is typically made with a discount for early payment rather an explicit interest charge.
  - o An offer of "3/10, net 40." means that the selling firm offers a 3 percent discount if the buyer pays the full amount of the purchase in cash within 10 days of the invoice date.
    - ▪ Otherwise, the buyer has 40 days to pay the balance in full from the date of delivery.
- To calculate the cost, we need to determine the interest rate the buyer is paying and convert it to an equivalent annual rate.
- The formula for calculating the EAR for a problem like this is shown below, in Equation 14.4:

$$\text{Effective annual rate} = \left(1 + \frac{\text{Discount}}{\text{Discounted price}}\right)^{365/\text{days credit}} - 1$$

- Trade credit is a loan from the supplier, and it can be a very costly form of credit.

B. ***Aging Accounts Receivables***

- A common tool that credit managers use is called an ***aging schedule***.
- The aging schedule shows the breakdown of the firm's accounts receivable by their date of sale—how long has the account not been paid in days.
- Its purpose is to identify and then track delinquent accounts and to see that they are paid.
- Aging schedules are also an important financial tool for analyzing the quality of a company's receivables.

14.5 Inventory Management

- Inventory management is largely a function of operations management, not financial management.
- Manufacturing companies generally carry three types of inventory: raw materials, work in process, and finished goods.

A. *Economic Order Quantity*

- The economic order quantity (EOQ) mathematically determines the minimum total inventory cost taking into account *reorder costs* and *inventory carrying costs.*
- The optimal order size strikes the balance between these two costs.

B. *Just-in-Time Inventory Management*

- In this system, the exact day-by-day, or even hour-by-hour raw material needs are delivered by the suppliers, who deliver the goods "just in time" for them to be used on the production line.
- A big advantage of this system is that there are essentially no raw inventory costs and no chance of obsolescence or loss to theft.
- On the other hand, if the supplier fails to make the needed deliveries, then production shuts down.
- If the system works for a firm, it cuts down their investment in working capital dramatically.

14.6 Cash Management and Budgeting

A. *Reasons for Holding Cash*

- Two reasons exist for holding a cash balance. First, it facilitates transactions with suppliers, customers, and employees.
- The second reason for holding cash is simply that most banks require firms to hold minimum cash balances, or **compensating balances**, in exchange for the services they provide.

B. *Cash Collection*

- Collection time, or **float**, is the time between when a customer makes a payment and when the cash becomes available to the firm.
- Collection time can be broken down into three components.
  - First is delivery time, or mailing time.
    - When a customer mails payment, it may take several days before that payment arrives.
  - Second is processing delay.
    - Once the payment is received, it must be opened, examined, accounted for, and deposited at the firm's bank.
  - Finally, there is a delay between the time of the deposit and the time when the cash is available for withdrawal.
  - Payments in cash at the point of sale reduce the collection time to zero.
    - Payments by checks or credit cards at the point of sale eliminates the mail time but not the processing time.
  - A ***lockbox*** system allows geographically dispersed customers to send their payments to a post office box close to them.
  - With a concentration account, a post office box is replaced by a local branch, which receives the mailings, processes the payments, and makes the deposits.
  - Either approach will reduce the collection time to an extent, but there is a cost associated with it.
  - Another increasingly popular means of reducing cash collection time is through the use of ***electronic funds transfers***. Such payments reduce cash collection times in every phase.

14.7 Financing Working Capital

A. *Strategies for Financing Working Capital*

- Exhibit 14.7 shows the three basic strategies that a firm can follow to finance its working capital and fixed assets.
  - Each of the three panels shows: (1) the total long-term financing needed, which consists of long-term debt and equity, and (2) the seasonal needs for working capital that fluctuates with the level of sales.
- The **maturity matching strategy** is shown in Figure A of Exhibit 14.7.
  - All working capital is funded with short-term borrowing and, as the level of sales varies seasonally, short-term borrowing fluctuates between some minimum and maximum level.
  - All fixed assets are funded with long-term financing.

- The "matching of maturities" is one of the most basic techniques used by financial managers to reduce risk when financing assets.
- The **long-term funding strategy** is shown in Figure B in Exhibit 14.7.
- This strategy relies on long-term debt to finance *both* capital assets and working capital.
- This strategy reduces the risk of funding current assets because there is no need to worry about refinancing assets since all funding is long term.
- Figure C in Exhibit 14.7 shows the **short-term funding strategy** where all working capital and a portion of fixed assets are funded with short-term debt.
- While this lowers the cost under some interest rate scenarios, it forces the firm to continually refinance the funding of the long-term assets in a changing interest rate environment.

B. *Financing Working Capital in Practice*

- Many financial managers try to match the maturities of assets and liabilities when funding the firm.
  - That is, short-term assets are funded with short-term financing, and long-term assets are funded with long-term financing.
- Most financial managers like to fund some of their current assets with long-term debt as shown in Figure A of Exhibit 14.7, so-called **permanent working capital**.
- In recent years, a number of large, well-known firms of the highest credit standing have been funding some of their long-term fixed assets with short-term debt sold in the commercial paper market.

C. *Sources of Short-Term Financing*

- Accounts payable (trade credit), bank loans, and commercial paper are common sources of short-term financing.
- Between 1990 and 2003, **accounts payable** constituted 37 percent of total current liabilities for all publicly traded manufacturing firms.
  - The buyer needs to figure out whether it makes financial sense to pay early and take advantage of the discount or to wait and pay in full when the account is due.
- Between 1990 and 2003, **short-term bank loans** accounted for 19 percent of total current liabilities for all publicly traded manufacturing firms.
  - An **informal line of credit** is a verbal agreement between the firm and the bank, allowing the firm to borrow up to an agreed-upon upper limit.
  - In exchange for providing the line of credit, a bank may require that the firm holds a **compensating balance** with them.
  - A **formal line of credit** is also known as "revolving credit," where the bank has a legal obligation to lend to the firm an amount of money up to a preset limit.
  - The firm pays a yearly fee, in addition to the interest expense on the amount they borrow.
  - If the firm backs the loan with an asset, the loan is defined as secured; otherwise, the loan is unsecured.
  - Secured loans allow the borrower to borrow at a lower interest rate, all else being equal.
- **Commercial paper** is a promissory note issued by large financially secure firms, which have high credit ratings.
  - Commercial paper is not "secured," which means that the issuer is not pledging any assets to the lender in the event of default.
  - However, most commercial paper is backed by a credit line from a commercial bank.
  - Therefore the default rate on commercial paper is very low, resulting in an interest rate that is usually lower than what a bank would charge on a direct loan.
- For medium-size and small businesses, **accounts receivable financing** is an important source of funds.
  - A company can secure a bank loan by pledging the firm's accounts receivable as security.
  - A second way for a business to finance itself with accounts receivables is to *sell* the receivables to a factor at a discount.
  - The firm that sold the receivables has no further legal obligation to the factor.

II. Suggested Approach to Material

This chapter focuses on short-term financial decisions that involve cash inflows and outflows that will occur within a year or less. Examples include the purchase of raw materials, paying for the purchases of raw materials, selling finished inventory, and the collection of cash for sales made on credit. This chapter focuses on these types of decisions, which are called *working capital management.*

The chapter begins by reviewing some basic definitions and concepts that are necessary to further our study of working capital management. Next, the authors examine the individual working capital accounts and then learn how to construct and analyze the operating and cash conversion cycles. They next examine how the different working capital accounts are managed: the cash account, accounts receivables, and inventory. Finally, the different financing options that financial managers consider, and the risks involved are discussed.

III. Chapter Glossary

Trade credit	Credit extended by one business to another.
Consumer credit	Credit extended by a business to consumers.
Cash conversion cycle	The length of time from the point at which a company pays for raw materials until the point at which it receives cash from the sale of finished goods made from those materials.
Operating cycle	The average time between purchasing raw materials and receiving cash for the sale of finished goods made from those materials.
Flexible current asset investment strategy	Current asset investment strategy that involves keeping high balances of current assets on hand.
Inventory carrying costs	Expenses associated with maintaining inventory, including interest forgone on money invested in inventory, storage costs, taxes, and insurance.
Restrictive current asset investment strategy	Current asset investment strategy that involves keeping the level of current assets at a minimum.
Shortage costs	Costs incurred because of lost production and sales or illiquidity.
Economic order quantity (EOQ)	Order quantity that minimizes the total variable costs incurred to order and hold inventory.
Compensating balances	Bank balances that firms must maintain to at least partially compensate banks for loans or services rendered.
Float	The time between when a customer makes a payment and when the cash becomes available to the firm.
Permanent working capital	The minimum level of working capital that a firm will always have on its books.
Maturity matching strategy	Financing strategy that matches the maturities of liabilities and assets.
Long-term funding strategy	Financing strategy that relies on long-term debt to finance both fixed assets and working capital.
Short-term funding strategy	Financing strategy that relies on short-term debt to finance all seasonal working capital and a portion of permanent working capital and fixed assets.
Informal line of credit	A verbal agreement between a bank and a firm under which the firm can borrow an amount of money up to an agreed-on limit.
Formal line of credit	A contractual agreement between a bank and a firm under which the bank has a legal obligation to lend funds to the firm up to a preset limit.
Commercial paper	Short-term debt in the form of promissory notes issued by large, financially secure firms with high credit ratings.
Factor	An individual or a financial institution, such as a bank or a business finance company, which buys accounts receivable without recourse.

IV. Summary of Key Equations

Equation	Description	Formula
14.1	Operating cycle	Operating cycle = DSO + DSI
14.2	Cash conversion cycle	Cash conversion cycle = DSO + DSI − DPO
14.3	Cash conversion cycle	Cash conversion cycle = Operating cycle − DPO
14.4	Effective annual rate (EAR)	$\text{EAR} = \left(1 + \frac{\text{Discount}}{\text{Discounted price}}\right)^{365/\text{days credit}} - 1$
14.5	Economic order quantity (EOQ)	$\text{EOQ} = \sqrt{\frac{2 \times \text{Reorder costs} \times \text{Sales per period}}{\text{Carrying costs}}}$

V. True or False Questions

1. One of the key issues in working capital management is how current assets should be financed.
   a. True
   b. False

2. Net working capital is all current assets less cash.
   a. True
   b. False

3. Working capital efficiency refers to the length of time between when a working capital asset is acquired and when it is converted into cash.
   a. True
   b. False

4. The operating cycle is the length of time between the cash outflow for materials and the cash inflow from sales.
   a. True
   b. False

5. The cash conversion cycle is calculated by summing the days' sales outstanding and the days' sales in inventory and subtracting the days' payables outstanding.
   a. True
   b. False

6. The flexible strategy has a *low* percent of current assets to sales, whereas a restrictive policy has a *high* percent of current assets to sales.
   a. True
   b. False

7. Current assets are kept at a maximum in the restrictive strategy.
   a. True
   b. False

8. Trade credit is typically made with a discount for early payment rather an explicit interest charge.
   a. True
   b. False

9. The economic order quantity mathematically determines the minimum total inventory cost taking into account reorder costs and inventory carrying costs.
   a. True
   b. False

10. A lockbox system allows a firm to pay off suppliers using the electronic fund transfer system.
   a. True
   b. False

VI. Multiple-Choice Questions and Problems

1. Working capital management involves two key issues of
   a. the appropriate amount and mix of current assets for the firm to hold
   b. how the current assets should be financed
   c. a and b
   d. None of the above.

2. Which one of the following statements is NOT true?
   a. Gross working capital is the funds invested in a company's cash account, account receivables, inventory, and other current assets.
   b. Net working capital refers to the sum of current assets and current liabilities.
   c. Liquidity is the ability of a company to convert assets—real or financial—into cash quickly without suffering a financial loss.
   d. Working capital management involves making decisions regarding the use and sources of current assets.

3. Two tools to measure the working capital management efficiency are the
   a. inventory cycle and the operating cycle.
   b. receivables cycle and the inventory cycle.
   c. operating cycle and the cash conversion cycle.
   d. None of the above.

4. When managing working capital accounts, financial managers want to do all of the following EXCEPT
   a. maintain minimal raw material inventories without causing manufacturing delays.
   b. use as little labor as possible to manufacture the product while producing a quality product.
   c. speed up paying accounts payable to avoid suffering any penalties.
   d. offer customers the most attractive credit terms possible on trade credit to maximize sales while minimizing the risk of nonpayment.

5. Which ONE of the following statements is true?
   a. Operating cycle = DSO + DSI
   b. Operating cycle = DSO − DSI
   c. Operating cycle = DPO − DSI
   d. None of the above.

6. The higher carrying costs associated with the flexible current asset investment result from
   a. the diversion of resources from the high return long-term assets to the low return inventory
   b. high warehousing and storage costs associated with high levels of inventory
   c. a and b
   d. None of the above.

7. Which one of the following about the flexible current asset investment strategy is NOT true?
   a. The restrictive strategy is a low-risk, low-return alternative to the flexible strategy.
   b. The flexible strategy calls for management to invest large amounts in cash, marketable securities, and inventory.
   c. The advantage of the flexible strategy is the large working capital balances the firm holds.
   d. The flexible strategy is perceived be a low-risk and low-return course of action for management to follow.

8. The document called the *terms of sale* specifies
   a. the terms and conditions of the sale.
   b. when the cash payment is due.
   c. the amount of any discount if early payment is made.
   d. All of the above.

9. Which one of the following statements about the long-term financing strategy is NOT true?
   a. It relies on short-term debt to finance *both* capital assets and working capital.
   b. The strategy reduces the risk of funding current assets.
   c. There is no need to worry about refinancing assets since all funding is long term.
   d. It relies on long-term debt to finance *both* capital assets and working capital.

10. Which ONE of the following statements is true?
    a. Accounts payable (trade credit), bank loans, and commercial paper are common sources of short-term financing.
    b. An informal line of credit is a verbal agreement between the firm and the bank, allowing the firm to borrow up to an agreed-upon upper limit.
    c. A formal line of credit is also known as "revolving credit."
    d. All of the above.

11. Naron Company, a men's designer firm, has an operating cycle of 105 days. The firm's days' sales in inventory is 53 days. How much does the firm have in receivables if it has credit sales of $133,450? Round to the nearest dollar.
    a. $19,012
    b. $21,252
    c. $27,501
    d. $14,233

12. Ferris Corp. estimates that it takes the company 32 days on average to pay off its suppliers. It also knows that it has days' sales in inventory of 43 days and days sales' outstanding of 35 days. What is its cash conversion cycle?
    a. 46 days
    b. 35 days
    c. 37 days
    d. 26 days

13. West Handicrafts, Inc., has net sales of $423,000 with 30 percent of it being credit sales. Its cost of goods sold is $324,000. The firm's cash conversion cycle is 47.9 days. The firm's operating cycle is 86.3 days. What is the firm's accounts payable? Round to the nearest dollar.
    a. $34,087
    b. $126,900
    c. $71,203
    d. $56,322

14. Serengeti Travels has borrowed $50,000 at a stated APR of 8.5 percent. The loan calls for a compensating balance of 8 percent. What is the effective interest rate for this company?
    a. 9.24%
    b. 8.50%

c. 8.00%

d. 16.50%

15. Trend, Inc., has just set up a formal line of credit of $5 million with First National Bank. The line of credit is good for up to three years. The bank will be charging the company an interest rate of 7.5 percent on the loan, and in addition the firm will pay an annual fee of 50 basis points on the unused balance. The firm borrowed $2,300,000 on the first day the credit line became available. What is the firm's effective interest rate on this line of credit? Round to one decimal place.

a. 8.5%

b. 7.25%

c. 9.0%

d. 8.1%

16. Santiago Corp. has daily sales of $23,400. The financial manager determined that a lockbox would reduce the collection time by 2.1 days. Assuming the company can earn 5 percent interest per year, what are the savings from the lockbox? Round to the nearest dollar.

a. $3,200

b. $2,457

c. $3,620

d. $1,100

17. Senter Corp. sells its goods with terms of 2/10 EOM, net 30. What is the implicit cost of the trade credit?

a. 18.50%

b. 30.00%

c. 44.59%

d. 21.89%

18. Xinhua Inc. sells $100,000 of its accounts receivable to factors at 3 percent discount. The firm's average collection period is one month. What is the simple annual interest cost of the factors loan?

a. 37.1%

b. 32.9%

c. 27.8%

d. 31.1%

The following information applies to the next two problems.

Jensen Autos, one of the largest car dealers in Eau Claire, sells about 700 vehicles a year. The cost of placing an order with their supplier is $1,100, and the inventory carrying costs are $120 for each car. Most of their sales are in late fall of each year.

19. What is the number of cars per order?

a. 80 cars

b. 101 cars

c. 58 cars

d. 113 cars

20. How many orders will the dealer need to place this year?

a. 4 orders

b. 5 orders

c. 6 orders

d. 7 orders

Answers to True or False Questions

1. a	**2.** b	**3.** a	**4.** a	**5.** a
6. b	**7.** b	**8.** a	**9.** a	**10.** b

Answers to Multiple-Choice Questions

1. c	**2.** b	**3.** c	**4.** c	**5.** a
6. c	**7.** a	**8.** d	**9.** a	**10.** d
11. a	**12.** a	**13.** a	**14.** a	**15.** d
16. b	**17.** c	**18.** a	**19.** d	**20.** c

Solutions to Multiple-Choice Problems

11. Solution:

Operating cycle = 105 days

DSI = 53 days

Operating cycle = DSO + DSI

DSO = OC − DSI = 105 − 53 = 52 days

Credit sales = $133,450

$$\text{DSO} = \frac{\text{Accounts receivable}}{\text{Credit sales}/365} = \frac{\text{Accounts receivable}}{\$133{,}450/365} = 52 \text{ days}$$

Accounts receivable = 52 × $365.62 = **$19,012.05**

12. Solution:

DPO = 32 days

DSI = 43 days

DSO = 35 days

Ferris's cash conversion cycle =

$$\begin{aligned}\text{Cash conversion cycle} &= \text{DSO} + \text{DSI} - \text{DPO}\\ &= 35 + 43 - 32\\ &= \mathbf{46\ days}\end{aligned}$$

13. Solution:

Net sales = $423,000

Credit sales = (0.3 × $423,000) = $126,900

Cash conversion cycle = 47.9 days

Operating cycle = 86.3 days

Cost of goods sold = $324,000

$$\begin{aligned}\text{Cash conversion cycle} &= (\text{DSO} + \text{DSI}) - \text{DPO}\\ 47.9 &= 86.3 - \text{DPO}\\ \text{DPO} &= \mathbf{38.4\ days}\end{aligned}$$

$$\text{DPO} = \frac{\text{Accounts payable}}{\text{COGS}/365} = \frac{\text{Accounts payable}}{\$324{,}000/365} = 38.4 \text{ days}$$

Accounts payable = 38.4 × \$887.67 = **\$34,086.53**

The firm has accounts payables of **\$34,087**.

14. Solution:

Amount to be borrowed = \$50,000

Stated annual interest rate = 8.5%

Compensating balance = 8%

Amount deposited as compensating balance = \$50,000 × 0.08 = \$4,000

Effective borrowing amount = \$50,000 − \$4,000 = \$46,000

Interest expense = \$50,000 × 0.085 = \$4,250

$$\text{Effective interest rate} = \frac{\text{Interest expense}}{\text{Effective borrowing amount}} = \frac{\$4{,}250}{\$46{,}000} = \mathbf{9.24\%}$$

15. Solution:

Line of credit limit = \$5,000,000

Loan rate = 7.5%

Annual fee on used balance = 0.5%

Amount borrowed = \$2,300,000

Unused balance = \$2,700,000

Annual fee = \$2,700,000 × 0.005 = \$13,500

Interest expense = \$2,300,000 × 0.075 = \$172,500

$$\text{Effective interest rate} = \frac{\text{Interest expense} + \text{Annual fee}}{\text{Borrowed amount}}$$

$$= \frac{(\$172{,}500 + \$13{,}500)}{\$2{,}300{,}000} = \mathbf{8.09\%}$$

16. Solution:

Average daily sales = \$23,400

Collection time saved = 2.1 days

Savings from mail float = 2.1 days × \$23,400= \$49,140

Savings if invested = \$49,140 × (0.05) = **\$2,457**

17. Solution:

Credit terms = 2/10 EOM, net 30

$$\text{Effective annual rate} = \left(1 + \frac{\text{Discount}}{\text{Discounted price}}\right)^{365/\text{days credit}} - 1$$

$$= (1 + 2/98)^{365/20} - 1$$

$$= (1.0204)^{18.2500} - 1$$

$$= 1.4459 - 1$$

= 0.4459, or **44.59 percent**

18. Solution:

Accounts receivable sold = \$100,000

Factor discount = 3%

Average collection period = 1 month

Dollar cost of factoring per month = \$100,000 × 0.03 = **\$3,000**

Simple monthly interest cost of factoring = 3/97= 0.03093

Simple interest cost of factoring = 0.03093 × 12 = **37.1%**

19. Solution:

Annual sales = 700 units

Cost of placing an order = \$1,100

Inventory carrying cost = \$120

$$\text{EOQ} = \sqrt{\frac{2 \times \text{Reorder costs} \times \text{Sales per period}}{\text{Carrying costs}}}$$

$$= \sqrt{\frac{2 \times \$1{,}100 \times 700}{\$120}} = 113.3$$

Economic order quantity = 113 cars.

20. Solution:

Number of orders = 700/113≅6

CHAPTER 15

How Firms Raise Capital

LEARNING OBJECTIVES

1. Explain what is meant by bootstrapping and why it is important.
2. Explain the role of venture capital firms in the economy, and discuss how they reduce their risk when investing in start-up businesses.
3. Discuss the advantages and disadvantages of going public, and be able to compute the proceeds from an IPO.
4. Explain why, when underwriting new security offerings, investment bankers prefer that the securities be underpriced, and compute the total cost of an IPO.
5. Explain the costs of bringing a general cash offer to market, and be able to compute the total cost of issuing a general cash offer.
6. Explain why a firm that has access to the public markets might elect to raise money through a private placement.
7. Review some advantages of borrowing from a commercial bank rather than selling securities in financial markets, and discuss bank term loans.

I. Chapter Outline

15.1 Bootstrapping

A. *How New Businesses Get Started*

- Most businesses are started by an entrepreneur who has a vision for a new business or product and a passionate belief in the concept's viability.
- The process by which many entrepreneurs raise "seed" money and obtain other resources necessary to start their businesses is often called **bootstrapping.**
- The initial "seed" money usually comes from the entrepreneur or other founders.
- The seed money, in most cases, is spent on developing a prototype of the product or service and a business plan.

15.2 Venture Capital

- The bootstrapping period usually lasts no more than one or two years.
- At some point, the founders will have developed a prototype of the product and a business plan, which they can "take on the road" to seek venture capital funding to grow the business.
- **Venture capitalists** are individuals or firms that help new businesses get started and provide much of their early-stage financing.

A. *Why Venture Capital Funding Is Different*

- Venture capital is important because entrepreneurs have only limited access to traditional sources of funding.
  - o Three reasons exist as to why traditional sources of funding do not work for new or emerging businesses: *the high degree of risk, types of productive assets, and informational asymmetry problems.*

B. ***How Venture Capitalists Reduce Their Risk***

- Venture capitalists know that only a handful of new companies will survive to become successful firms.
- They use a number of tactics when they invest in new ventures, including funding the ventures in stages, requiring entrepreneurs to make personal investments, syndicating investments, and maintaining in-depth knowledge about the industry in which they specialize.
  - ***Staged Funding.*** The key idea behind staged funding is that each funding stage gives the venture capitalist an opportunity to reassess the management team and the firm's financial performance.
  - ***Personal Investment.*** Venture capitalists often require an entrepreneur to make a substantial personal investment in the business.
  - ***Syndication.*** It is a common practice to syndicate seed- and early-stage venture capital investments.
  - ***In-depth Knowledge.*** Another factor that reduces risk is the venture capitalist's in-depth knowledge of the industry and technology.

C. ***The Exit Strategy***

- Every venture capital agreement includes provisions identifying who has the authority to make critical decisions concerning the exit process.
- Venture capital firms exit venture-backed companies in three principal ways: selling to a strategic buyer, selling to a financial buyer, and offering stock to the public.

D. ***Venture Capitalists Provide More Than Financing***

- The extent of the venture capitalists' involvement in management of the firm depends on the experience and depth of the management team.
- One of their most important roles is to provide advice to entrepreneurs.

E. ***The Cost of Venture Capital Funding***

- The cost of venture capital funding is very high, but the high rates of return earned by venture capitalists are not unreasonable.
- A typical venture capital fund may generate annual returns of 15 to 25 percent on the money that it invests, compared with an average annual return for the S&P 500 of about 12 percent.

15.3 Initial Public Offering

- One way to raise larger sums of cash or to facilitate the exit of a venture capitalist is through an **initial public offering,** or **IPO,** of the company's common stock.
- A firm's decision to go public depends on an assessment of whether the advantages outweigh the disadvantages.
- Going public has a number of potential advantages.
  - Larger amounts of equity capital can be raised in the public equity markets.
  - Going public can enable an entrepreneur to fund a growing business without giving up control.
  - After the IPO, there is an active secondary market in which stockholders can buy and sell its shares.
  - Publicly traded firms find it easier to attract top management talent and to better motivate current managers if a firm's stock is publicly traded.
- There are several disadvantages to going public.
  - One disadvantage of going public is the high cost of the IPO itself.
  - The costs of complying with ongoing SEC disclosure requirements also represent a disadvantage of going public.
  - The transparency that results from this compliance can be costly for some firms.
  - Finally, SEC requirements encourage managers to focus on short-term profits rather than long-term wealth maximization.

A. ***Investment Banking Services***

- To complete an IPO, a firm will need the services of investment bankers, who are experts in bringing new securities to market.
- Investment bankers provide three basic services when bringing securities to market—origination, underwriting, and distribution.
- Securing the services of an investment banking firm with a reputation for quality and honesty will improve the market's receptivity and help ensure a successful IPO.
- *Origination* includes giving the firm financial advice and getting the issue ready to sell.

- *Underwriting* is the risk-bearing part of investment banking.
  - The securities can be underwritten in two ways: (1) on a firm-commitment basis or (2) on a best-effort basis.
    - In the **firm-commitment underwriting,** which is more typical, the investment banker guarantees the issuer a fixed amount of money from the stock sale.
    - With a **best-effort underwriting,** the investment banking firm makes no guarantee to sell the securities at a particular price.
  - Before the shares are sold, representatives from the underwriting syndicate hold a due diligence meeting with representatives of the issuer.
  - Investment bankers hold due diligence meetings to protect their reputations and to reduce the risk of investors' lawsuits in the event the investment goes sour later on.
- *Distribution* involves reselling the securities to the public.
  - Once the due diligence process is complete, the underwriters and the issuer determine the final offer price in a *pricing call.*
  - If management finds the price acceptable, the issuer files an amendment to the registration statement with the SEC, which contains the terms of the offering and the final prospectus.
    - Once the securities are registered with the SEC, they can be sold to investors.
  - The syndicate's primary concern is to sell the securities as quickly as possible at the offer price.
  - At the *closing* of a firm-commitment offering, the issuing firm delivers the security certificates to the underwriter and the underwriter delivers the payment for the securities, net of the underwriting fee, to the issuer.

15.4 IPO Pricing and Cost

A. *The Underpricing Debate*

- The issuer prefers the stock price to be as high as realistically possible while the underwriters prefer some degree of underpricing.
- **Underpricing** is defined as offering new securities for sale at a price below their true value.
- In a firm-commitment offering, the underwriters will suffer a financial loss if the offer price is set too high; under a best-effort agreement, the issuing firm will lose.
- If the underpricing is significant, the investment banking firm will suffer a loss of reputation for failing to price the new issue correctly and raising less money for its client than it could have.

15.5 General Cash Offer by a Public Company

- If a public firm has a high credit rating, the lowest-cost source of external funds is often a **general cash offer,** also referred to as a *registered public offering*.
- A general cash offer is a sale of *debt or equity,* open to all investors, by a registered public company that has previously sold stock to the public.

A. *Competitive or Negotiated Sale*

- In a general cash offer, management must decide whether to sell the securities on a competitive or a negotiated basis.
  - In a *competitive sale,* the firm specifies the type and amount of securities it wants to sell and hires an investment banking firm to do the origination work.
  - In a *negotiated sale,* the issuer selects the underwriter at the beginning of the origination process.
- For debt issues, most experts believe that competitive sales are the least costly method of selling so-called vanilla bonds when market conditions are stable.
- For equity securities, negotiated sales provide the lowest-cost method of sale.

B. *Shelf Registration*

- Since November 1983, the SEC has allowed some two thousand large corporations the option of using **shelf registration.**
- Shelf registration allows a firm to register an inventory of securities for a two-year period.
- Corporations gain two important benefits from shelf registration.
  - First is the greater flexibility in bringing securities to market. Securities can be taken off the shelf and sold within minutes.
  - Second, shelf registration allows firms to periodically sell small amounts of securities, raising money as it is actually needed, rather than banking a large amount of money from a single security sale and spending it over time.

15.6 Private Markets and Bank Loans

A. ***Private versus Public Markets***

- For many smaller firms and firms of lower credit standing that have limited access, or no access, to the public markets, the cheapest source of external funding is often the private markets.
- Many private companies that are owned by entrepreneurs, families, or family foundations and are sizable companies of high credit quality prefer to sell their securities in the private markets even though they can access public markets.

B. ***Private Placements***

- **Private placement** occurs when a firm sells unregistered securities directly to investors such as insurance companies, commercial banks, or wealthy individuals.
- About half of all corporate debt is sold through the private placement market.
- Private placements have a number of advantages, relative to public offerings, for certain issuers.
  - Net of transaction costs, lower cost of funds.
  - Private lenders are more willing to negotiate changes to a bond contract.
  - If a firm suffers financial distress, the problems are more likely to be resolved without going to a bankruptcy court.
  - Other advantages include the speed of private placement deals and flexibility in issue size.
- The biggest drawback of private placements involves restrictions on the resale of the securities.

C. ***Private Equity Firms***

- Like venture capitalists, private equity firms pool money from wealthy investors, pension funds, insurance companies, and other sources to make investments.
- Private equity firms invest in more mature companies, and they often purchase 100 percent of a business.
- Private equity firm managers look to increase the value of the firms they acquire by closely monitoring their performance and providing better management.
- Once value is increased, they sell the firms for a profit after holding investments typically for three to five years.
- Private equity investors focus on firms that have stable cash flows because they use a lot of debt to finance their acquisitions.
- When a large amount of leverage is used to take over a company, the transaction is called a *leveraged buyout.*

D. ***Private Investments in Public Equity***

- *Private investment in public equity* (PIPE) transactions are transactions in which a public company sells unregistered stock to an investor—often a hedge fund or some other institutional investor.
- In a PIPE transaction, investors purchase securities (equity or debt) directly from a publicly traded company in a private placement.
- Because the securities sold in a PIPE transaction are not registered with the SEC, they are "restricted securities."
- The major advantage of a PIPE transaction to issuers is that it gives them faster access to capital and a lower funding cost than a registered public offering.
- PIPE transactions involving a healthy firm can also be executed without the use of an investment bank, resulting in a cost saving of 7 to 8 percent of the proceeds.

E. ***Commercial Bank Lending***

- Almost every company has a working relationship with at least one bank, and smaller companies depend on them for funding and for financial advice.
- **Prime-rate loan** are loans in which the borrowing rate is based on the *prime rate of interest,* which is historically the loan rate that banks charge their most creditworthy customers.
- In determining the interest rate to charge on a loan, the bank takes the prime rate plus two other factors into account. The calculation, called the bank loan pricing model, is shown in Equation 15.1.
- **Term loans** are defined as business loans with maturities greater than one year.
  - Term loans are the most common form of intermediate-term financing provided by commercial banks.
  - Bank term loans may be secured or unsecured, and the funds can be used to buy inventory or to finance plant and equipment.
- Before making a loan, the bank conducts a credit analysis of the customer.
  - To determine the customer's credit category (DRP), banks usually look at five to seven credit risk categories, which look very much like bond ratings.
  - Those with the highest credit rating borrow at the prime rate or below, while others have to pay a default risk premium over and the prime rate.

II. Suggested Approach to Material

This chapter is about how firms raise capital so that they can acquire the productive assets needed to grow and remain profitable. The chapter begins by examining how many new businesses acquire their first equity funding through "bootstrapping" and the role venture capitalists play in providing equity to help firms get started. Once a firm is successfully launched, the venture capitalists' job is done and they exit the scene. At this juncture, management has a number of other funding options, and we discuss those options in the remainder of the chapter.

The chapter next explains how firms sell their first issue of common stock in the public markets and the role of investment banks in completing these sales. First-time equity sales are known as initial public offerings, or IPOs. The role that private markets play in funding business firms and factors that managers consider when deciding between a public and a private market sale is then discussed. The chapter closes with a discussion of the importance of commercial banks in providing short-term and intermediate-term financing.

III. Chapter Glossary

Venture capitalists	Individuals or firms that invest purchase equity in new businesses and often provide the entrepreneurs with business advice.
Angels (angel investors)	Wealthy individuals who invest their own money in new ventures.
Initial public offering (IPO)	A company's first sale of stock in the public markets.
Seasoned public offering	The sale of securities to the public by a firm that already has publicly traded securities outstanding.
Preliminary prospectus	The initial registration statement filed with the SEC by a company preparing to issue securities in the public market; it contains detailed information about the issuer and the proposed issue.
Firm-commitment underwriting	Underwriting agreement in which the underwriter purchases securities for a specified price and resells them.
Best-effort underwriting	Underwriting agreement in which the underwriter does not agree to purchase the securities at a particular price but promises only to make its "best effort" to sell as much of the issue as possible above a certain price.
Underwriting syndicate	A group of underwriters that joins forces to reduce underwriting risk.
Underpricing	Offering new securities for sale at a price below their true value.
General cash offer	A sale of debt or equity, open to all investors, by a company that has previously sold stock to the public.
Shelf registration	A type of SEC registration that allows firms to register to sell securities over a two-year period and, during that time, take the securities "off the shelf" and sell them as needed.
Term loan	A business loan with a maturity greater than one year.

IV. Summary of Key Equations

Equation	Description	Formula
15.1	Bank loan pricing model	$k_l = \text{PR} + \text{DRP} + \text{MAT}$

V. True or False Questions

1. Most businesses are started by an entrepreneur who has a vision for a new business or product and a passionate belief in the concept's viability.
   a. True
   b. False

2. The initial "seed" money usually comes from banks.
   a. True
   b. False

3. Venture capitalists are individuals or firms that help new businesses get started and provide much of their early-stage financing.
   a. True
   b. False

4. Angel investors are typically wealthy individuals who invest their own money in emerging businesses at the very early stages in small deals.
   a. True
   b. False

5. Nearly $50 billion was invested in venture capital funds in 2005 and 2006 combined.
   a. True
   b. False

6. Modern venture capital firms tend to specialize in a specific line of business, such as hospitality, food manufacturing, or medical devices.
   a. True
   b. False

7. Traditional sources of funding do not work for new or emerging businesses because of the high degree of risk involved in starting a new business.
   a. True
   b. False

8. No informational asymmetry exists in entrepreneurial businesses.
   a. True
   b. False

9. A common way for venture capitalists to exit is to sell part of the firm's equity to a strategic buyer in the private market.
   a. True
   b. False

10. Publicly traded firms find it easier to attract top management talent and to better motivate current managers if a firm's stock is publicly traded.
    a. True
    b. False

11. The costs of complying with ongoing SEC disclosure requirements do not represent a disadvantage of going public.
    a. True
    b. False

12. Securing the services of an investment banking firm with a reputation for quality and honesty will improve the market's receptivity and help ensure a successful IPO.
    - a. True
    - b. False

13. With a **best-effort underwriting,** the investment banking firm makes no guarantee to sell the securities at a particular price.
    - a. True
    - b. False

14. Participating in a syndicate entitles each underwriter to receive a portion of the underwriting fee as well as an allocation of the securities to sell to its own customers.
    - a. True
    - b. False

15. In a firm-commitment offering, the underwriters will suffer a financial loss if the offer price is set too high.
    - a. True
    - b. False

16. A general cash offer is a sale of equity but not debt securities, that is open to all investors, by a registered public company that has previously sold stock to the public.
    - a. True
    - b. False

17. Shelf registration allows a firm to register an inventory of securities for a two-year period and during that time, the firm can take the securities "off the shelf" and sell them as needed.
    - a. True
    - b. False

18. In a traditional private placement, the issuer sells the securities directly to investors.
    - a. True
    - b. False

19. When a large amount of leverage is used to take over a company, the transaction is called a *leveraged buyout.*
    - a. True
    - b. False

20. The major advantage of a PIPE transaction to issuers is that it gives them faster access to capital and a lower funding cost than a registered public offering.
    - a. True
    - b. False

VI. Multiple-Choice Questions and Problems

1. The process by which many entrepreneurs raise "seed" money and obtain other resources necessary to start their businesses is called
    - a. bootstepping.
    - b. bootstrapping.
    - c. shoestrapping.
    - d. shoestepping.

2. Which one of the following statements is **NOT** true?
   a. The bootstrapping period usually lasts more than five years.
   b. Venture capitalists are individuals or firms that help new businesses get started and provide much of their early-stage financing.
   c. Individual venture capitalists are typically wealthy individuals who invest their own money in emerging businesses at the very early stages in small deals.
   d. The seed money, in most cases, is spent on developing a prototype of the product or service and a business plan.

3. Three reasons why traditional sources of funding do not work for new or emerging businesses are:
   a. Types of productive assets, informational asymmetry problems, and the low level of return.
   b. Low levels of return, informational asymmetry problems, and the high degree of risk.
   c. Types of productive assets, informational asymmetry problems, and the high degree of risk
   d. None of the above.

4. Which one of the following statements is **NOT** true?
   a. It is a common practice to syndicate late-stage venture capital investments.
   b. Syndication occurs when the originating venture capitalist sells a percentage of a deal to other venture capitalists.
   c. It increases the diversification of the originating venture capitalist's investment portfolio.
   d. The willingness of other venture capitalists to share in the investment provides independent corroboration that the investment is a reasonable decision.

5. The principal way(s) in which venture capital firms exit venture-backed companies are:
   a. selling to a strategic buyer.
   b. selling to a financial buyer.
   c. offering stock to the public.
   d. All of the above.

6. Advantages of going public include
   a. a larger amount of capital can be raised this way than the amount that can be raised through private sources.
   b. additional equity capital can usually be raised through follow-on seasoned public offerings at a low cost.
   c. going public can enable an entrepreneur to fund a growing business without giving up control.
   d. All of the above.

7. Disadvantages of going public include
   a. the high cost of the IPO itself.
   b. the costs of complying with ongoing SEC disclosure requirements.
   c. the transparency that results from this compliance can be costly for some firms.
   d. All of the above.

8. Basic services provided by investment bankers when bringing securities to market include
   a. origination.
   b. underwriting.
   c. distribution.
   d. All of the above.

9. Origination includes
   a. giving the firm financial advice.
   b. getting the issue ready to sell.
   c. helping the firm determine whether it is ready for an IPO.
   d. All of the above.

10. Which one of the following statements is **NOT** true about a best efforts underwriting agreement?

- **a.** Underwriters may combine to form a group called an underwriting syndicate.
- **b.** The issuing firm does not bear the price risk associated with underwriting the issue.
- **c.** Compensation is based on the number of shares sold.
- **d.** The investment banking firm makes no guarantee to sell the securities at a particular price.

11. The three basic costs associated with issuing stock in an IPO are

- **a.** price premium, out-of-pocket expenses, and underpricing.
- **b.** underwriting spread, out-of-pocket expenses, and underpricing.
- **c.** underwriting spread, price premium, and underpricing.
- **d.** None of the above.

12. If a public firm has a high credit rating, the lowest-cost source of external funds is

- **a.** a general cash offer.
- **b.** an IPO.
- **c.** unregistered public offering.
- **d.** None of the above.

13. Benefits from shelf registration include all **EXCEPT**:

- **a.** Greater flexibility in bringing securities to market.
- **b.** Shelf registration allows firms to periodically sell small amounts of securities and raise capital as needed.
- **c.** A shelf registration statement can cover multiple securities, but there is a penalty if authorized securities are not issued.
- **d.** Costs associated with selling the securities are reduced because only a single registration statement is required.

14. Advantages of private placements include:

- **a.** Possibly lower cost of funds.
- **b.** Greater willingness of private lenders to negotiate changes to a bond contract.
- **c.** The speed of private placement deals and flexibility in issue size.
- **d.** All of the above.

15. Private equity firms improve the performance of firms in which they invest by:

- **a.** making sure that the firms have the best possible management teams.
- **b.** closely monitoring each firm's performance and providing advice and counsel to the firm's management team.
- **c.** facilitating mergers and acquisitions that help improve the competitive positions of the companies in which they invest.
- **d.** All of the above.

16. Quixote, Inc., issues a $25 million IPO priced at $20 per share, and the price at which it was sold to the public is $12.50 per share. The firm's legal fees, SEC registration fees, and other administrative costs are $200,000. The firm's stock price increases 15 percent on the first day. What is the total cost of issuing the securities to the firm?

- **a.** $9.375 million
- **b.** $13.325 million
- **c.** $25 million
- **d.** None of the above

17. When Johnston Corp. went public in 2009, the offer price was $21.00 per share and the closing price at the end of the first day was $25.20. The firm issued 3 million shares. What was the loss to the company due to underpricing?

- **a.** $12.6 million
- **b.** $20.8 million

c. $14.2 million

d. $22.8 million

18. Shumacher Corp. wants to borrow money from Oxford Bank for a period of five years. The firm's credit standing calls for a premium of 2.5 percent over the prime rate. The current prime rate is 6.25 percent, the 30-year Treasury bond yield is 5.875 percent, the three-month Treasury bill yield is 3.5 percent, and the 5-year Treasury note yield is 4.75 percent. What is the appropriate loan rate for this customer?

a. 8.75%

b. 7.25%

c. 10%

d. None of the above

19. General Corporation is planning a production line and needs to raise $15 million to finance it. The company plans to raise the money through a general cash offering priced at $21.50 a share. Star's underwriters charge a 6 percent spread. How many shares does the company have to sell to achieve its goal?

a. 742,207 shares

b. 697,674 shares

c. 512,350 shares

d. None of the above

20. Fortune Hotels issues an IPO sold on a best-effort basis. The company's investment bank demands a spread of 20 percent. Five million shares are issued. However, the bank was overly optimistic and could not sell at the offer price of $31. If the net proceeds to the issuer is $110 million, how much did the investment bank receive?

a. $22.0 million

b. $27.5 million

c. $31.0 million

d. None of the above

Answers to True or False Questions

1. a	2. b	3. a	4. a	5. a
6. a	7. a	8. b	9. a	10. a
11. b	12. a	13. a	14. a	15. a
16. b	17. a	18. a	19. a	20. a

Answers to Multiple-Choice Questions

1. b	2. a	3. c	4. a	5. d
6. d	7. d	8. d	9. d	10. b
11. b	12. a	13. c	14. d	15. d
16. b	17. a	18. c	19. a	20. b

VIII. Solutions to Multiple-Choice Problems

16. Solution:

Stock price at end of first day = \$20(1.15) = \$23.00

First-day underpricing = (\$23.00 − \$20) = \$3.00 per share.

Number of shares outstanding = (\$25 million/\$20 per share) = 1.25 million.

Total underpricing = (\$3.00 per share × 1,250,000 shares of stock) = **\$3,750,000**

Underwriter's gross spread (\$20 − \$12.50) =\$7.50 per share.

Underwriting cost = (\$7.50 per share × 1.25 million shares) = **\$9,375,000**

Total cost to the firm of selling the IPO = \$3,750,000 + \$200,000 + \$9,375,000
= **\$13,325,000**

17. Solution:

Change in price on first day = \$25.20 − \$21.00 = \$4.20

Number of shares outstanding = 3.0 million

Loss due to underpricing = \$4.20 × 3,000,000 = **\$12.6 million**

18. Solution:

Prime rate =PR = 6.25%;

Default risk premium = DRP = 2.5%

Maturity risk premium = MAT = $k_{5\text{-year}} - k_{\text{T-bill}}$ = 4.75% − 3.5% = 1.25%

Borrowing rate for firm A = k = PR +DRP+ MAT
= 6.25% + 2.5% + 1.25% = **10%**

19. Solution:

Underwriter's spread = 6 %

Price per share the firm gets = [\$21.50*(1 − 0.06)] = \$20.21

Therefore, to raise \$15 million, the company needs to issue:

\$15,000,000 / \$20.21 = **742,207 new shares**

20. Solution:

Number of shares issued = 5 million

Net proceeds to issuer = \$110 million

Underwriting spread = 20%

Gross proceeds from offer = \$110,000,000 / 0.80 = \$137.5 million

Proceeds to underwriter = \$137.5 million × 0.20 = **\$27.5 million**

CHAPTER 16

Capital Structure Policy

LEARNING OBJECTIVES

1. Describe the two Modigliani and Miller propositions, the key assumptions underlying them, and their relevance to capital structure decisions.
2. Discuss the benefits and costs of using debt financing.
3. Describe the trade-off and pecking order theories of capital structure choice, and explain what the empirical evidence tells us about these theories.
4. Discuss some of the practical considerations that managers are concerned with when they choose a firm's capital structure.

I. Chapter Outline

16.1 Capital Structure and Firm Value

- A firm's **capital structure** is the mix of financial securities used to finance its activities.
  - o The mix will always include common stock and will often include debt and preferred stock.
  - o The fraction of the total financing that is represented by debt is a measure of the financial leverage in the firm's capital structure.
    - ▪ A higher fraction of debt indicates a higher degree of financial leverage.
      - The amount of financial leverage in a firm's capital structure is important because it affects the value of the firm.

A. *The Optimal Capital Structure*

- Managers at a firm choose a capital structure so that the mix of securities making up the capital structure minimizes the cost of financing the firm's activities.
  - o This mix is the optimal capital structure because the capital structure that minimizes the cost of financing the firm's projects is also the capital structure that maximizes the total value of those projects and, therefore, the overall value of the firm.

B. *The Modigliani and Miller Propositions*

- **M&M Proposition 1**
  - o States that the capital structure decisions a firm makes will have no effect on the value of the firm if:
    1. there are no taxes,
    2. there are no information or transaction costs, and
    3. the real investment policy of the firm is not affected by its capital structure decisions.
       - ▪ The real investment policy of the firm includes the criteria that the firm uses in deciding which real assets (projects) to invest in.

- o The market value of the debt plus the market value of the equity must equal the value of the cash flows produced by the firm's assets, which is the value of the firm.
  - ▪ M&M Proposition 1 essentially says that the combined value of the equity and debt claims (represented by the present value of free cash flows the firm's assets are expected to produce in the future) does not change when you change the capital structure of the firm if no one other than the stockholders and the debt holders is receiving cash flows.
- o Such a change is called a financial restructuring in which a combination of financial transactions occur that change the firm's capital structure without affecting its real assets.

- **M&M Proposition 2**
  - o M&M's Proposition 2 states that the cost (required return on) of a firm's common stock is directly related to the debt-to-equity ratio.
    1. This can be seen by looking at Equation 16.3:
       - ▪ $k_{cs} = k_{Assets} + \left(\frac{V_{Debt}}{V_{cs}}\right)(k_{Assets} - k_{Debt})$
       - ▪ The first source of risk is the underlying risk of the assets, which is reflected in the expected return on the firm's asset and is known as the business risk of the firm.
         - It is the risk associated with the characteristics of the firm's business activities.
       - ▪ The second source of risk is the capital structure of the firm, which reflects the effect of the firm's financing decisions on the riskiness of the cash flows that the stockholders will receive.
         - Financial risk is associated with required payments to a firm's lenders.
- **What the M&M Propositions Tell Us**
  - o The value of the M&M analysis is that it tells us exactly where we should look if we want to understand how capital structure affects firm value and cost of equity.
    1. If financial policy matters as we know that it does, it must be because of one or more of the following:
       1. Taxes matter,
       2. Information or transaction costs matter, or
       3. Capital structure choices affect a firm's real investment policy.

16.2 The Benefits and Costs of Using Debt

A. *Interest Tax Shield Benefit*

- The most important benefit from including debt in a firm's capital structure stems from the fact that firms can deduct interest payments for tax purposes but cannot deduct dividend payments.
  - o This makes it less costly to distribute cash to security holders through interest payments than through dividends.
- The total dollar amount of interest paid each year, and, therefore, the amount that will be deducted from the firm's taxable income, is

$$D \times k_{Debt}.$$

  - o This will result in a reduction in taxes paid of

$$D \times k_{Debt} \times t,$$

  where t is the firm's marginal tax rate that applies to the interest expense deduction.
- If this reduction will continue in perpetuity, the perpetuity model, to calculate the present value of the tax savings from debt:
  - o $V_{Tax\ savings\ debt} = PVA_{\infty} = \frac{CF}{i} = \frac{D \times k_{Debt} \times t}{i}$
- Since the firm will benefit from the interest tax shield only if it is able to make the required interest payments, the cash savings associated with the tax shield are about as risky as the cash flow stream associated with the interest payments:
  - o $V_{Tax\ savings\ debt} = \frac{D \times k_{Debt} \times t}{k_{Debt}} = D \times t$
  - o The perpetuity model assumes that
    - (1) the firm will continue to be in business forever,
    - (2) the firm will be able to realize the tax savings in the years in which the interest payments are made (the firm's EBIT will always be at least as great as the interest expense), and
    - (3) the firm's tax rate will remain constant.

B. ***Other Benefits***

- Underwriting spreads and out-of-pocket costs are more than three times as large for stock sales as they are for bond sales.
- Debt provides managers with incentives to focus on maximizing the cash flows that the firm produces since interest and principal payments must be made when they are due.
  - The incentives occur because managers must make these payments or face the prospect of bankruptcy, which can destroy a manager's career.
- Debt can be used to limit the ability of bad managers to waste the stockholders' money on things such as fancy jet aircraft, plush offices, and other negative-NPV projects that benefit the managers personally.

C. ***The Costs of Debt***

- Financial managers limit the amount of debt in their firms' capital structures because there are costs that can become quite substantial at high levels of debt.
  - At low levels of debt, the benefits are greater than the costs, and adding more debt increases the overall value of the firm.
  - At some point, the costs begin to exceed the benefits, and adding more debt financing destroys firm value.
  - Financial managers want to add debt just to the point at which the value of the firm is maximized.
- **Bankruptcy costs,** also referred to as **costs of financial distress,** are costs associated with financial difficulties that a firm might get into because it uses debt financing.
  - The term *bankruptcy cost* is used rather loosely in capital structure discussions to refer to costs incurred when a firm gets into financial distress.
    - Therefore, firms can incur bankruptcy costs even if they never actually file for bankruptcy.
  - **Direct bankruptcy costs** are out-of-pocket costs that a firm incurs as a result of financial distress.
    - These costs include things such as fees paid to lawyers, accountants, and consultants.
  - **Indirect bankruptcy costs** are costs associated with changes in the behavior of people who deal with a firm in financial distress.
    - Some of this firm's potential customers will decide to purchase a competitor's products because:
      - of concerns that the firm will not be able to honor its warranties.
      - parts or service may likely not be available in the future.
      - some customers will demand a lower price for the product to compensate them for these risks.
    - When suppliers learn that a firm is in financial distress, they worry about not being paid; to protect against losses for future shipments, they often begin to require cash on delivery.
    - Employees at a distressed firm worry that their jobs or benefits are in danger, and some start looking for new jobs.
    - If the firm enters into the formal bankruptcy process, it incurs another indirect bankruptcy cost because a bankruptcy judge must approve all investments made by the firm.
  - **Agency costs** result from conflicts of interest between principals and agents where one party, known as the principal, delegates its decision-making authority to another party, known as the agent.
    - The agent is expected to act in the interest of the principal, but agents sometimes have interests that conflict with those of the principal.
    - **Stockholder-manager agency costs** occur to the extent that the incentives of the managers are not perfectly identical to those of the stockholders.
      - Managers will make some decisions that benefit themselves at the expense of the stockholders.
      - Using debt financing provides managers with incentives to focus on maximizing the cash flows that the firm produces and limits the ability of bad managers to waste the stockholders' money on negative-NPV projects.
        - This amounts to a reduction in the agency costs associated with the principal-agent relationship between stockholders and managers.
      - Whereas the use of debt financing can reduce agency costs, it can also increase these costs by altering the behavior of managers who have a high proportion of their wealth riding on the success of the firm through their stockholdings, future income, and reputations.
        - The use of debt increases the volatility of a firm's earnings and the probability that the firm will get into financial difficulty.
        - Increased risk causes managers to make more conservative decisions.
      - ***Stockholder-lender agency costs*** can occur when investors lend money to a firm and delegate authority to the stockholders to decide how that money will be used.
        - Lenders expect that the stockholders, through the managers they appoint, will invest the money in a way that enables the firm to make all of the interest and principal payments that have been promised.

- o However, stockholders may have incentives to use the money in ways that are not in the best interests of the lenders.
- o Lenders know that stockholders have incentives to distribute some or all of the funds that they borrow as dividends, and so they protect themselves against this sort of behavior by including provisions in the lending agreements that limit the ability of stockholders to pay dividends and other behavior.
  - ▪ These protections are not foolproof in that they cannot totally eliminate a problem.
- o One type of this behavior is known as the **asset substitution problem** where once a loan has been made to a firm, the stockholders have an incentive to substitute less risky assets for more risky assets such as negative-NPV projects.
- o Another type of behavior is known as the **underinvestment problem,** and it occurs in a financially distressed firm when the value that is created by investing in a positive-NPV project is likely to go to the lenders instead of the stockholders; therefore, the firm foregoes financing and undertaking the project.

16.3 Two Theories of Capital Structure

A. ***Trade-Off Theory***

- The **trade-off theory** of capital structure says that managers choose a specific target capital structure based on the trade-offs between the benefits and the costs of debt.
  - o The theory states that managers will increase debt to the point at which the costs and benefits of adding another dollar of debt are exactly equal because this is the capital structure that maximizes firm value.

B. ***The Pecking Order Theory***

- The pecking order theory recognizes that different types of capital have different costs. This leads to a pecking order in the financing choices that managers make by choosing the least expensive capital first and then moving to increasingly more costly capital when the lower cost sources of capital are no longer available.
  - o Managers view internally generated funds, or cash on hand, as the cheapest source of capital.
  - o Debt is more costly to obtain than internally generated funds but is still relatively inexpensive.
  - o Raising money by selling stock is the most expensive.

C. ***The Empirical Evidence***

- When researchers compare the capital structures in different industries, they find evidence that supports the trade-off theory.
  - o Industries with a large amount of tangible assets typically use relatively large amounts of debt, whereas industries with more intangible assets use relatively little debt.
- Some researchers argue that, on average, debt levels appear to be lower than the trade-off theory suggests they should be.
- More general evidence also indicates that the more profitable a firm is, the less debt it tends to have, which is exactly opposite of what the trade-off theory suggests we should see.
  - o This evidence is consistent with the pecking order theory.
- The pecking order theory is also supported by the fact that, in an average year, public firms actually repurchase more shares than they sell.
  - o In the United States, internally generated funds represent the largest source of financing for new investments, and debt represents the largest source of external financing.
- Both the trade-off theory and the pecking order theory offer some insights into how managers choose the capital structures for their firms, but neither is able to explain all of the capital structure choices that we observe.

16.4 Practical Considerations in Choosing a Capital Structure

- Managers don't think only in terms of a trade-off or a pecking order but are concerned about how their financing decisions will influence the practical issues that they must deal with when managing a business.
- Financial flexibility is an important consideration in many capital structure decisions.
  - o Managers must ensure that they retain sufficient financial resources in the firm to take advantage of unexpected opportunities as well as unforeseen problems.
    - ▪ They try to manage their firms' capital structures in a way that limits the risk to a reasonable level.
  - o Managers think about leverage and the effect that interest expense has on the reported dollar value of net income.
  - o Managers consider control implications when choosing between equity and debt financing of the firm.

II. Suggested Approach to Material

Chapter 16 discusses capital structure and how it affects firm value. It introduces the Modigliani and Miller (M&M) theory of capital structure as well the three major assumptions required for the theorem to hold. These assumptions are (1) that neither the firm nor the investor is subject to taxes, (2) there are no information or transactions costs, and (3) the way in which the firm is financed does not affect its real investment policy. M&M proves that firm value is unaffected by the firm's choice of capital structure. The chapter then proceeds to relax the no-tax assumption to discuss the value of the tax shield to the firm. At that point, the theory predicts that firms should have greater leverage than what we see in practice. The chapter then discusses benefits and costs of leverage that further relax the assumptions of M&M in order to discuss a more realistic understanding of capital structure.

The chapter then discusses two theories of capital structure. Trade-off theory suggests that firms will adjust their capital structure to maximize the value of the firm. Pecking order theory suggests that firms will always select the cheapest form of capital to finance a project. The empirical evidence does not completely support either theory. The chapter concludes with a practical discussion of capital structure.

Although the material tends to be a bit theoretical, the discussion is accompanied by a number of examples to help the student understand the arguments and their implications. While the material might appear in a purely theoretical chapter, it does touch upon issues that many executives will one day have to understand and deal with. As such, the material does have practical applications.

III. Chapter Glossary

Capital structure	The mix of financial securities that are used to finance a firm's activities.
Financial leverage	The use of debt in a firm's capital structure; the more debt, the higher the degree of financial leverage.
Optimal capital structure	The capital structure that minimizes the cost of financing a firm's activities.
Real investment policy	The policy relating to the criteria the firm uses in deciding which real assets (projects) to invest in.
Firm value, or enterprise value	The total value of the firm's assets; it equals the value of the equity financing plus the value of the debt financing used by the firm.
Financial restructuring	A combination of financial transactions that changes the capital structure of the firm without affecting its real assets.
Business risk	The risk in the cash flows to stockholders that is associated with uncertainty due to the characteristics of the business itself.
Financial risk	The risk in the cash flows to stockholders that is due to the way in which the firm has financed its activities.
Bankruptcy costs, or costs of financial distress	Costs associated with financial difficulties a firm might experience because it uses debt financing.
Direct bankruptcy costs	Out-of-pocket costs that a firm incurs when it gets into financial distress.
Indirect bankruptcy costs	Costs associated with changes in the behavior of people who deal with a firm when the firm gets into financial distress.
Asset substitution problem	The incentive that stockholders in a financially leveraged firm have to substitute more risky assets for less risky assets.
Underinvestment problem	The incentive that stockholders in a financially leveraged firm have to turn down positive-NPV projects when the firm is in financial distress.
Trade-off theory	The theory that managers trade off the benefits against the costs of using debt to identify the optimal capital structure for a firm.
Pecking order theory	The theory that in financing projects, managers first use retained earnings, which they view as the least expensive form of capital, then debt, and finally externally raised equity, which they view as the most expensive.

IV. Summary of Key Equations

Equation	Description	Formula
16.1	Value of the firm as the sum of the debt and equity values	$V_{Firm} = V_{Assets} = V_{Debt} + V_{Equity}$
16.2	Formula for weighted average cost of capital (WACC) for a firm with only common stock and no taxes	$WACC = x_{Debt}k_{Debt} + x_{cs}k_{cs}$
16.3	Cost of common stock in terms of the required return on assets and the required return on debt	$k_{cs} = k_{Assets} + \left(\frac{V_{Debt}}{V_{cs}}\right)(k_{Assets} - k_{Debt})$
16.4	Value of the tax savings of debt (upper bound)	$V_{Tax\ savings\ debt} = D \times t$

V. True or False Questions

1. Free cash flow does not include the effect of interest and principal repayments.

a. True

b. False

2. The WACC accounts for how a firm's projects are financed.

a. True

b. False

3. Under the assumptions of M&M Proposition 1, increasing the amount of debt in a firm's capital structure may increase the firm's value.

a. True

b. False

4. M&M Proposition 1 demonstrates how individuals can "undo" the capital structure decisions of firms.

a. True

b. False

5. Under the conditions outlined in M&M Proposition 1, capital structure decisions do not affect the level, timing, or risk of cash flows.

a. True

b. False

6. The expected return on a firm's assets reflects both the business and financial risk of the firm.

a. True

b. False

7. More leverage increases the firm's flexibility when choosing projects such as capital expenditures and R&D.

a. True

b. False

8. Indirect bankruptcy costs will vary by industry.

a. True

b. False

9. Because of career concerns, managers usually prefer riskier investments than equity holders.
   a. True
   b. False

10. When a firm announces that it will issue stock, the equity price usually increases since this is a signal that the firm has positive-NPV projects.
   a. True
   b. False

VI. Multiple-Choice Questions and Problems

1. The capital structure that minimizes the cost of financing the firm's projects is called
   a. the generic capital structure.
   b. the optimal capital structure.
   c. the issue M&M capital structure.
   d. none of the above.

2. A firm's enterprise value is given by
   a. the value of equity plus the value of debt.
   b. the value of equity minus the value of debt.
   c. the value of equity minus the value of debt plus the value of future projects.
   d. none of the above.

3. The weighted average cost of capital (WACC) excludes
   a. the cost of options.
   b. the cost of preferred equity.
   c. the cost of common equity.
   d. the cost of debt.

4. M&M Proposition 2 states that the cost of a firm's common stock increases
   a. as the dollar amount of common equity increases.
   b. as the proportion of the firm that is financed with debt increases.
   c. decreases as the debt-to-value ratio decreases.
   d. none of the above.

5. The value of a single year's cash flow from the interest tax shield increases
   a. as the amount of debt increases.
   b. as the tax rate increases.
   c. as the interest rate on the debt increases.
   d. all of the above.

6. Academic studies have estimated that the tax benefit of debt realized by firms is approximately
   a. 10% of firm value.
   b. a 10% reduction in WACC.
   c. a 10% reduction in the cost of debt
   d. 10% of debt value.

7. Which of the following is usually an indirect bankruptcy cost?
   a. Lawyers fees
   b. Accountants fees

c. Higher supplier financing fees

d. None of the above

8. Which of the following is an example of the asset substation problem?

 a. A firm raising funds for a soft drink project and then financing a bottled water project.

 b. A firm raising funds for a soft drink project and then financing a biotech project.

 c. A firm raising funds for a soft drink project and then financing a soft drink project.

 d. None of the above.

9. The underinvestment problem occurs in a financially distressed firm when

 a. the value of investing in a positive–NPV project is likely to go to debt holders instead of equity holders.

 b. the value of investing in a positive–NPV project is likely to go to equity holders instead of debt holders.

 c. management invests in negative–NPV projects to reduce their own risk.

 d. issuing equity becomes difficult due to increased risk.

10. Which of the following is more likely to support the existence of an optimal capital structure?

 a. Trade-off theory

 b. Pecking order theory

 c. Mortensen and Mikail theory

 d. a and b above

11. Stratego Consulting believes that it can generate annual cash flows of $185 per year. What is the value of Stratego if its cost of capital is 12 percent? Round your answer to the nearest dollar.

 a. $1,850

 b. $1,542

 c. $925

 d. None of the above

12. Barrell Dynamics believes that it can generate annual cash flows of $185 per year. What is the value of Barrell's equity if the firm has annual interest payments of $25 and the cost of equity is 15 percent? Round your answer to the nearest dollar.

 a. $1,542

 b. $1,233

 c. $1,067

 d. None of the above

13. Prada Bell believes that it can generate annual cash flows of $185 per year. What is the value of Prada's debt if the firm has annual interest payments of $25 and the cost of equity is 15 percent? The WACC for the firm is 12 percent. Round your answer to the nearest dollar.

 a. $1,542

 b. $1,067

 c. $475

 d. None of the above

14. UVA55 currently has a capital structure that is 30% debt and 70% equity. If the firm's cost of equity is 15%, the cost of debt is 10%, what is the appropriate WACC?

 a. 11.5%

 b. 12.5%

 c. 13.5%

 d. None of the above

15. FourMica, Inc., has a WACC of 12%, a cost of debt of 8%, and a cost of equity of 16%. What must the debt-to-equity ratio be?

 a. 1

 b. 1/2

 c. 1/4

 d. None of the above

16. Myron's Irons has a capital structure with 20% debt and 80% equity. Its pre–tax cost of debt is 5%, and its cost of equity is 15%. The firm's marginal corporate income tax rate is 40%. What is the appropriate WACC?

 a. 9.00%

 b. 12.60%

 c. 13.0%

 d. None of the above

17. A firm has $500mm in outstanding debt and $1,500mm in outstanding equity. Its cost of equity is 20%, and its cost of debt is 8%. What is the appropriate WACC?

 a. 11%

 b. 14%

 c. 17%

 d. None of the above

18. A firm plans to issue $1,500,000 worth of debt at a YTM of 10%. The debt is trading at par. The firm's marginal corporate tax rate is 36%, while its average tax rate is 25%. By how much will this debt issuance reduce the firm's annual tax liability?

 a. $54,000

 b. $60,000

 c. $96,000

 d. None of the above

19. A firm plans to issue $3 million worth of debt at a YTM of 11%. The debt is trading at par. The firm's marginal corporate tax rate is 39%. What is the present value of the tax savings in perpetuity?

 a. $128,700

 b. $1,170,000

 c. $1,830,000

 d. None of the above

20. Suppose that Scheister, Inc., has debt with a face value of $1,000,000 and assets worth $900,000. Firm management has just identified a project that will require an initial outlay of $80,000 and will return a NPV of $32,000 with probability of 0.4 and an NPV of $12,000 with probability of.6. The firm currently has no cash. What would be the expected cash flow to shareholders if they took on this project?

 a. −$80,000

 b. $0

 c. $4,800

 d. $7,200

Answers to True or False Questions

1. a	**2.** a	**3.** b	**4.** a	**5.** a
6. b	**7.** b	**8.** a	**9.** b	**10.** b

Answers to Multiple-Choice Questions

1. b	**2.** a	**3.** a	**4.** b	**5.** d
6. a	**7.** c	**8.** b	**9.** a	**10.** a
11. b	**12.** c	**13.** c	**14.** c	**15.** a
16. b	**17.** c	**18.** a	**19.** b	**20.** c

Solutions to Multiple-Choice Problems

11. Solution:

$V_{Firm} = CF/i = \$185/0.12 = \$1541.67$

12. Solution:

Cash flows to shareholders = Cash flows − Interest payments
= \$185 − \$25
= \$160

Value of equity is then \$160 /0.15 = \$1,066.67

13. Solution:

Cash flows to shareholders = Cash flows − Interest payments
= \$185 − \$25
= \$160

Value of equity is then \$160 / 0.15 = \$1,066.67

Value of debt = \$1,541.67 − \$1,066.67 = \$474

14. Solution:

$\text{WACC} = x_{Debt}\, k_{Debt} + x_{Equity}\, k_{Equity} = 0.3 \times 0.10 + 0.70 \times 0.15 = 0.13.5$

15. Solution:

$\text{WACC} = x_{Debt}\, k_{Debt} + x_{Equity}\, k_{Equity}$
$= x_{Debt} \times 0.08 + x_{Equity} \times 0.16 = 0.12$

Also, D + E = 1 by definition.

Therefore, substituting gives you: $x_{Debt} \times 0.08 + (1 - x_{Debt}) \times 0.16 = 0.12$.

Solving for x_{Debt} gives you 1/2, which means that x_{Equity} must be 1/2. Therefore, the D/E is 1.

16. Solution:

$\text{WACC with taxes} = x_{Debt}\, k_{Debt\ pretax}\, (1 - t) + x_{Equity}\, k_{Equity}$
$= 0.2 \times 0.05 \times (1 - 0.4) + 0.8 \times 0.1 = 0.126$

17. Solution:

$\text{WACC} = x_{Debt}\, k_{Debt} + x_{Equity}\, k_{Equity} = (500/2000) \times 0.08 + (1{,}500/2000) \times 0.2 = 0.17$

18. Solution:

$\text{Tax shield} = D \times k_{debt} \times t = \$1{,}500{,}000 \times 0.1 \times 0.36 = \$54{,}000$

19. <u>Solution:</u>

$V_{\text{Tax-savings debt}} = D \times t = \$3{,}000{,}000 \times 0.39 = \$1{,}170{,}000$

20. <u>Solution:</u>

The payoff to stockholders will be equal to:

$0.40 \times (\$80{,}000 + \$32{,}000 - \$100{,}000) + 0.60 \times \text{maximum}(\$0, \$80{,}000 + \$12{,}000 - \$100{,}000)$
$= 0.40 \times (\$12{,}000) + 0.60 \times \text{maximum}(\$0, -\$8{,}000) = 0.40 \times (\$12{,}000) + \$0 = \$4{,}800$

CHAPTER 17

Dividends and Dividend Policy

LEARNING OBJECTIVES

1. Explain what a dividend is, and describe the different types of dividends and the dividend payment process.
2. Explain what a stock repurchase is and how companies repurchase their stock.
3. Discuss the benefits and costs associated with dividend payments, and compare the relative advantages and disadvantages of dividends and stock repurchases.
4. Define stock dividends and stock splits, and explain how they differ from other types of dividends and from stock repurchases.
5. Describe factors that managers consider when setting the dividend policies for their firms.

I. Chapter Outline

17.1 Dividends

- The term **dividend policy** is generally used to refer to a firm's overall policy regarding distributions of value to stockholders.
- A **dividend** is something of value that is distributed to a firm's stockholders on a pro-rata basis—that is, in proportion to the percentage of the firm's shares that they own.
  - o A dividend can involve the distribution of cash, assets, or something else, such as discounts on the firm's products that are available only to stockholders.
  - o When a firm distributes value through a dividend, it reduces the value of the stockholders' claims against the firm.
    - ▪ A dividend reduces the stockholders' investment in a firm by returning some of that investment to them.
    - ▪ The value that stockholders receive through a dividend was already theirs, and so a dividend simply takes this value out of the firm and returns it to stockholders.

A. ***Types of Dividends***

- The most common form is the regular cash dividend, which is a cash dividend that is paid on a regular basis.
  - o These dividends are generally paid quarterly and are a common means by which firms return some of their profits to stockholders.
- The size of a firm's regular cash dividend is typically set at a level that management expects the company to be able to maintain in the long run, barring some major change in the fortunes of the company.
  - o Management does not like to reduce the dividend because dividend reduction is often viewed negatively by the stock market.
- Management can afford to err on the side of setting the regular cash dividend too low because it always has the option of paying an **extra dividend** if earnings are higher than expected.

- Extra dividends are often paid at the same time as regular cash dividends and are used by some companies to ensure that a minimum portion of earnings is distributed to stockholders each year without setting an expectation of a higher regular cash dividend.
- A special dividend, like an extra dividend, is a one-time payment to stockholders.
  - Special dividends tend to be considerably larger than extra dividends and to occur less frequently.
  - They are used to distribute unusually large amounts of cash such as the proceeds from the sale of a major asset or business.
- A **liquidating dividend** is a dividend that is paid to stockholders when a firm is liquidated.
  - A firm is liquidated when its assets are sold.
- Distributions of value to stockholders can also take the form of discounts on the company's products, free samples, and the like.
  - These noncash distributions are not thought of as dividends, in part because the value received by stockholders is not in the form of cash and in part because the value received by individual stockholders does not often reflect their proportional ownership in the firm.

B. *The Dividend Payment Process*

- **The Board Vote:** The process begins with a vote by a company's board of directors to pay a dividend.
  - As stockholder representatives, the board must approve any distribution of value to stockholders.
- **The Public Announcement:** The date on which the dividend announcement is made is known as the declaration date, or announcement date, of the dividend.
  - The announcement typically includes the amount of value that stockholders will receive for each share of stock that they own, as well as the other dates associated with the dividend payment process.
  - The price of a firm's stock often changes when a dividend is announced because the public announcement sends a signal to the market about what management thinks the future performance of the firm will be.
    - A. If the signal differs from what investors expected, they will adjust the prices at which they are willing to buy or sell the company's stock accordingly.
    - B. This means that a dividend decision sends information to investors and that information is incorporated into stock prices at the time of the public announcement.
- **The Ex-Dividend Date:** The ex-dividend date is the first date on which the stock will trade without rights to the dividend.
  - An investor who buys shares before the **ex-dividend date** will receive the dividend, while an investor who buys the stock on or after the ex-dividend date will not.
  - Before the ex-dividend date, a stock is said to be trading cum dividend, or with dividend.
  - On or after the ex-dividend date, the stock is said to trade ex dividend.
  - The price of the firm's shares changes on the ex-dividend date even if there is no new information about the firm.
    - A. This drop simply reflects the difference in the value of the cash flows (after taxes if applicable) that the stockholders are entitled to receive before and after the ex-dividend date.
- **The Record Date:** The **record date** typically follows the ex-dividend date by two days.
  - The record date is the date on which an investor must be a stockholder of record (that is, officially listed as a stockholder) in order to receive the dividend.
  - The ex-dividend day precedes the record date because it takes time to update the stockholder list when someone purchases shares.
- **The Payable Date:** The final date in the dividend payment process is the **payable date**, when the stockholders of record actually receive the dividend.
  - The divided payment process is not as well defined for private companies as it is for public companies, because in private companies shares are bought and sold less frequently, there are fewer stockholders, and no stock exchange is involved in the dividend payment process.

17.2 Stock Repurchases

- With a **stock repurchase,** a company buys some of its shares from stockholders.

A. *How Stock Repurchases Differ from Dividends*

- Stock repurchases differ from dividends in four ways.
  - First, they do not represent a pro-rata distribution of value to the stockholders because not all stockholders participate.
    - Individual stockholders decide whether they want to participate in a share repurchase.

- o Second, when a company repurchases its own shares, it removes them from circulation.
  - ▪ This reduces the number of shares of stock that are held by investors, thereby removing a large number of shares from circulation can change the proportional ownership characteristics of the firm.
- o Third, stock repurchases are taxed differently than dividends.
  - ▪ The total value of dividends is normally taxed.
  - ▪ Conversely, when a stockholder sells shares back to the company, the stockholder is taxed only on the profit from the sale.
- o Fourth, the way in which we account for dividends and stock repurchases on a company's balance sheet is also different.
  - ▪ When the company pays a cash dividend, the cash account on the assets side of the balance sheet and the retained earnings account on the liabilities and stockholders' equity side of the balance sheet are reduced.
  - ▪ In contrast, when a company uses cash to repurchase stock, the cash account on the assets side of the balance sheet is reduced, while the treasury stock account on the liabilities and stockholders' equity side of the balance sheet is increased.

B. *How Stock Is Repurchased*

- Companies repurchase stock in three general ways.
  - o First, they can simply purchase shares in the market, much as you would. These kinds of purchases are known as **open-market repurchases,** which are a very convenient way of repurchasing shares on an ongoing basis.
    - ▪ Open-market repurchases can be cumbersome because the government limits the number of shares that a company can repurchase on a given day.
      - These limits, which are intended to restrict the ability of firms to influence their stock price through trading activity, mean that it could take months for a company to distribute a large amount of cash using open-market repurchases.
    - ▪ When the management of a company wants to distribute a large amount of cash at one time and does not want to use a special dividend, it can repurchase shares using a **tender offer,** which is an open offer by a company to purchase shares.
      - There are two types of tender offers: fixed price and Dutch auction.
        - o With a fixed-price tender offer, management announces the price that will be paid for the shares and the maximum number of shares that will be repurchased.
          - ▪ Interested stockholders then tender their shares by letting management know how many shares they are willing to sell.
        - o With a Dutch auction tender offer, the firm announces the number of shares that it would like to repurchase and asks the stockholders how many shares they would sell at a series of prices, ranging from just above the price at which the shares are currently trading to some higher number.
          - ▪ Stockholders then tell the company how many of their shares they would sell at the various offered prices.
    - ▪ The third general way in which shares are repurchased is through direct negotiation with a specific stockholder where **targeted stock repurchases** are typically used to buy blocks of shares from large stockholders.
    - ▪ These repurchases can benefit stockholders because managers may be able to negotiate a per-share price that is below the current market price because the stockholder who owns a large block of shares might have to offer the shares for a below-market price in order to sell them all in the open market.

17.3 Dividend Policy and Firm Value

- Dividend policy can affect the value of a firm.
- The general conditions under which capital structure policy does not affect firm value are as follows:
  1. There are no taxes.
  2. There are no information or transaction costs.
  3. The real investment policy of the firm is fixed.
- Dividend policy does not matter under the above conditions because a stockholder can "manufacture" any dividends he or she wants at no cost when these conditions hold.
- A stockholder could also undo a company's dividend policy by simply reinvesting the dividends that the company pays in new shares.
- If investors could replicate a company's dividend policy on their own at no cost, they would not care whether or not the company paid a dividend.

A. *Benefits and Costs of Dividends*

- One benefit of paying dividends is that it attracts investors who prefer to invest in stocks that pay dividend yields.
- While it is true that the investor could simply sell some stock each month to cover expenses, in the real world it may be less costly—and it is certainly less trouble—to simply receive regular cash dividend payments instead.
  - Recall that under the M&M conditions, there are no transaction costs.
  - In the real world, however, the retiree or institutional investor will have to pay brokerage commissions each time he or she sells stock.
  - The dividend check, in contrast, simply arrives each quarter.
    - Of course, the retiree will have to consider the impact of taxes on the value of dividends versus the value of proceeds from the sale of stock; but it is quite possible that receiving dividends might, on balance, be more appealing.
- Other investors may have no current need for income from their investment portfolios and prefer not to receive dividends.
- Some argue that a large regular dividend indicates that a company is financially strong because the "signal" of strength can result in a higher stock price.
  - This argument is based on the assumption that a company that is able to pay a large dividend, rather than holding on to cash for future investments, is a company that is doing so well that it has more money than it needs to fund its available investments.
  - The problem with this line of reasoning is that it ignores the possibility that a company might have more than enough money for all its future investment opportunities because it does not have many future investment opportunities.
- If the board of directors of a company votes to pay the stockholders dividends that amount to more than the excess cash that the company is producing from its operations, then the money to pay the dividends will have to come from selling equity periodically in the public markets.
  - The need to raise equity in the capital markets will help align the incentives of managers with those of stockholders because it increases the cost to managers of operating the business inefficiently.
- There are costs to the firm associated with dividends.
  - Taxes are among the most important costs.
  - Owners of stocks that pay dividends often have to pay brokerage fees if they want to reinvest the proceeds.
    - To eliminate this cost, some companies offer **dividend reinvestment programs (DRIPs)**. Through a DRIP, a company sells new shares, commission free, to dividend recipients who elect to automatically reinvest their dividends in the company's stock.
  - To the extent that a company uses a lot of debt financing, paying dividends can increase the cost of debt.
- Using the cash flow identity of sources and uses of cash, we can see that an expected increase in the cash flow from operations is a good signal, and investors will interpret it as suggesting that cash flows to stockholders will increase in the future.
- The cash flow identity suggests that managers will change dividend polices when something fundamental has changed in the business and it is this fundamental change that causes the stock price to change.
  - The dividend announcement is really just the means by which investors find out about the fundamental change.
- Stock repurchases are an alternative to dividends as a way of distributing, and they have some distinct advantages over dividends.
  - Stock repurchases give stockholders the ability to choose when they receive the distribution, which affects the timing of the taxes they must pay as well as the cost of reinvesting funds that are not immediately needed.
  - Stockholders who sell shares back to a company pay taxes only on the gains they realize, and historically these capital gains have been taxed at a lower rate than dividends.
  - From management's perspective, stock repurchases provide greater flexibility in distributing value.
    - Even when a company publicly announces an ongoing open-market stock repurchase program, as opposed to a regular cash dividend, investors know that management can always quietly cut back or end the repurchases at any time.
    - This means that if future cash flows are not certain, managers are likely to prefer to distribute extra cash today by repurchasing shares through open-market purchases because this enables them to preserve some flexibility.
    - Since most ongoing stock repurchase programs are not as visible as dividend programs, they cannot be used as effectively to send a positive signal about the company's prospects to investors.
    - A more subtle issue concerns the fact that managers can choose when to repurchase shares in a stock repurchase program.
      - Just like other investors, managers prefer purchasing shares when they believe that the shares are undervalued in the market.

- The problem is that since managers have better information about the company's prospects than do other investors, they can take advantage of this information to the detriment of other investors.
  - o Management is supposed to act in the *best* interest of all its stockholders, and this may not always be the case with stock repurchases.

17.4 Stock Dividends and Stock Splits

A. ***Stock Dividends***

- One type of "dividend" that does not involve the distribution of value is known as a **stock dividend**.
  - o When a company pays a stock dividend, it distributes new shares of stock on a pro-rata basis to existing stockholders.
  - o The only thing that happens when the stock dividend is paid is that the number of shares each stockholder owns increases and their value goes down proportionately.
    - ▪ The stockholder is left with exactly the same value as before.

B. ***Stock Splits***

- A **stock split** is quite similar to a stock dividend, but it involves the distribution of a larger multiple of the outstanding shares.
  - o We can often think of a stock split as an actual division of each share into more than one share.
- Besides their size, a key distinction between stock dividends and stock splits is that stock dividends are typically regularly scheduled events, like regular cash dividends, while stock splits tend to occur infrequently during the life of a company.

C. ***Reasons for Stock Dividends and Splits***

- The most often cited reason for stock dividends or splits is known as the trading range argument, which proposes that successful companies use stock dividends or stock splits to make their shares more attractive to investors.
  - o It has historically been more expensive for investors to purchase odd lots of less than 100 shares than round lots of 100 shares.
  - o Odd lots are less liquid than round lots because more investors want to buy round and it is relatively expensive for companies to service odd-lot owners.
  - o Researchers have found little support for this explanation.
  - o The transaction costs argument no longer carries much weight, as there is now little difference in the costs of purchasing round lots and odd lots.
- One real benefit of stock splits is that they can send a positive signal to investors about the outlook that management has for the future, and this, in turn, can lead to a higher stock price.
  - o Management is unlikely to want to split the stock of a company two-for-one or three-for-one if it expects the stock price to decline.
- Reverse stock splits may be undertaken to satisfy exchange requirements.
  - o The New York Stock Exchange generally requires listed shares to trade for more than \$5, and the NASDAQ requires shares to trade for at least \$1.

17.5 Setting a Dividend Policy

- The best-known survey of dividend policy was published in 1956, more than 50 years ago, by John Lintner. The survey asked managers at 28 industrial firms how they set their firms' dividend policies.
  - o The key conclusions from the Lintner study are as follows:
    1. Firms tend to have long-term target payout ratios.
    2. Dividend changes follow shifts in long-term sustainable earnings.
    3. Managers focus more on dividend changes than on the absolute level (dollar amount) of the dividend.
    4. Managers are reluctant to make dividend changes that might have to be reversed.
- A more recent study, by Brav, Graham, Harvey, and Michaely published in 2005, updates Lintner's findings.
  - o The link between earnings and dividends is weaker today than when Lintner conducted his survey.
  - o They found that rather than setting a target level for repurchases, managers tend to repurchase shares using cash that is left over left over after investment spending.
  - o In addition, many managers prefer repurchases because repurchase programs are more flexible than dividend programs and because they can be used to time the market by repurchasing shares when management considers a company's stock price too low.

- Finally, the managers who were interviewed appeared to believe that institutional investors do not prefer dividends over repurchases or vice versa.
  - In other words, the choice between these two methods of distributing value does not have much of an effect on who owns the company's stock.

A. *Practical Considerations in Setting a Dividend Policy*

- A company's dividend policy is largely a policy about how the excess value in a company is distributed to its stockholders.
- It is extremely important that managers choose their firms' dividend polices in a way that enables them to continue to make the investments necessary for the firm to compete in its product markets.
- Managers should consider several practical questions when selecting a dividend policy:
  1. Over the long term, how much does the company's level of earnings (cash flows from operations) exceed its investment requirements? How certain is this level?
  2. Does the firm have enough financial reserves to maintain the dividend payout in periods when earnings are down or investment requirements are up?
  3. Does the firm have sufficient financial flexibility to maintain dividends if unforeseen circumstances wipe out its financial reserves when earnings are down?
  4. Can the firm quickly raise equity capital if necessary?
  5. If the company chooses to finance dividends by selling equity, will the increased number of stockholders have implications for the control of the company?

II. Suggested Approach to Material

Chapter 17 discusses dividends and other methods of distributing value to stockholders. The discussion begins with a definition of a dividend as well as some practical details that are needed to study the topic. The chapter then turns to stock repurchases as an alternative to delivering value to stockholders and then to how a firm's dividend policy might affect firm value. A brief discussion of dividend splits and stock dividends is then discussed, and finally the chapter ends by discussing the practical matters associated with setting a dividend policy.

Although this may be the student's first exposure to this material, the discussion of dividend policy will look familiar because the Modigliani and Miller arguments are similar to these same researchers' arguments used in the capital structure chapter. It is important to understand the Modigliani and Miller arguments in order to understand the practical importance of how dividends actually affect firm value, versus the theoretical discussion.

III. Chapter Glossary

Dividend policy	The overall policy concerning the distribution of value from a firm to its stockholders.
Dividend	Something of value distributed to a firm's stockholders on a pro-rata basis—that is, in proportion to the percentage of the firm's shares that they own.
Regular cash dividend	A cash dividend that is paid on a regular basis, typically quarterly.
Extra dividend	A dividend that is generally paid at the same time as a regular cash dividend to distribute additional value.
Special dividend	A one-time payment to stockholders that is normally used to distribute a large amount of value.
Liquidating dividend	The final dividend that is paid to stockholders when a firm is liquidated.
Declaration date	The date on which a dividend is publicly announced.
Ex-dividend date	The first day on which a stock trades without the rights to a dividend.
Record date	The date by which an investor must be a stockholder of record in order to receive a dividend.
Payable date	The date on which a company pays a dividend.

Stock repurchase	The purchase of stock by a company from its stockholders; an alternative way for the company to distribute value to the stockholders.
Open-market repurchase	The repurchase of shares by a company in the open market.
Tender offer	An open offer by a company to purchase shares.
Targeted stock repurchase	A stock repurchase that targets a specific stockholder.
Dividend reinvestment program (DRIP)	A program in which a company sells new shares, commission free, to dividend recipients who elect to automatically reinvest their dividends in the company's stock.
Stock dividend	A distribution of new shares to existing stockholders in proportion to the percentage of shares that they own (pro rata); the value of the assets in a company does not change with a stock dividend.
Stock split	A pro-rata distribution of new shares to existing stockholders that is not associated with any change in the assets held by the firm; stock splits involve larger increases in the number of shares than stock dividends.

IV. Summary of Key Equations

The chapter is primarily a qualitative chapter and does not have a relevant summary of key equations.

V. True or False Questions

1. A liquidating dividend occurs when a going-concern liquidates all of its assets and pays out the proceeds to its shareholders.
   a. True
   b. False

2. Consider an investor who purchases a dividend-paying stock of a public company the day prior to the dividend record date. We would expect this investor to receive a dividend distribution.
   a. True
   b. False

3. Dividends do not affect the level of the stockholder's investment in the firm.
   a. True
   b. False

4. Stock repurchases are best for stockholders who are subject to high capital gains rates.
   a. True
   b. False

5. A small regular dividend could signal that a firm has many new project alternatives.
   a. True
   b. False

6. Fixed price tender offer stock repurchases always take place at a price higher than the market price of the stock.
   a. True
   b. False

7. Open-market stock repurchases are limited in the rate in which the firm can repurchase shares.
   a. True
   b. False

8. All three conditions of Modigliani and Miller for dividend policy do not hold because it appears that dividend policy does matter for firm value.
   a. True
   b. False

9. Suppose that the government raises short- and long-term capital gains taxes while leaving all other taxes unchanged. This tax rate change would discourage companies to increase the use of stock repurchases rather than issuing dividends.
   a. True
   b. False

10. Stock splits must add value to the firm since we usually see the price of a stock increase after such a split.
    a. True
    b. False

VI. Multiple-Choice Questions and Problems

1. Consider a company that had a large amount of extra cash last quarter because it sold a division. Which type of dividend is the company likely to use?
   a. Regular cash dividend
   b. Extra dividend
   c. Special dividend
   d. Liquidating dividend

2. Which step in the dividend payment process for a public company usually results in a change in the company's stock price? Assume the dividend has changed from the last dividend paid.
   a. Public announcement
   b. Ex-dividend date
   c. Payable date
   d. Both a and b

3. Which one of these examples could meet the strict definition for a dividend?
   a. Steel Gen Corp regularly distributes $0.05 to each shareholder for every share they own.
   b. Chalone Vineyards once offered their investors discounts on wine in proportion to the number of shares they owned.
   c. Churchill Downs, Inc., which operates several horse racing tracks including the location for the Kentucky Derby, distributes two free general admission tickets to every investor who holds more then 100 shares in the company (as of 2008).
   d. Both a and b meet the definition.

4. Which of the following is a possible result of a stock repurchase?
   a. Removing a large number of shares from circulation can change the ability of certain shareholders to control the firm.
   b. If the number of remaining shares is relatively small, the remaining shares will be less liquid.
   c. The company will decrease its leverage ratio (debt-to-equity ratio).
   d. Both a and b.

5. Which type of stock repurchase often takes place at a price above the current market price of the stock?
   a. Open-market repurchase
   b. Dividend reinvestment program
   c. Debt conversion program
   d. Targeted stock repurchase

6. Which of the following explanations is a possible benefit of dividends?
   a. Dividends can be used to legally pay shareholders before interest obligations are due the owners of the firm's debt.
   b. Paying out large regular dividends can force management to regularly raise more capital. The extra scrutiny involved in raising capital can increase the incentives of management to run the company efficiently.
   c. Dividends signal a large number of investment alternatives for the firm.
   d. Paying dividends reduces the probability that the firm will enter financial distress.

7. In early 2003 the U.S. government cut the tax rate on dividends to a flat 15 percent instead of treating divided payments as other income. All else being equal, how would we expect the number of companies paying dividends to change?
   a. We would expect the number of dividend-paying companies to increase.
   b. We would expect the number of dividend-paying companies to decrease.
   c. We would expect the number of dividend-paying companies to stay relatively constant.
   d. None of the above.

8. Suppose you own shares of Dividor, Inc., which has just announced a 3-for-1 stock split. Immediately after the announcement, the price of the company's shares rose by 5 percent. You don't expect any new information about the company until after the stock split. Ignoring any discounting for time, if you intend to sell your shares soon you should:
   a. Sell the stock now—the single share you have now is likely to be worth more than the three shares you'll have after the split.
   b. Sell the stock after the split—typically, the market reacts positively to stock splits. The three shares you'll have after the split will be worth more then the single share you have now.
   c. Sell the stock now—the stock is likely to be more liquid before the split when there are fewer shares.
   d. It doesn't matter when the stock is sold. If there is no new information about the stock, then the value of three shares after the split should be the same as the value of the single share you hold now.

9. Given the general reason that management undertakes a reverse stock split, what would be a reasonable interpretation for how management expects the price of the shares to perform?
   a. They expect the price of the shares to increase.
   b. They have no expectation for how the shares should perform.
   c. They do not expect the price of the shares to increase in the near term.
   d. Reverse stock splits are not related to the future price of the shares.

10. Which one of these actions could by itself have an impact on control of the firm?
    a. A tender offer stock repurchase
    b. A special dividend payment
    c. A stock split
    d. A regular cash dividend payment

11. MoStock, Inc., has announced a 3-to-1 stock split. If the company currently has 1 million shares outstanding, how many outstanding shares will it have after the split?
    a. 4 million
    b. 3 million
    c. 2 million
    d. 1 million

12. Split-Div, Inc., has issued quarterly dividends of $0.20 per share each quarter over the last few years. This quarter Split-Div initiated a 4-for-1 stock split. What is the minimum quarterly dividend the board of Split-Div should approve to avoid sending a bad signal to investors?
    a. $0.02 per share
    b. $0.05 per share
    c. $0.10 per share
    d. $0.20 per share

13. You own 1,200 shares of Politico Co. The company has recently announced a 1-for-4 reverse stock split. How many shares will you own after the reverse split?
    a. 300 shares
    b. 400 shares
    c. 3,600 shares
    d. 4,800 shares

14. Belevu Co. has announced that it will pay its regular cash dividend of $0.45 per share. If dividends are taxed at 20 percent, about how much do you expect the price of Belevu to drop on the ex-dividend day?
    a. $0.09
    b. $0.36
    c. $0.45
    d. $0.52

15. Sandlot Co is currently trading at $45.00 per share. The company is paying a regular cash dividend of $0.50 per share and an extra dividend of $0.20 per share. Tomorrow is the ex-dividend day. The tax rate on dividends is 25 percent. Assuming there is no new information released about the company, how much do you expect the companies' stock to trade for tomorrow?
    a. $44.20
    b. $44.30
    c. $44.48
    d. $45.00

16. PhxRealState. is being liquidated. The company's assets can be sold for $30 million. It will cost $25 million for the company to meet all its previous obligations and to pay off debt holders. The company has 20 million shares outstanding. If you own 3,000 shares, how much do you expect to receive in liquidating dividends? Ignore taxes.
    a. $250
    b. $750
    c. $1,000
    d. $1,200

17. You own 10,000 shares of stock in FinGood, Inc., which has just sold one of its large resort hotels for $400 million. Management intends to return the entire revenue from the sale to shareholders by issuing a special dividend. If FinGood has 50 million shares outstanding, how large a dividend payment do you expect to receive?
    a. $8
    b. $40,000
    c. $80,000
    d. $100,000

18. You purchased 2,000 shares of The Beer Co. four years ago at $20 per share. You have just received a mailing from the company announcing a fixed-price tender offer stock repurchase at $28 per share. Capital gains are taxed at 20 percent. If you participate in the repurchase, how much will you receive?
    a. $12,800
    b. $21,400

c. $52,800

d. $56,000

19. ZYX Co has 5 million shares outstanding. The shares are currently selling for $48. If the firm repurchases $20 million at market prices, approximately how much will the stock be worth after the repurchase? Ignore taxes.

a. $40

b. $44

c. $48

d. $52

20. You purchased 2,000 shares of Zero Technologies several years ago at $50 per share. The company does not pay a regular cash dividend. You want to "manufacture" your own dividend by selling a little bit of stock each quarter. The company's stock is currently trading at $75. If capital gains are taxed at 15 percent, how many shares would you have to sell to receive $3,420 in cash?

a. 27 shares

b. 46 shares

c. 48 shares

d. 51 shares

Answers to True or False Questions

1. a	**2.** a	**3.** b	**4.** b	**5.** a
6. a	**7.** a	**8.** a	**9.** a	**10.** b

Answers to Multiple-Choice Questions

1. c	**2.** d	**3.** d	**4.** d	**5.** a
6. b	**7.** a	**8.** d	**9.** c	**10.** a
11. b	**12.** b	**13.** a	**14.** b	**15.** c
16. b	**17.** c	**18.** c	**19.** c	**20.** c

Solutions to Multiple-Choice Problems

11. **Solution:**

The company had 1 million shares outstanding and is issuing a 3-for-1 stock split.

3×1 million = 3 million.

12. **Solution:**

To avoid sending a bad signal to investors, the company needs to pay out the same dividend relative to the number of outstanding shares. After a 4-for-1 split, the equivalent regular cash dividend would be $0.20 / 4 = $0.05.

13. **Solution:**

You own 1,200 shares. After a 4-for-1 reverse stock split, you would own:

1,200 / 4 = 300 shares.

14. Solution:

The price would be expected to drop by the amount investors receive after taxes:

$0.45 × 80% = $0.36

15. Solution:

The price would be expected to drop by the amount investors receive after taxes:

($0.50 + 0.20) × 75% = $0.525. The new stock price would be $45.00 − $0.525 = $44.48.

16. Solution:

Shareholders will receive the residual claim after other claimholders have been paid:

$30 million − $25 million = $5 million. That $5 million will be distributed pro rata. As a holder of 3,000 shares you will receive:

$5 million × (3,000 shares / 20 million shares) = $750

17. Solution:

The 400 million will be distributed pro rata. You will receive:

$400 million × (10,000 shares / 50 million shares) = $80,000

18. Solution:

You will only be taxed on the capital gain. So you will receive:

2,000 shares × ($20 + (($28 − $20) × 0.80)) = $52,800

19. Solution:

Before the repurchase the firm was worth:

$48 per share × 5 million shares = $240 million

The firm repurchased $20,000,000 at the market price of $48 = 416,666.67 shares. After the repurchase the firm has:

$240 million − $20 million = $220 million

The number of remaining shares is 4,583,333.33. So each share is worth:

$220,000,000 / 4,583,333.33 = $48

20. Solution:

Each share you sell will yield ($50 + (($75 − $50) × 0.85)) = $71.25.

To raise $3,420 you must sell $3,420 / $71.25 = 48 shares.

CHAPTER 18

Business Formation, Growth, and Valuation

LEARNING OBJECTIVES

1. Explain why the choice of organizational form is important, and describe two financial considerations that are especially important in starting a business.
2. Describe the key components of a business plan, and explain what a business plan is used for.
3. Explain the three general approaches to valuation, and be able to value a business with commonly used business valuation approaches.
4. Explain how valuations can differ between public and private companies and between young and mature companies, and discuss the importance of control and key person considerations in valuation.

I. Chapter Outline

18.1 Starting a Business

- Regardless of their motivation, the first decision anyone must make is whether they want to found a business or acquire an existing business.
- Starting a business is inherently more risky than buying and growing a business that someone else has already established.
- The founder of a company must start from scratch and make several critical decisions.
- As the business is being built, the founder must also manage the day-to-day operations to ensure that his or her overall plan is being implemented.

A. *Making the Decision to Proceed*

- o Businesses fail for a number of different reasons, including lack of acceptance of the products by customers, poorly thought-out strategy, poor management skills to properly execute a good strategy, and underestimating how much money it will take to get their businesses up and running.
- o Chances of succeeding in a business can improve if one does not jump into a business without careful thought, or overanalyze opportunities to the point where you are just convincing yourself not to proceed, but takes on calculated risks.

B. *Choosing the Right Organizational Form*

- An LLC is a hybrid of a limited partnership and a corporation.
  - o It was first developed in Wyoming in 1977.
  - o An LLC provides limited liability.
  - o All investors retain the tax advantages of a limited partnership.
  - o Limited partnerships are more costly to form than sole proprietorships.
  - o The lives of partnerships and LLCs are flexible.
  - o Limited partners and LLCs are less constrained than general partnerships for additional capital.

- An *S-corporation* is a variation of the *C-corporation* form that is used by public corporations.
  - o With approval from the IRS, any C-corporation can become an S-corporation.
  - o Allows the stockholders to avoid double taxation but places limits on the ownership of the firm's stock.
  - o All profits of an S-corporation pass directly to the stockholders as they would pass to the partners in a partnership.
  - o Currently, an S-corporation can have
    - ▪ no more than 100 stockholders
    - ▪ only one class of common stock
    - ▪ individuals who are U.S. citizens or residents as stockholders (no corporations or partnerships can own shares).
  - o A sole proprietorship is the least expensive type of business to start.
  - o The life of a sole proprietorship is limited to the life of the proprietor.
  - o Sole proprietorships must rely on equity contributions from the proprietor and debt or lease financing.

C. *Financial Considerations*

- Two tools are particularly useful in understanding the cash requirements of a business and in estimating how much financing a new business will require—**cash flow break-even analysis** and the **cash budget**.
  - o Cash flow break-even analysis focuses the entrepreneur's attention on the importance of maximizing a product's per unit contribution and minimizing its associated overhead costs.
  - o The cash budget is also a very useful planning tool for entrepreneurs. It summarizes the cash flows into and out of a firm over a period of time.

18.2 The Role of the Business Plan

A. *Why Business Plans Are Important*

- A **business plan** is like a road map for a business.
- A business plan is a tool that can
  - o help raise capital,
  - o help an entrepreneur set the goals and objectives for the company,
  - o serve as a benchmark for evaluating and controlling the company's performance, and
  - o communicate the entrepreneur's ideas to managers, outside directors, customers, suppliers, and others.

B. *The Key Elements of a Business Plan*

- A well-developed business plan includes the following:
  - o An *executive summary,* which summarizes the key issues presented in the report.
  - o A *market analysis,* which discusses the industry and highlights the important characteristics of the industry as they relate to the company.
  - o A *company overview,* which describes what the company does and what its comparative advantages are.
  - o A detailed description or the *product(s) and services* the company will sell, its current state of development or market penetration, competitive advantages, product life cycle, and any patents or legal protections that might provide a competitive advantage.
  - o A detailed discussion of the *marketing and sales* activities that will enable the business to achieve the sales and margin levels reflected in the financial forecasts.
  - o A detailed discussion of the *operations* of the business.
  - o Detailed information on the *management team and ownership* of the business.
  - o A detailed discussion of *capital requirements and uses*.
  - o A business plan also presents historical *financial results* when they are available and *financial forecasts*.
  - o The end of a business plan often includes *appendixes,* which contain information providing detailed support for the analyses presented earlier in the report.

18.3 Valuing a Business

- The value of a business is determined by the ***magnitude*** of the cash flows that it is expected to produce, the ***timing*** of those cash flows, and the ***likelihood*** that the cash flows will be realized.

A. *Fundamental Business Valuation Principles*

- There are two important valuation principles.
  - o The first principle is that the value of a business changes over time.
  - o The second valuation principle is that there is no such thing as *the* value for a business.

- The value of a business can be different to different investors.
  - A *strategic investor* is one who has an interest in acquiring the business. The **investment value** of the firm to a strategic investor will take into consideration the benefits that can accrue from the acquisition and hence is likely to carry a higher value.
  - A *financial investor,* on the other hand, is only interested in financial performance of the firm and not in acquiring the business.

B. *Business Valuation Approaches*

- Business valuation methods can be classified into one of three general categories: (1) cost approaches, (2) market approaches, and (3) income approaches.

C. *Cost Approaches*

- The **replacement cost** of a business is the cost of duplicating the assets, including the intangible assets, of the business in their present form as of the valuation date.
- The **adjusted book value** approach involves restating the value of the individual assets in a business to reflect their fair market values.
  - The adjusted book value approach is useful in estimating a floor value for a business under certain circumstances: (1) it is especially difficult to forecast the cash flows that a business is likely to produce, (2) you suspect that the going-concern value of the business is negative, and (3) liquidation is being explicitly considered.

D. *Market Approaches*

- **Multiples analysis** uses stock price or other value multiples that are observed for public companies to estimate the value of a company's stock or an entire business.
- The process calls for:
  - identifying publicly traded companies engaged in business activities that are similar to those of the company being analyzed, and
  - using the prices at which shares of those *comparables* are trading, along with accounting data, to estimate the value of the company of interest.
- Price/earnings (P/E) and price/revenue multiples (ratios) are commonly used to directly estimate the value of the stock in a company.
- In the **transaction approach,** analysts use the information on what someone has paid for a comparable company in a merger or an acquisition to estimate a value for the firm.
- This transaction information is used to compute the same types of multiples that are used in a multiples analysis, and these multiples are used in the same way to value the company of interest.
- Since transaction data reflect the price that a particular investor paid for an entire company, it provides an estimate of the *investment* value to that investor.

E. *Income Approaches*

- The most direct approaches for estimating the value of the cash flows a business is expected to produce are the income approaches, which, like NPV analysis, directly estimate the value of those cash flows.
- These approaches provide the intrinsic value for the firm, which can be different from the market value. While market value reflects what people are willing to pay for the firm, the intrinsic value reflects what the firm is truly worth.
- In the **free cash flow from the firm (FCFF) approach,** an analyst values the free cash flows that the assets of the firm are expected to produce in the future.
  - In this approach the total value of the firm, V_F, is computed as the present value of the FCFF, discounted by the firm's WACC,
  - When analysts use the WACC approach to value a business, they must make an assumption about how the firm's operations will be financed in the future.
- The **free cash flow to equity (FCFE) approach** uses only the portion of the cash flows that are available for distribution to stockholders.
  - Stripping out the cash flows to or from the lenders leaves the cash flows available to stockholders.
  - Three specific cash flows associated with lenders are not included—the interest expense on existing debt, the repayment of debt principal, and the proceeds from new debt issues.
- The **dividend discount model (DDM) approach** estimates the value of equity directly by discounting cash flows to stockholders.
  - In contrast to the FCFE approach, which values cash flows that are *available for distribution* to stockholders, the DDM approach values the stream of cash flows that stockholders *expect to receive* through dividend payments. The firm may or may not be expected to distribute all available cash flows in any particular year.

18.4 Important Issues in Valuation: Public versus Private Companies

A. ***Financial Statements***
- Incomplete and unreliable financial statements can complicate the process of valuing a private business, making it more difficult to accurately assess its value.

B. ***Marketability***
- The shareholder of a private firm may have to spend considerable resources (both money and time) to sell his or her shares.
- This must be taken into account in the form of a marketability discount when estimating the value of any claim to the cash flows of a firm.

C. ***Young versus Mature Companies***
- Young, rapidly growing companies tend to be more difficult to value than mature, stable companies.
- The cash flows will be negative until the business becomes profitable and its investment expenditures are less than those profits. This means that the positive cash flows, which represent the value of the business, are further into the future and are, therefore, less certain.

D. ***Controlling Interest versus Minority Interest***
- The amount of stock that is required for an investor to exercise control can vary depending on the ownership structure of the company. Whether a controlling ownership interest is being sold has important implications for a valuation analysis.
- An adjustment must be made to reflect the benefits of control if one used multiples based on public stock market prices to estimate the value of a controlling interest.

E. ***Key People***
- Analysts must also consider whether it is appropriate to adjust the estimated value of the business for the likelihood that these "key people" may not remain with the firm as long as expected.
- If an analyst believes that those customers may go to another firm if the CEO departs, then a **key person discount** may be appropriate.

II. Suggested Approach to Material

The earlier chapters discussed how businesses are organized and how financial managers make long-term investment decisions, manage working capital requirements, and finance the investments and activities of their businesses. In this chapter these concepts are reexamined in the context of a discussion of business formation, growth, and valuation. This chapter provides an integrated perspective on how financial managers' decisions affect firm value.

The authors begin by considering the decision by an entrepreneur to start a business and how the business should be organized. They then discuss financial considerations that must concern managers of young, rapidly growing firms.

Next, they focus on the role that a carefully prepared business plan plays in raising capital for a young, rapidly growing business and in providing a road map of where the business is going for use in managerial decision making. The last two sections of this chapter address business valuation concepts. The discussions in these sections provide a broad overview of the business valuation approaches that financial managers use and how differences in the characteristics of public and private companies and of young, rapidly growing, and mature companies affect valuation analyses. The impact of control considerations and key people on business valuations is also considered.

III. Chapter Glossary

Business plan	A document that describes the details of how a business will be developed over time.
Valuation date	The date on which a value estimate applies.
Investment value	The value of a business to a specific investor.
Fair market value	The value of a business to a typical investor.

Replacement cost	The cost of duplicating the assets of a business in their present form on the valuation date.
Adjusted book value	The sum of the fair market values of the individual assets in a business.
Going-concern value	The difference between adjusted book value and the value of a business as a going concern (the present value of the expected cash flows).
Multiples analysis	A valuation approach that uses stock price or other value multiples for public companies to estimate the value of another company's stock or its entire business.
Transactions analysis	A valuation approach that uses transactions data from the sale of businesses to estimate the value of a company's stock or its entire business.
Enterprise value	The value of a company's equity plus the value of its debt; also the present value of the total cash flows the company's assets are expected to generate in the future.
Nonoperating assets (NOA)	Cash or other assets that are not required to support the operations of a business.
Terminal value	The value of the expected free cash flows beyond the period over which they are explicitly forecast.
Free cash flow from the firm (FCFF) approach	An income approach to valuation in which all free cash flows the assets are expected to generate in the future are discounted to obtain the enterprise value.
Free cash flow to equity (FCFE) approach	An income approach to valuation in which all cash flows that are expected to be available for distribution to stockholders in the future are discounted to obtain the value of the equity.
Dividend discount model (DDM) approach	An income approach to valuation in which all dividends that are expected to be distributed to stockholders in the future are discounted to obtain the value of the equity.
Control premium	An adjustment that is made to a business value estimate to reflect value associated with control that is not already reflected in the analysis.
Key person discount	An adjustment to a business value estimate that is made to reflect the potential loss of value associated with the unexpected departure of a key person.

IV. Summary of Key Equations

Equation	Description	Formula
18.1	Price/earnings multiple based on constant-growth model	$\frac{P_0}{E_1} = \frac{b}{k_{cs} - g}$
18.2	Implementing the income approach to business valuation	$V_F = PV(FCF_T) + PV(TV_T) + NOA$
18.3	FCFF approach	$V_F = \sum_{t=0}^{\infty} \frac{FCFF_t}{(1 + WACC)^t}$
18.4	FCFE approach	$V_E = \sum_{t=0}^{\infty} \frac{FCFE_t}{(1 + k_E)^t}$

V. True or False Questions

1. Starting a business is more risky than buying and growing a business that someone else has already established.
   a. True
   b. False

2. It is the founder's responsibility to manage the day-to-day operations to ensure that his or her overall plan is being implemented.
   a. True
   b. False

3. Businesses fail because of a lack of management skills to execute a good strategy.
   a. True
   b. False

4. A business has a better chance to succeed if one takes no risks.
   a. True
   b. False

5. A Limited Liability Corporation (LLC) is a hybrid of a limited partnership and a corporation.
   a. True
   b. False

6. An *S-corporation* is a variation of the *C-corporation* form that is used by public corporations.
   a. True
   b. False

7. The life of a sole proprietorship is limited to the life of the proprietor.
   a. True
   b. False

8. C-corporations can have an unlimited number of stockholders.
   a. True
   b. False

9. The cash budget helps identify how much money will be needed to launch a new product or business.
   a. True
   b. False

10. The financing plan presents the results from a strategic planning process that focuses on how the business will be developed over time.
    a. True
    b. False

11. A business plan communicates the entrepreneur's ideas to managers, outside directors, customers, suppliers, and others.
    a. True
    b. False

12. A financial investor is one who is interested in buying the firm.
    a. True
    b. False

13. Business valuation methods include cost approaches, market approaches, and discount approaches.
    - a. True
    - b. False

14. **Multiples analysis** is a market approach to valuing a business.
    - a. True
    - b. False

15. All companies, both public and private, are required to file audited financial statements with the SEC.
    - a. True
    - b. False

VI. Multiple-Choice Questions and Problems

1. Businesses fail because of
    - a. lack of acceptance of the products by customers.
    - b. poor management skills to properly execute a good strategy.
    - c. underestimating how much money it will take to get their businesses up and running.
    - d. All of the above

2. Chances of succeeding in a business can improve if one
    - a. does not jump into a business without careful thought.
    - b. doesn't overanalyze opportunities to the point where you are just convincing yourself not to proceed.
    - c. takes on calculated risks.
    - d. all of the above.

3. Different organizational forms include all but
    - a. C-corporations
    - b. S-corporations
    - c. Z-corporations
    - d. Partnerships

4. A limited liability company (LLC) is
    - a. more costly to form than sole proprietorships.
    - b. less costly to form than sole proprietorships.
    - c. equally costly to form as sole proprietorships.
    - d. None of the above

5. An S-corporation can have
    - a. no more than 100 stockholders.
    - b. only one class of common stock.
    - c. only individuals who are U.S. citizens or residents as stockholders.
    - d. All of the above are true.

6. Which ***one*** of the following statements is true?
    - a. Two tools are particularly useful in understanding the cash requirements of a business and in estimating how much financing a new business will require—**cash flow break-even analysis** and the **cash budget.**
    - b. The cash flow break-even point calculation brings into focus the importance of maximizing a product's per unit contribution.

c. The cash flow break-even point tells the entrepreneur how much money will be needed to launch a new product or business.

d. All of the above are true.

7. A business plan does all of the following **EXCEPT**

a. provide a roadmap for the business,

b. serve as the only document needed to register with the SEC.

c. present the results from a strategic planning process that focuses on how the business will be developed over time.

d. can help raise capital.

8. The value of a business is determined by

a. the magnitude of the cash flows that it is expected to produce.

b. the timing of those cash flows.

c. the likelihood that the cash flows will be realized.

d. All of the above

9. Business valuation methods can be classified into

a. cost approaches, market approaches, and income approaches.

b. cost approaches, market approaches, and discount approaches

c. discount approaches, market approaches, and income approaches.

d. None of the above

10. The adjusted book value approach is useful in estimating a floor value for a business when

a. it is especially difficult to forecast the cash flows that a business is likely to produce.

b. you suspect that the going-concern value of the business is negative.

c. liquidation is being explicitly considered.

d. All of the above

11. Which ***one*** of the following statements about transaction approach is **NOT** true?

a. In the transaction approach, analysts use the information on what someone has paid for a comparable company in a merger or an acquisition to estimate a value for the firm.

b. the types of multiples that are used in this approach are different from those used in a multiples analysis.

c. it provides an estimate of the *investment* value to that investor.

d. Transaction information is obtained from the financial statements of public companies that have acquired other companies.

12. When using the income approach to valuing a business, it is important to remember that

a. it is difficult to estimate the life of a business.

b. businesses often have cash or other assets that are not necessary for operations that can complicate the valuation.

c. both a and b

d. None of the above.

13. In the **free cash flow from the firm (FCFF)** approach, the total value of the firm, V_F, is computed as the present value of the FCFF,

a. discounted by the firm's cost of equity.

b. discounted by the firm's WACC.

c. discounted by the firm's cost of debt.

d. None of the above.

14. The **free cash flow to equity (FCFE) approach** uses only the portion of the cash flows that are available

a. for distribution to bondholders.

b. for distribution to bondholders and stockholders.

c. for distribution to stockholders.

d. None of the above.

15. Important issues that one must consider in valuing private firms include

a. incomplete and unreliable financial statements.

b. the higher transaction costs associated with the stock at the private firm that will result in a lower price for that investment.

c. difficulty in valuing a young, rapidly growing company.

d. All of the above.

16. Shriver, Inc., makes designer gold bracelets. Their annual costs include shop rent of $12,500, salaries for two jewelers of $118,000, design software costs of $10,000, and other overhead costs of $13,000. An average bracelet is priced at $4,000. It costs $2,000 in raw material, $1,250 in labor, and $250 in other expenses. What is the minimum number of bracelets that need to be sold to earn a profit?

a. 38

b. 44

c. 307

d. 614

17. Turnbull Corp. has debt of $230 million and generated a net income of $121 million in the last fiscal year. In attempting to determine the total value of the firm, an investor identified a similar firm in Jacobs, Inc., an all-equity firm. This firm had 150 million shares outstanding, a share price of $14.25, and net income of $182 million. What is the total value of Turnbull Corp.? Round to the nearest million dollars.

a. $1,421 million

b. $1,651 million

c. $1,191 million

d. $1,715 million

18. You are valuing the equity of a company using the FCFE approach and have estimated that the FCFE in the next three years will be $6.25, $7.70, and $8.36 million, respectively. Beginning in year 4, you expect the cash flows to increase at a rate of 4 percent per year for the indefinite future. You estimate that the cost of equity is 12 percent. What is the value of equity in this company?

a. $77 million

b. $95 million

c. $109 million

d. $60 million

19. Sigma, Inc., a tech firm, is expected to grow rapidly in the next three years and then have a level growth rate for the foreseeable future. The firm expects free cash flows of $3.425 million, $5.123 million, and $7.50 million over the next three years, and thereafter its cash flows will grow at a steady rate of 8 percent per annum. The company has no nonoperating assets (NOA). If the appropriate WACC is 10.5 percent, what is the enterprise value of this business? Round to the nearest million.

a. $253 million

b. $240 million

c. $324 million

d. $13 million

20. Kristi Sims is interested in investing in a private company. Based on earnings multiples of similar publicly traded firms, she estimates the value of the private company's stock to be $23.25 per share. He plans to acquire a majority of the shares in the company. The expected control premium is 15 percent. Kristi estimates the marketability discount for such a firm to be 15 percent. The discount for the key person, one of the founders who may leave the firm upon Kristi control of the firm, is 20 percent. What price should she be willing to pay for these shares?

a. $18.18

b. $35.36

c. $17.68

d. $36.36

Answers to True False Questions

1. a	**2.** a	**3.** a	**4.** b	**5.** a
6. a	**7.** a	**8.** a	**9.** b	**10.** b
11. a	**12.** b	**13.** b	**14.** a	**15.** b

Answers to Multiple-Choice Questions

1. d	**2.** d	**3.** c	**4.** a	**5.** d
6. d	**7.** b	**8.** d	**9.** a	**10.** d
11. b	**12.** c	**13.** b	**14.** c	**15.** d
16. c	**17.** b	**18.** b	**19.** a	**20.** a

Solutions to Multiple-Choice Problems

16. Solution:

Fixed costs = $12,500 + $118,000 + $10,000 + $13,000 = $153,500

Unit variable costs = $2,000 + $1,250 + $250 = $3,500

Unit selling price = $4,000

Therefore,

$$\text{Break-even point} = \frac{\text{Fixed costs}}{\text{Price} - \text{Unit Variable cost}}$$

$$= \frac{\$153{,}500}{\$4{,}000 - \$3{,}500} = 307 \textbf{ bracelets}$$

The firm needs to sell at least 307 bracelets annually before they can make a profit.

17. Solution:

The P/E multiple for Jacobs Inc. is:

$$\text{P/E} = \frac{\text{Total equity}}{\text{Net income}} = \frac{(\$14.25 \times 150{,}000{,}000)}{\$182{,}000{,}000} = 11.74$$

Implied equity value for Turnbull:

V_E = P/E × Net income = 11.74 × $121,000,000

= $1,420,540,000

Value of Turnbull's debt = V_D = $230 million

Therefore, the implied total value of Turnbull is:

$V_F = V_E + V_D = \$1{,}420.54 + \$230.00 = \mathbf{\$1{,}650.54\ million}$

18. **Solution:**

Cost of equity $= k_E = 12.0\%$

The present value of the cash flows expected over the next five years is:

$$PV(FCFF_3) = \frac{\$6.25}{(1.12)} + \frac{\$7.70}{(1.12)^2} + \frac{\$8.36}{(1.12)^3}$$
$$= \$17.67 \text{ million}$$

The terminal value is:

$$TV_3 = \frac{FCFE_3 \times (1+g)}{k_E - g} = \frac{\$8.36 \times (1.04)}{0.12 - 0.04} = \$108.68 \text{ million}$$

The present value of the terminal value is:

$$PV(TV_3) = \frac{TV_3}{(1+k_E)^3} = \frac{\$108.68}{(1.12)^3} = \$77.36 \text{ millions}$$

Therefore, if there are no non-operating assets, the value of the equity is:

$V_F = \$17.67 + \$77.36 = \mathbf{\$95.03\ million}$

19. **Solution:**

Cost of capital = WACC = 10.5%

The present value of the cash flows in the first three years is:

$$PV(FCFF_3) = \frac{\$3.425}{(1.105)} + \frac{\$5.123}{(1.105)^2} + \frac{\$7.50}{(1.105)^3}$$
$$= \$3.10 + \$4.20 + \$5.56$$
$$= \$12.86 \text{ million}$$

Free cash flows in year 4 = \$7.50(1.08) = \$8.10 million

$$\text{Terminal value} = TV = \frac{\$8.10}{0.105 - 0.08} = \$324 \text{ million}$$

The present value of the terminal value is:

$$PV(TV_3) = \frac{TV_3}{(1+WACC)^3} = \frac{\$324}{(1.105)^3} = \$240.14 \text{ millions}$$

Total enterprise value is, therefore

$$V_F = PV(FCF_T) + PV(TV_T) + NOA = \$12.86 + \$240.14 + \$0$$
$$= \mathbf{\$253\ million}$$

20. **Solution:**

Value per share = Share value * [(1 + Control premium) * (1 − Marketability discount) * (1 − Key person discount)

= \$23.25 * (1 + 15%) * (1 − 15%) * (1 − 20%)

= **\$18.18**

CHAPTER 19

Financial Planning and Forecasting

LEARNING OBJECTIVES

1. Explain what a financial plan is and why financial planning is so important.
2. Discuss how management uses financial planning models in the planning process, and explain the importance of sales forecasts in the construction of financial planning models.
3. Discuss how the relation between projected sales and balance sheet accounts can be determined, and be able to analyze a strategic investment decision using a percent of sales model.
4. Describe the conditions under which fixed assets vary directly with sales, and discuss the impact of so-called lumpy assets on this relation.
5. Explain what factors determine a firm's sustainable growth rate, discuss why it is of interest to management, and be able to compute the sustainable growth rate for a firm.

I. Chapter Outline

19.1 Financial Planning?

A. ***The Planning Documents***

- Financial planning relates to the identification of the kinds of projects that a firm needs to undertake and the ways of financing those projects. This results in a **financial plan.** The plan extends over a three- to five-year period called the planning horizon.
- A financial plan addresses four main issues:
  - **Strategic Plan**—Where is the company headed?
  - **Investment Plan**—What capital resources does the management need to get there?
  - **Financing Plan**—How is the firm going to pay for the resources needed?
  - **Cash Budget**—How is the firm going to pay its day-to-day bills?

1. The Strategic Plan

- The plan describes the vision of the firm, documents the firm's long-term goals, the strategies that management will use to achieve the goals, and the capabilities the firm needs to sustain its competitive position.
- The planning is done by the firm's top management with the financial manager providing key input, and it has to be approved by the board of directors.
- The strategic plan identifies:
  - The line of business in which the firm will compete.
  - Major areas of investment in real assets.
  - Capital expenditures
  - Acquisitions and new lines of business
  - Mergers, alliances, and divestitures that may happen in the near future.

2. The Investment Plan (Capital Budget)
- It is the part of the investment plan that describes the firm's outlay for plant and equipment.
- Three steps are involved in the capital budgeting process:
  - Management identifies a list of potential projects that are consistent with the business strategy.
  - Senior management ranks the projects according to the value they would create for the shareholders.
  - Finally, the proposed capital budget schedule is reviewed by senior management for funding and that sets the capital budget.

3. The Financing Plan
- Once the capital budget is ready, management needs to decide how to fund them.
- The firm will use a combination of internally generated funds and externally raised funds to finance the capital expenditures.
- Depending on the level of internally generated funds available to the firm, the firm will seek to raise funds in the form of either debt or equity.
- There are three elements to a financing plan:
  - First, a financing plan identifies the *dollar amount* of funds that has to be raised externally and the sources of funds available to the firm.
  - Second, the plan states management's *desired capital structure* for the firm.
  - Finally, the financing plan states the firm's *dividend policy,* which is relevant because it dictates the amount of funds that have to be raised in the capital markets.

4. Divisional Business Plans
- The business plans prepared by the firm's various business divisions are also part of the firm's financial plans.
- They identify how the various divisions will strive to achieve the corporate goals.
- They also identify the resources needed by each of the divisions to implement their strategies.

5. Cash Budget
- An overall cash budget for the firm is generated based on all the divisional cash budgets and that of the corporate offices.
- It focuses on the cash inflows and outflows of the firm.
- It allows the firm to determine whether any borrowing is necessary.
- A poorly developed cash budget could lead to serious cash shortages.

B. *The Financial Plan—Putting It All Together*

The strategic plan, the investment plan, and the financing plan are brought together by a firm's financial plan.

- The plan focuses on the two major decisions that management will make: (1) the investment decision and (2) the financing decision.
- Next, each of the firm's business divisions' plans is integrated.
- One important tool used in this process is a financial planning model.
  - Such models provide management with the ability to prepare projected financial statements.
  - These projected statements can be used to analyze the investment alternatives and estimate the amounts of external funding needed.

C. *Benefits of Financial Planning*

- It helps management establish financial and operating goals for the firm and to communicate those goals throughout the firm.
- The financial plan can help align the actions of managers and their operating units with the firm's strategic goals.

19.2 Financial Planning Models

- They help management analyze investment and financing alternatives.
- Most sophisticated planning models are now created as software and make the process speedy and accurate.

A. *The Importance of Sales Forecast*

- Sales forecast techniques come in quite an array—from best estimates by the sales staff to complex multivariate forecast models.
- They are usually generated from within the company.
- Since sales are often correlated to the regional or national economy, macroeconomic forecast are incorporated into the model.

B. *Building the Model: Inputs and Outputs*

- Current financial statements, sales forecasts, the resulting changes in the firm's balance sheet and income statement items, and macroeconomic variables serve as the major inputs and become the baseline to compare the projected financial statements.
- Last, investment and financing decisions are incorporated as inputs.
- The outputs of the financial planning model are a series of pro forma financial statements and financial ratios based on these statements.
  - o These pro forma balance sheets may not be balanced. The difference between assets and liabilities and owners' equity, often referred to as the ***plug value,*** often represents the external funding needed.

C. *A Simple Planning Model*

- A very basic planning model is called the **percent of sales** model, where the driving factor of this model is the expected sales growth rate.
- All or most of the input variables (i.e., the income statement and balance sheet elements) vary directly with sales.

19.3 A Better Financial Planning Model

- Unlike the previously described model, this model takes a more realistic approach in its assumptions.
- Not all balance sheet and income statement items vary directly with sales.
  - o *All* variable costs and *most* current assets and current liabilities vary directly with sales.

A. *The Income Statement*

- The pro forma income statement is generated by recognizing that all variable costs change directly with sales.

B. *The Balance Sheet*

- Some balance sheet items vary directly with sales whereas others do not.
- To determine which accounts vary directly with sales, a trend analysis may be conducted on historic balance sheets of the firm.
- Typically, working capital accounts like inventory, accounts receivables, and accounts payables vary directly with sales.
- Fixed assets do not always vary directly with sales. It will do so only if the firm is operating at 100 percent capacity and fixed assets can be incrementally changed.
  - o Firms that are highly capital intensive are more risky than those that are not because a downturn can reduce sales sharply but fixed costs do not change rapidly.

C. *Liabilities and Equity*

- Only current liabilities are likely to vary directly with sales. The exception here is notes payables (short-term borrowings) that change as the firm pays it down or makes an additional borrowing.
- Long-term liabilities and equity accounts change as a direct result of managerial decisions like debt repayment, stock repurchase, and issuing new debt or equity.
- Retained earnings will vary as sales changes but not directly. It is affected by the firm's dividend payout policy.

D. *The Preliminary Pro Forma Balance Sheet*

- First, calculate the projected values for all the accounts that vary with sales.
- Second, calculate the projected value of any other balance sheet account for which an end-of-period value can be forecast or otherwise determined.
- Third, enter the current year's number for all the accounts for which the next year's figure cannot be calculated or forecast.
- At this point the balance sheet will be unbalanced. A plug value is necessary to get the balance sheet to balance.
  - o First, determine the retained earnings based on the firm's dividend policy.
  - o Next, the plug figure will represent the external financing necessary to make the total assets equal total liabilities and equity. This calls for management to choose a financing option—choosing debt, equity, or a combination—to raise the additional funds needed.

E. *The Management Decision*

- The first decision relates to the firm's dividend policy. Should the firm alter its dividend policy to increase the amount of retained earning?
- If external funding is still needed, should the firm issue new debt, or issue equity? Or should it be a mix of both?

- It is important to recognize that while financial planning models can identify the amount of external financing needed, the financing option is a managerial decision.

19.4 Beyond the Basic Planning Models

A. *Improving Financial Planning Models*
- The previously described models have several weaknesses.
- First, interest expense was not accounted for. It is difficult to do so until all the financing options are finalized.
- Second, all working capital accounts do not necessarily vary directly with sales, especially cash and inventory.
- Third, how fixed assets are adjusted plays a significant role.

19.5 Managing and Financing Growth

- Managers prefer rapid growth as a goal to capture market share and establish a competitive position.
- Most firms experiencing rapid growth fund the growth with debt, increasing the firm's leverage and putting it at risk.

A. *External Funding Needed*
- **External funding needed (EFN)** is defined as the additional debt or equity a firm needs to issue so that it can purchase additional assets to support an increase in sales.
- EFN is tied to new investments the management has deemed necessary to support the sales growth.
- The new investments are the projected capital expenditure plus the increase in working capital necessary to sustain increases in sales.
- Companies first resort to internally generated funds in the form of addition to retained earnings.
- Once internally generated funds are exhausted, the firm looks to raise funds externally. See Equations 19.5 and 19.6.

B. *Internal Growth Rate*
- The **internal growth rate (IGR)** is defined as the maximum growth rate that a firm can achieve without external financing. See Equations 19.7 and 19.8.
- The higher the retained earnings generated by a firm and the lower the total assets a firm has, the higher the growth possible without using external funding.

C. *The Sustainable Growth Rate*
- The **sustainable growth rate (SGR)** is the rate of growth that the firm can sustain without selling additional shares of equity.
- This measure is important to management because it helps them determine whether they can avoid issuing new equity. New equity issues are both expensive and cause dilution of earnings to existing shareholders.
- As Equation 19.9 shows, the SGR is a function of the plowback ratio and the ROE.

II. Suggested Approach to Material

The chapter begins with a discussion of what financial planning is all about. This discussion is followed by an overview of some simple financial planning models. Then the weaknesses in the simple models are identified, and some better planning models are discussed. The chapter concepts of internal growth rates and sustainable growth rates are introduced, and this is followed by coverage of external funding needed to facilitate growth in sales.

Financial planning is important for a firm's efforts to achieve its strategic goals. Planning, though often initiated from the top, has to integrate inputs from all the divisions of the firm. Hence, divisional budgets play an important role.

There is an important difference between growing fast and growing under control. Understanding what the internal growth rate and sustainable growth rate reveals to management is important whether it is a big business or a small business venture. One should also understand the role of the payout and plowback ratios in the determination of the SGR and IGR.

III. Chapter Glossary

Financial planning	The process by which management decides what types of investments the firm needs to make and how to finance those investments.
Financial plan	A plan outlining the investments a firm intends to make and how it will finance them.
Planning horizon	A time frame specified in a plan for the achievement of a goal or a course of action.
Strategic planning	The process by which management establishes the firm's long-term goals, the strategies that will be used to achieve the goals, and the capabilities that are needed to sustain the firm's competitive position.
Pro forma financial statements	Projected financial statements that reflect a set of assumptions concerning operating, investment, and financing decisions.
Plug value	A variable used to adjust a pro forma balance sheet so that it balances. Normally, the plug value is the amount of external financing needed.
Percent of sales model	A type of simple financial planning model that assumes that most income statement and balance sheet accounts vary proportionally with sales.
External funding needed (EFN)	The additional debt or equity a firm must raise from external sources to meet its total funding requirements.
Lumpy assets	Fixed assets added as large, discrete units; these assets may not be used to full capacity for some time, leaving the company with excess capacity.
Internal growth rate (IGR)	The maximum growth rate that a firm can achieve without external financing.
Sustainable growth rate (SGR)	The rate of growth that a firm can sustain without selling additional equity while maintaining the same capital structure.

IV. Summary of Key Equations

Equation	Description	Formula
19.1	Percent change in sales.	$\% \Delta S = \dfrac{(S_{t+1} - S_t)}{S_t}$
19.2	Percent of net income paid out	$\text{Dividend payout ratio} = \dfrac{\text{Cash dividends}}{\text{Net income}}$
19.3	Percent of net income retained	$\text{Retention ratio} = \dfrac{\text{Retained earnings}}{\text{Net income}}$
19.4	Level of assets needed to generate \$1 of sales	$\text{Capital intensity ratio} = \dfrac{\text{Total assets}}{\text{Net sales}}$
19.5 19.6	External funding needed to support growth in sales	EFN = New investments − Addition to retained earnings EFN = (Growth rate × Initial assets) − Addition to retained earnings
19.7 19.8	Internal growth rate (level of growth that can be supported without raising external funds)	IGR = Addition to retained earnings/Initial assets IGR = Plowback ratio × Return on equity × Measure of leverage

19.9	Sustainable growth rate (level of growth that can be supported without raising external equity or increasing current leverage)	SGR = Plowback ratio × ROE

V. True or False Questions

1. Financial planning relates to the identification of the kinds of projects a firm needs to undertake and the ways of financing those projects.
   a. True
   b. False

2. The strategic plan addresses the issue of what capital resources the management needs to get to achieve their goals.
   a. True
   b. False

3. The strategic plan documents the firm's long-term goals, the strategies that management will use to achieve the goals, and the capabilities the firm needs to sustain its competitive position.
   a. True
   b. False

4. The financial plan focuses on the investment decision and the financing decision.
   a. True
   b. False

5. Projected or *pro forma* statements can be used to analyze the investment alternatives but not to estimate the amounts of external funding needed.
   a. True
   b. False

6. While sales are often correlated to the regional or national economy, it is not necessary to incorporate macroeconomic forecasts into the model.
   a. True
   b. False

7. Capital intensity measures the dollar amount of total assets needed to generate a dollar of sales.
   a. True
   b. False

8. External funding needed (EFN) is defined as the additional debt or equity a firm needs to issue so that it can purchase additional assets to support an increase in sales.
   a. True
   b. False

9. The higher a firm's dividend payout ratio, the higher the firm's internal growth rate.
   a. True
   b. False

10. The higher a firm's plowback ratio, the higher the firm's sustainable growth rate.
    a. True
    b. False

VI. Multiple-Choice Questions and Problems

1. The financial plan addresses the following issue(s):

a. Where is the company headed?

b. What capital resources does the management need to get there?

c. How is the firm going to pay for the resources needed?

d. All of the above

2. The strategic plan

a. documents the firm's long-term goals.

b. defines the strategies that management will use to achieve the goals.

c. describes the capabilities the firm needs to sustain its competitive position.

d. All of the above.

3. Which one of the following is **NOT** true about the capital budgeting process?

a. Management identifies a list of potential projects that are consistent with the business strategy and ranks them according to the value they would create for the shareholders.

b. Senior management reviews the list.

c. Once the list is made, no management review can change it.

d. All of the above are true of the capital budgeting process.

4. The financial plan includes

a. the strategic plan, financing plan, and options plan.

b. the strategic plan, investment plan, and financing plan.

c. the financing plan, investment plan, and options plan.

d. none of the above.

5. The percent of sales method

a. is a basic planning model.

b. has the expected sales growth rate as the driving factor.

c. calls for all income statement accounts and balance sheet accounts to vary directly with sales.

d. All of the above are true of the percent of sales method.

6. Which statement is **NOT** true for a firm that is operating at full capacity?

a. Fixed assets vary directly with sales.

b. Fixed assets can never vary directly with sales.

c. Fixed assets can be incrementally changed.

d. All of the above are true

7. In using more sophisticated planning models, which one of the following statements is **NOT** true?

a. Current liabilities are likely to vary directly with sales.

b. Long-term liabilities and equity accounts change as a direct result of managerial decisions.

c. Retained earnings will vary directly as sales change.

d. All of the above are true

8. Which one of the following statements is **NOT** true?

a. The internal growth rate (IGR) is defined as the maximum growth rate that a firm can achieve without external financing.

b. The higher the retained earnings generated by a firm, the higher the growth possible without using external funding.

c. The lower the total assets a firm has, the higher the growth possible without using external funding.

d. All of the above are true.

9. The sustainable growth rate (SGR) is

a. the maximum growth rate that a firm can achieve without external financing.

b. the rate of growth that the firm can sustain without selling additional shares of equity.

c. the rate of growth that the firm can sustain by only selling equity and not debt.

d. None of the above.

10. Which one of the following statements about the sustainable growth rate (SGR) is **NOT** true?

a. The higher a firm's ROE, the higher the SGR.

b. The higher the plowback ratio, the larger the proportion of net income retained in the firm and the greater the firm's SGR.

c. The higher a firm's ROE, the lower the SGR.

d. None of the above.

11. Tangent, Inc., has revenues of $4,375,233 and costs of $2,467,321, and pays a tax rate of 34 percent. If the firm pays out 60 percent of its earnings as dividends every year, what is the amount of retained earnings?

a. $171,254.18

b. $755,533.15

c. $503,688.77

d. None of the above.

12. A firm paid out $163,961.60 as dividends on net income of $298,112. What is the firm's retention ratio?

a. 55%

b. 45%

c. 50%

d. None of the above.

13. Comacho Traders has total assets of $513,480 and sales of $723,062. What is the firm's capital intensity ratio?

a. 1.41

b. 0.71

c. 1.23

d. None of the above.

14. The Gary Sobers Sporting Goods Co. has assets of $412,332. What would the revenues have to be for the capital intensity to be at 0.75?

a. $412,332

b. $549,776

c. $309,249

d. None of the above.

15. Mercantile Company has net income of $3,413,500 on assets of $16,109,445 and retains 55 percent of its income every year. What is the company's internal growth rate?

a. 21.2%

b. 8.6%

c. 11.7%

d. 9.4%

16. The Highway 66 Motel has net income of $866,500 on assets of $2,337,682 and retains 40 percent of its income every year. What is the company's internal growth rate?

    a. 21.2%

    b. 8.6%

    c. 14.83%

    d. 9.4%

17. Nederland Finance Company has total assets worth $9,751,223. It is expecting to grow its revenue at a rate of 20 percent next year. At year-end it had a net income of $2,213,564 and paid out 65 percent as dividends. What is the external financing needed by this firm to meet its growth expectations?

    a. $1,020,547.72

    b. $511,428.00

    c. No external funding needed.

    d. None of the above

18. Ontario Manufacturing Company has total assets worth $13,442,902. It is expecting to grow its revenue at a rate of 20 percent next year. At year-end it had a net income of $6,431,768 and paid out 70 percent as dividends. What is the external financing needed by this firm to meet its growth expectations?

    a. $373,143.92

    b. $2,688,580

    c. No external funding needed.

    d. None of the above

19. If Newell Corp. has a ROE of 18.6 percent and a dividend payout ratio of 60 percent, what is its sustainable growth rate?

    a. 7.44%

    b. 2.15%

    c. 0.47%

    d. 8.20%

20. If Charter Corp. has a ROE of 15.7 percent and a dividend payout ratio of 50 percent, what is its sustainable growth rate?

    a. 7.40%

    b. 31.4%

    c. 0.47%

    d. 7.85%

Answers to True or False Questions

1. a	**2.** b	**3.** a	**4.** a	**5.** b
6. b	**7.** a	**8.** a	**9.** b	**10.** a

Answers to Multiple-Choice Questions

1. d	**2.** d	**3.** c	**4.** b	**5.** d
6. b	**7.** c	**8.** d	**9.** b	**10.** c
11. c	**12.** b	**13.** b	**14.** b	**15.** c
16. c	**17.** a	**18.** a	**19.** a	**20.** d

Solutions to Multiple-Choice Problems

11. Solution:

Revenue = \$4,375,233 Costs = \$2,467,321;

Tax rate = 34% Payout ratio = 60%

$$\text{Net income} = (\$4{,}375{,}233 - \$2{,}467{,}321)(1 - 0.34) = \$1{,}259{,}221.92$$

$$\text{Retained earnings} = 1{,}259{,}221.92\ (1 - 0.60) = \mathbf{\$503{,}688.77}$$

12. Solution:

Dividends = \$163,961.60 Net income = \$298,112.

$$\text{Dividend payout ratio} = \frac{\text{Dividends}}{\text{Net income}} = \frac{\$163{,}961.60}{\$298{,}112.00} = 55\%$$

$$\text{Retention} = (1 - \text{Dividend payout ratio}) = (1 - 0.55) = \mathbf{45\%}$$

13. Solution:

Total assets = \$513,480 Sales = \$723,062

$$\text{Capital intensity ratio} = \frac{\text{Total assets}}{\text{Net sales}} = \frac{\$513{,}480}{\$723{,}062} = \mathbf{71.01}\%$$

14. Solution:

Total assets = \$412,332 Capital intensity ratio = 0.75

$$\text{Capital intensity ratio} = \frac{\text{Total assets}}{\text{Net sales}}$$

$$0.75 = \frac{\$412{,}332}{\text{Net sales}}$$

$$\text{Net sales} = \frac{\$412{,}332}{0.75} = \mathbf{\$549{,}776}$$

15. Solution:

Net income = \$3,413,500

Total assets = \$16,109,445

Plowback ratio = 55%

$$\begin{aligned}\text{Internal growth rate (IGR)} &= \text{Plowback ratio} \times \text{ROE} \times \text{Equity ratio} \\ &= \text{Plowback ratio} \times \frac{\text{Net income}}{\text{Equity}} \times \frac{\text{Equity}}{\text{Total assets}} \\ &= \text{Plowback ratio} \times \frac{\text{Net income}}{\text{Total assets}} \\ &= 0.55 \times \frac{\$3{,}413{,}500}{\$16{,}109{,}445} \\ &= \mathbf{11.65}\%\end{aligned}$$

16. Solution:

Net income = \$866,500

Total assets = \$2,337,682

Plowback ratio = 40%

$$\text{Internal growth rate (IGR)} = \text{Plowback ratio} \times \text{ROE} \times \text{Equity ratio}$$
$$= \text{Plowback ratio} \times \frac{\text{Net income}}{\text{Equity}} \times \frac{\text{Equity}}{\text{Total assets}}$$
$$= \text{Plowback ratio} \times \frac{\text{Net income}}{\text{Total assets}}$$
$$= 0.40 \times \frac{\$866{,}500}{\$2{,}337{,}682}$$
$$= \mathbf{14.83}\%$$

17. Solution:

Total assets = \$9,751,223

Net income = \$2,213,564

Expected net income = \$2,213,564 (1.20) = \$2,656,276.80

Addition to retained earnings = \$2,656,276.80 × (1 − 0.65) = \$929,696.88

EFN = (Initial assets × Growth rate) − Addition to retained earnings

= (\$9,751,223 × 0.20) − \$929,696.88

= \$1,950,244.60 − \$774,747.40 = **\$1,020,547.72**

18. Solution:

Total assets = \$13,442,902

Net income = \$6,431,768

Expected net income \$6,431,768 (1.20) = \$7,718,121.60

Addition to retained earnings = \$7,718,121.60 × (1 − 0.70) = \$2,315,436.48

EFN = (Initial assets × Growth rate) − Addition to retained earnings

= (\$13,442,902 × 0.20) − \$2,315,436.48

= \$2,688,580.40 − \$1,929,530.40 = **\$373,143.92**

19. Solution:

ROE = 18.6%

Payout ratio = 60%

Plowback ratio = (1 − Payout ratio) = (1 − 0.60) = 40%

SGR = Plowback ratio × ROE

= 0.40 × 0.186 = **7.44**%

20. Solution:

ROE = 15.7%

Payout ratio = 50%

Plowback ratio = (1 − Payout ratio) = (1 − 0.50) = 50%

SGR = Plowback ratio × ROE

= 0.50 × 0.157 = 7.85%

CHAPTER 20

Options and Corporate Finance

LEARNING OBJECTIVES

1. Define a *call option* and a *put option,* and describe the payoff function for each of these options.
2. List and describe the factors that affect the value of an option.
3. Name some of the real options that occur in business, and explain why traditional NPV analysis does not accurately incorporate their value.
4. Describe how the agency costs of debt and equity are related to options.
5. Explain how options can be used to manage a firm's exposure to risk.

I. Chapter Outline

20.1 Financial Options

- A **financial option** is a **derivative security** because its value is derived from the value of another asset.
- The owner of a financial option has the right, but not the obligation, to buy or sell an asset on or before a specified date for a specified price.
- The asset that the owner has a right to buy or sell is known as the **underlying asset.**
- The last date on which an option can be exercised is called the **exercise date** or **expiration date,** and the price at which the option holder can buy or sell the asset is called the **exercise price** or **strike price.**

A. ***Call Options***

- A call option gives the owner the right to buy, or "call," the underlying asset.
- Once the asset price increases above the exercise price, the value of the call option at exercise increases dollar for dollar in tandem with the price of the underlying asset.
- The buyer pays the seller a fee to purchase the option.
  - o This fee, which is known as the **call premium,** makes the total return to the seller positive when the price of the underlying asset is near or below the exercise price.

B. ***Put Options***

- The owner of a **put option** has the right to *sell* the underlying asset at a pre-specified price.
- The payoff function for the owner of a put option is similar to that for a call option, but it is the reverse in the sense that the owner of a put option profits if the price of the underlying asset is *below* the exercise price.
  - o The owner of a put option will not want to exercise that option if the price of the underlying asset is above the exercise price.
  - o When the value of the underlying asset is below the exercise price, however, the owner of the put option will find it profitable to exercise the option.

- The payoff for the seller of the put option is negative when the price of the underlying asset is below the exercise price.
- The seller of a put option hopes to profit from the fee, or **put premium,** that he or she receives from the buyer of the put option.

C. *American, European, and Bermudan Options*

- *European options* can only be exercised on the expiration date.
- *American options* can be exercised at any point in time on or before the expiration date.
- *Bermudan* options can be exercised only on specific dates during the life of the option.

D. *More on the Shapes of Option Payoff Functions*

- The payoff functions for options are not straight lines for all possible values of the underlying asset.
  - Each payoff function has a "kink" at the exercise price, which exists because the owner of the option has a right, but not the obligation, to buy or sell the underlying asset. If it is not in the owner's interest to exercise the option, he or she can simply let it expire.

20.2 Option Valuation

- It is more complicated to determine the value of an option at a point in time before the expiration date because we don't know exactly how the value of the underlying asset will change over time, and therefore we don't know if it will make sense to exercise the option.

A. *Limits on Option Values*

- We know that the value of a call option can never be less than zero, since the owner of the option can always decide not to exercise it if doing so is not beneficial.
- The value of a call option can never be greater than the value of the underlying asset since it would not make sense to pay more for the right to buy an asset than you would pay for the asset itself.
- The value of a call option prior to expiration will never be less than the value of that option at expiration because there is always a possibility that the value of the underlying asset will be greater than it is today at some time before the option expires.
- When we consider the value of a call option at some time prior to expiration, we must compare the current value of the underlying asset with the *present value of the exercise price,* discounted at the *risk-free rate.*
  - The present value of the exercise price is the amount that an investor would have to invest in risk-free securities at any point prior to the expiration date to ensure that he or she would have enough money to exercise the option when it expired.

B. *Variables That Affect Option Values*

- The higher the current value of the underlying asset, the more likely it is that the value of the asset will be above the exercise price when the call option expires.
  - The higher the current value of the asset, the greater the likely difference between the value of the asset and the exercise price when the option expires.
  - This means that, holding the exercise price constant, investors will pay more for a call option if the underlying asset value is higher, because the expected value of the option at expiration is higher.
- The opposite relation applies to the exercise price in that the lower the exercise price, the more likely that the value of the underlying asset will be higher than the exercise price when the option expires.
- The greater the volatility of the underlying asset value, the higher the value of a call option prior to valuation.
  - The intuition is that the value of an option will increase more when the value of the underlying asset goes up than it will decrease when the value of the underlying asset goes down. This means that a greater potential change in the underlying price will be more beneficial to the value of the option.
- The greater the time to maturity, the more the value of the underlying asset is likely to change by the time the option expires; this increases the value of an option.
  - The time until the expiration affects the value of a call option through its effect on the volatility of the value of the underlying asset.
- The value of a call option increases with the risk-free rate.
  - Exercising a call option involves paying cash in the future for the underlying asset.
  - The higher the interest rate, the lower the present value of the amount that the owner of a call option will have to pay to exercise it, which translates into value for the owner of the option.

C. *The Binomial Pricing Model*

- This simple model assumes that the underlying asset will have one of only two possible values when the option expires.
  - The value of the underlying asset will either increase to some value above the exercise price or decrease to some value below the exercise price.
- To solve for the value of the call option using this model, we must assume that investors have no arbitrage opportunities with regard to this option.
  - **Arbitrage** is the act of buying and selling assets in a way that yields a return above that suggested by the Security Market Line (SML).
- To value the call option in our simple model, we first create a portfolio that consists of the asset underlying the call option and a risk-free loan.
  - The relative investments in these two assets will be selected so that the combination of the asset and the loan has the same cash flows as the call option when it expires, regardless of whether the value of the underlying asset goes up or down.
  - This is called a *replicating* portfolio, since it replicates the cash flows of the option.
  - The replicating portfolio will consist of:
    - x shares of the underlying stock, and
    - a risk-free loan with a face value of y.
  - The value of the call option can be calculated.
    - Solve for the values of x and y.
    - Multiply the current cost of the underlying stock by x.
    - Subtracting y from the above amount will yield the value of the call option.

D. *Put-Call Parity*

- Although there are other methods to value a put option, the value of a put option can be calculated by examining the relationship of a put option to a call option with the same maturity and exercise price.
  - This relation is called **put-call parity.**
  - The formula for put-call parity is:

$$P = C + Xe^{-rt} - V$$

where P is the value of the put option,
C is the value of the call option,
X is the exercise price,
V is the current value of the underlying asset, and
e is the exponential function.

20.3 Real Options

- **Real options** are options on real assets.
- NPV analysis does not adequately reflect the value of real options, and while it might not always be possible to directly estimate the value of the real options associated with a project, it is important to recognize that they exist when we perform a project analysis.

A. *Options to Defer Investment*

- An example is as stated in the text concerning the Russian government and an oil field development project where the Russian government waited to see what happened to the price of oil before it decided to exercise its option to acquire an ownership interest in the Sakhalin II project.
  - The underlying asset in this option is the stream of cash flows that the developed oil field would produce, while the exercise price from the company's perspective is the amount of money that the company would have to spend to develop it (drill the well and build any necessary infrastructure).
- The value of an option to defer investment is not reflected in an NPV analysis because NPV analysis does not allow for the possibility of deferring an investment decision.

B. *Options to Make Follow-On Investments*

- Some projects introduce future business opportunities that would not otherwise be available. This type of real option is an *option to make follow-on investments.*

- Options to make follow-on investments are inherently difficult to value because, at the time we are evaluating the original project, it may not be obvious what the follow-on projects will be.
  - Even if we know what the projects will be, we are unlikely to have enough information to estimate what they are worth.
  - Projects that lead to investment opportunities that are consistent with a company's overall strategy are more valuable than otherwise similar projects that do not lead to additional investment opportunities.

C. *Options to Change Operations*

- Options to change operations are related to the flexibility managers have once an investment decision has been made. These options include the opportunity to change operations and to abandon a project; they also affect the NPV of a project and must be taken into account at the time the investment decision is made.
  - The changes that managers might make can involve something as simple as reducing output if prices decline or increasing output if prices increase.

D. *Options to Abandon Projects*

- An *option to abandon a project* is the ability to choose to terminate a project by shutting it down.
  - Management will save money that would otherwise be lost if the project kept going. The amount saved represents the gain from exercising this option.

E. *Concluding Comments on NPV Analysis and Real Options*

- In order to use NPV analysis to value such a real option, we would not only have to estimate all the cash flows associated with the expansion but would also have to estimate the probability that we would actually undertake the expansion and determine the appropriate rate at which to discount the value of the expansion back to the present.

20.4 Agency Costs

- Agency conflicts between stockholders and debt holders and between stockholders and managers arise because the interests of stockholders, lenders (creditors), and managers are not perfectly aligned.
- One reason is that the claims that they have against the cash flows produced by the firm have payoff functions that look like different types of options.

A. *Agency Costs of Debt*

- The payoff functions for stockholders and lenders (creditors) differ, as do the payoff functions for different options.
- The payoff function for the stockholders of a firm that has issued debt looks exactly like that for the owner of a call option, where the exercise price is the amount owed on the loan and the underlying asset is the firm itself.
  - If the value of the firm exceeds the exercise price, the stockholders will choose to exercise their option; if it does not exceed the exercise price, they will let their option expire unexercised.
- One way to think about the payoff function for the lenders is that when they lend money to the firm, they are essentially selling a put option to the stockholders.
  - This option gives the stockholders the right to "put" the assets to the lenders for an exercise price that equals the amount they owe.
  - When the value of the firm is less than the exercise price, the stockholders will exercise their option by defaulting.
- **The Dividend Payout Problem:** The incentives that stockholders of a leveraged firm have to pay themselves dividends arise because of their option to default.
  - If a company faces some realistic risk of going bankrupt, the stockholders might decide that they are better off taking money out of the firm by paying themselves dividends.
  - This situation can arise because the stockholders know that the bankruptcy laws limit their possible losses.
- **The Asset Substitution Problem:** When bankruptcy is possible, stockholders have an incentive to invest in very risky projects, some of which might even have negative NPVs.
  - Stockholders have this incentive because they receive all of the benefits if things turn out well but do not bear all of the costs if the outcome is poor.
- **The Underinvestment Problem:** Stockholders have incentives to turn down positive-NPV projects when all of the benefits are likely to go to the lenders. The problem arises from the differences in the payoff functions.

B. ***Agency Costs of Equity***

- Managers are hired to manage the firm on behalf of the stockholders, but they do not always act in the stockholders' best interest.
- The payoff function for a manager can be quite different from that for stockholders. In fact, it can look a lot like that for a lender.
  - If a company gets into financial difficulty and a manager is viewed as responsible, that manager could lose his or her job and find it difficult to obtain a similar job at another company.
    - The most obvious way for a company to get into financial difficulty is to default on its debt.
    - So as long as a company is able to avoid defaulting on its debt, a manager has a reasonable chance of retaining his or her job.
- The fact that the payoff function for a manager resembles that for a lender means that managers, like lenders, have incentives to invest in less risky assets and to distribute less value through dividends and stock repurchases than the stockholders would like them to.

20.5 Options and Risk Management

- Risk management typically involves hedging, or reducing a firm's financial risks.
- Options, along with other derivative instruments, such as forwards, futures, and swaps, are commonly used to reduce risks associated with commodity prices, interest rates, foreign exchange rates, and equity prices.
- One interesting benefit of using options in this way is that they provide downside protection but do not limit the upside.
  - This is just like buying insurance.
    - Many insurance contracts are little more than specialized put options.
- Options and other derivative instruments help to manage commodity price risks, large swings in interest rates, risks associated with foreign exchange rates, as well as to manage risks associated with equity prices as occurs within defined benefit pension plans.

II. Suggested Approach to Material

Chapter 20 considers the description, valuation, and use of options. The discussion begins with financial options and how they are valued within a simple binomial model. The chapter then turns to options on real assets, known as real options. Real options often occur within corporate investment decisions, such as the right to delay investing in a project, expanding a project, and abandoning a project, or a change in the technology employed in a project. This framework provides a valuation tool that is not properly reflected in an NPV analysis.

The chapter then revisits the agency costs of debt discussed earlier in Chapter 16. The option-like payoffs that are embedded in the payoff to equity investors contribute to the problems of asset substitution, underinvestment, dividend payout, and claim dilution. The discussion then follows with how option-like payoffs contribute to conflicts between stockholders and the managers. The chapter concludes with a discussion of the ways in which managers use financial options to alter their companies' exposures to various types of risks.

Although this chapter may be considered advanced for a first course in finance, the subject matter is handled in a simple real-world discussion. The concepts are both easy to grasp and interesting, considering the common occurrence of option discussions in the popular press.

III. Chapter Glossary

Financial option	The right to buy or sell a financial security, such as a share of stock, on or before a specified date for a specified price.
Derivative security	A security that derives its value from the value of another asset; an option is an example of a derivative security.
Underlying asset	The asset from which the value of an option is derived.

Exercise (expiration) date	The last date on which an option can be exercised.
Exercise (strike) price	The price at which the owner of an option has the right to buy or sell the underlying asset.
Option payoff function	The function that shows how the value of an option varies with the value of the underlying asset.
Call option	An option to buy the underlying asset.
Call premium	The price that the buyer of a call option pays the seller for that option.
Put option	An option to sell the underlying asset.
Put premium	The price that the buyer of a put option pays the seller for that option.
Arbitrage	Buying and selling assets in a way that takes advantage of price discrepancies and yields a profit greater than that which would be expected based solely on the risk of the individual investments.
Put-call parity	The relation between the value of a call option on an asset and the value of a put option on the same asset that has the same exercise price.
Real option	An option for which the underlying asset is a real asset.

IV. Summary of Key Equations

Equation	Description	Formula
20.1	Put-call parity	$P = C + Xe^{-rt} - V$

V. True or False Questions

1. The owner of a call option on a stock is obligated to buy the stock when the option expires.
   a. True
   b. False

2. Consider a portfolio of one put option and one call option on the same asset, with the same strike price. The payoff from this portfolio will be identical to the payoff from the underlying asset.
   a. True
   b. False

3. A put option with a strike price of $25 should be priced higher than an otherwise identical put option with a strike price of $20, holding other items the same.
   a. True
   b. False

4. An American option should always be worth at least as much as a European option with the same strike price.
   a. True
   b. False

5. A stock is currently priced at $50. The risk-free interest rate is 0 percent. A call option on the stock with an exercise price of $45 expires in two months. Without arbitrage this call option cannot be priced at less then $5.
   a. True
   b. False

6. The buyer of a put option and the seller of a call option could both benefit when the price of the underlying asset goes down.
   a. True
   b. False

7. Consider two call options that are equal in all respects, except for the exercise price. The call option with the higher exercise price will be worth more.
   a. True
   b. False

8. If the volatility of the value of an underlying asset goes up, we would expect the price of call and put options on the underlying asset to increase.
   a. True
   b. False

9. An asset is currently selling for $40. A call option on the asset with a strike price of $45 is set to expire one year from now. The option is currently selling for $1. In six months if the price of the asset is once again $40, all else being equal, we would expect the price of the same call option (now six months from expiration) to be less then $1.
   a. True
   b. False

10. Evaluating the real options relevant to a project is an important tool for identifying sources of value that NPV analysis might miss.
   a. True
   b. False

VI. Multiple-Choice Questions and Problems

1. An investor (the buyer) purchases a call option from a seller. On the expiration date of a call option
   a. the buyer has the obligation to buy the underlying asset and the seller has the obligation to sell it.
   b. the buyer has the right to buy the underlying asset and the seller has the obligation to sell it.
   c. the buyer has the obligation to buy the underlying asset and the seller has the right to sell it.
   d. none of the above.

2. An investor (the buyer) purchases a put option from a seller. On the expiration date of a call option
   a. the buyer has the obligation to sell the underlying asset and the seller has the right to buy it.
   b. the buyer has the obligation to sell the underlying asset and the seller has the obligation to buy it.
   c. the buyer has the right to sell the underlying asset and the seller has the obligation to buy it.
   d. none of the above

3. Which one of the following statements is **NOT** true?
   a. The value of a call option can never be negative.
   b. The value of a call option can never be more then the value of the underlying asset.
   c. The value of a call option can never be worth less then the current value of the asset minus the present value of the strike price.
   d. The value of a call option can never be worth more then the strike price.

4. Suppose you own a call option on a stock with a strike price of $20, which expires today. The price of the underlying stock is $15. If you exercise the option and immediately sell the stock,
   a. you will earn $5.
   b. you will lose $5.

c. you will lose $15.

d. you will earn $15.

5. Suppose you own a put option on a stock with a strike price of $35, which expires today. The price of the underlying stock is $25. If you purchase the stock and exercise the put option,

a. you will earn $10.

b. you will lose $10.

c. you will earn $25.

d. you will lose $25.

6. Consider an American and a European call option on a dividend-paying stock, with otherwise identical features (same strike price, etc.). Which one of the following statements is true?

a. The American call option will never be worth less then the European call option.

b. The European call option will never be worth less then the American call option.

c. Both options should always have the same value.

d. None of the above statements are true.

7. Which of the following changes, when considered individually, will increase the value of a call option?

a. The value of the underlying asset becomes more volatile.

b. The price of the underlying asset goes down.

c. Getting closer to the expiration date (the passage of time).

d. A higher strike price.

8. If the price of the underlying asset increases, what happens to the value of call and put options?

a. Put options will be worth more, call options will be worth less.

b. Put options will be worth less, call options will be worth more.

c. Both call and put options will be worth more.

d. Both call and put options will be worth less.

9. With everything else constant, as the expiration date gets closer what happens to the value of call and put options?

a. Call options will be worth more, put options will be worth less.

b. Call options will be worth less, put options will be worth more.

c. Both call and put options will be worth more.

d. Both call and put options will be worth less.

10. With everything else held constant, what happened to the value of call and put options if the risk-free interest rate increases?

a. Call options will be worth more, put options will be worth less.

b. Call options will be worth less, put options will be worth more.

c. Both call and put options will be worth less.

d. Both call and put options will be worth more.

11. What is the payoff for a call option with a strike price of $45 if the underlying stock price at expiration is $75?

a. $30

b. $45

c. $75

d. None of the above

12. You own a put option on ABC. Co. stock with a strike price of $40. The current stock price is $40. You will benefit if

a. the stock price goes up.

b. the stock price goes down.

c. the stock price stays the same.

d. It doesn't matter; you are indifferent to changes in the stock price.

13. Consider a call option with a strike price of $20, which expires in one year. The risk-free rate of interest is 5 percent. The underlying stock price is $30. Without arbitrage, which of the following is a possible price for the call option?

a. $0

b. $8

c. $15

d. None of the above

14. Assume that the stock of RL Divisions, Inc., is currently trading for $20 and will either rise to $32 or fall to $15 in one month. The risk-free rate for one month is 0 percent. What is the value of a call option with a strike price of $25?

a. $6.58

b. $0.41

c. $7.06

d. $2.05

15. Assume that the stock of ABC, Inc., is currently trading for $45 and will either rise to $59 or fall to $44 in one year. The risk-free rate for one year is 5 percent. What is the value of a call option with a strike price of $55, which expires in one year?

a. $0

b. $0.83

c. $0.27

d. $0.52

16. Assume that the stock of ABC, Inc., is currently trading for $22 and will either rise to $31 or fall to $18 in one year. The risk-free rate for one year is 0 percent. What is the value of a put option with a strike price of $25?

a. $0

b. $1.85

c. $3

d. $4.85

17. Suppose you are creating a portfolio that consists of zero-interest bonds, stock from a single company, and call and put options on the stock. Holding which of the following combination of securities will give the payoff shown in the accompanying diagram?

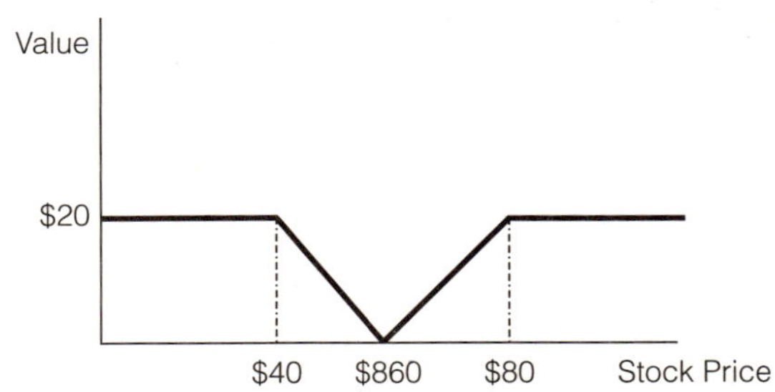

a. Buy one call option and one put option on the stock with a strike price of $60.

b. Buy one call option with a strike price of $60 and sell short one call option with a strike price of $80. Buy one put option at a strike price at $60 and sell short one put option with a strike price of $40.

c. Buy one share of the underlying stock. In addition buy two call options, one with a $40 strike price and one with a $80 strike price.

d. Buy one share of the underlying stock and a put option with a strike price of $60. Sell short two call options, one with a strike price of $40 and one with a strike price of $80.

18. Airbusy Aviation, Inc., is considering an investment in a new commercial airplane design. It is carefully taking everything into account when making a decision about the project. Which of the following considerations is **not** an example of a real option?

- **a.** If the project is successful, the technology the firm develops can reduce the cost of designing the next new military aircraft.
- **b.** The project requires doing a lot of research and building a large new manufacturing facility. The company plans to fund the research immediately, but will wait to see how much demand exists for the aircraft before building the large expensive manufacturing plant.
- **c.** If the economy slows, the revenues from the project are unlikely to exceed the costs of development. The project has a negative NPV.
- **d.** If the manufacturing facility is built, it will be a multiuse facility. If the project is not successful, the firm can sell the plant to other heavy equipment manufacturers in many different industries. The plant will cost more to build, but it will be easier to sell if things go poorly for the project.

19. Which of the following is **NOT** an example of the agency cost of debt?

- **a.** The dividend payout problem
- **b.** The underinvestment problem
- **c.** The asset substitution problem
- **d.** The negative NPV problem

20. Which type of risk cannot be managed by hedging with financial instruments?

- **a.** Foreign exchange rate risk
- **b.** The risk of higher input commodity prices
- **c.** The risk of lower output commodity prices
- **d.** All of these risks can be hedged.

Answers to True or False Questions

1. b	**2.** a	**3.** a	**4.** a	**5.** a
6. a	**7.** b	**8.** a	**9.** a	**10.** a

Answers to Multiple-Choice Questions

1. b	**2.** c	**3.** d	**4.** b	**5.** a
6. d	**7.** c	**8.** b	**9.** d	**10.** a
11. a	**12.** b	**13.** c	**14.** d	**15.** b
16. d	**17.** b	**18.** c	**19.** d	**20.** d

Solutions to Multiple-Choice Problems

12. **Solution:**

Without arbitrage, the value of the option must fall between $10.96 and $30. Out of the given choices, only $15 is a possible price for the option.

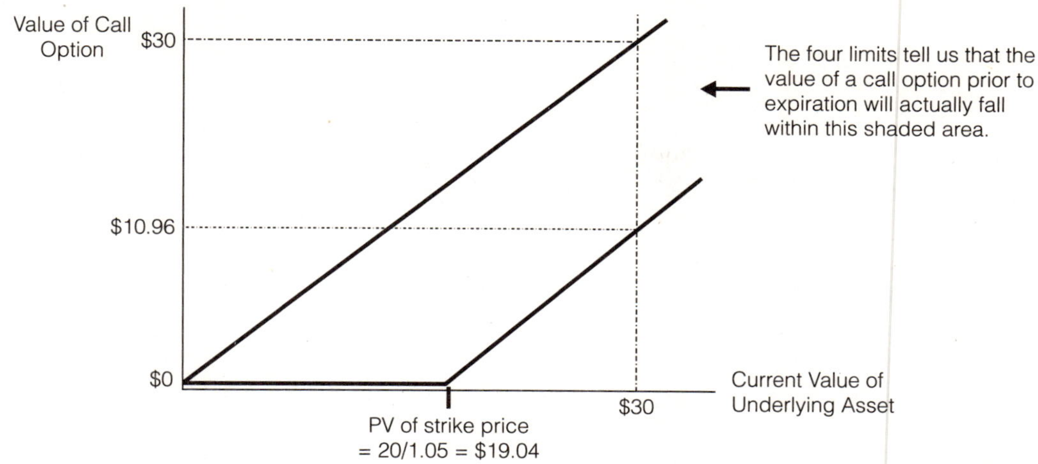

14. Solution:

The payoff from the call option is $7 if the stock price rises and $0 if the stock price falls. From the binomial pricing model we can create a replicating portfolio with the following two equations:

$\$7 = (\$32 \times x) + (1.00 \times y)$

$\$0 = (\$15 \times x) + (1.00 \times y)$

$x = 0.41$ shares of stock

$Y = -\$6.18$ of risk-free bonds.

The value of the option is the value of the replicating portfolio:

$(0.41 \times \$20) + (-0.618) = \$2.05$

15. Solution:

The payoff from the call option is $4 if the stock price rises and $0 if the stock price falls. From the binomial pricing model we can create a replicating portfolio with the following two equations:

$\$4 = (\$59 \times x) + (1.05 \times y)$

$\$0 = (\$44 \times x) + (1.05 \times y)$

$x = 0.267$ shares of stock

$Y = -\$11.17$ of risk-free bonds.

The value of the option is the value of the replicating portfolio:

$(0.267 \times \$45) + (-11.17) = \$0.83$

16. Solution:

The payoff from the put option is $0 if the stock price rises and $7 if the stock price falls. From the binomial pricing model we can create a replicating portfolio with the following two equations:

$\$0 = (\$31 \times x) + (1.00 \times y)$

$\$7 = (\$18 \times x) + (1.00 \times y)$

$x = -0.54$ shares of stock

$Y = \$16.69$ of risk-free bonds.

The value of the option is the value of the replicating portfolio:

$(-0.54 \times \$22) + (\$16.69) = \$4.85$

CHAPTER 21

International Financial Management

LEARNING OBJECTIVES

1. Discuss how the basic principles of finance apply to international financial transactions.
2. Differentiate among the spot rate, the forward rate, and the cross rate in the foreign exchange markets; make foreign exchange and cross rate calculations; and be able to hedge an asset purchase where payment is made in a foreign currency.
3. Identify the major factors that distinguish international from domestic capital budgeting, explain how the capital budgeting process can be adjusted to account for these factors, and compute the NPV for a typical international capital project.
4. Discuss the importance of the Euromarkets to large U.S. multinational firms, and calculate the cost of borrowing in the Eurobond market.
5. Explain how large U.S. money center banks make and price Eurocredit loans to their customers, and compute the cost of a Eurocredit bank loan.

I. Chapter Outline

21.1 Introduction to International Finance Management

A. *Globalization of the World Economy*

- **Globalization** refers to the removal of barriers to free trade and the closer integration of national economies.
- Consumers in many countries buy goods that are purchased from a number of countries, other than just their own.
- The production of goods and services has also become highly globalized.
- Like product markets, the financial system has also become highly integrated.

B. *The Rise of Multinational Corporations*

- A ***multinational corporation*** is a business firm that operates in more than one country but is headquartered or based in its home country.
- Multinationals are owned by a mixture of domestic and foreign stockholders.
- ***Transnational corporations,*** regardless of the location of their headquarters, are managed from a global perspective rather than the perspective of a firm residing in a particular country.

C. *Factors Affecting International Financial Management*

- Six factors can cause international business transactions to differ from domestic deals.
  - o The uncertainty of future exchange rate movements is called **foreign exchange rate risk,** or just **exchange rate risk.**
  - o Differences in legal systems and tax codes can also impact the way firms operate in foreign countries.
  - o Although English is the official business language, it is not the world's social language.

- Cultural views also shape business practices and people's attitudes toward business.
- An economic system determines how a country mobilizes its resources to produce goods and services needed by society, as well as how the production is distributed.
- **Country risk** refers to political uncertainty associated with a particular country.
  - At the extreme, a country's government may even expropriate—that is, take over—a business's assets within the country.
  - These types of actions clearly can affect a firm's cash flows and, thus, the value of the firm.

D. *Goals of International Financial Management*

- Stockholder wealth maximization is the accepted goal for firms in the United States, as well as in some other countries that share a similar heritage, such as the United Kingdom, Australia, India, and Canada.
- In Continental Europe, for example, countries such as France and Germany focus on maximizing corporate wealth.
  - The European manager's goal is to earn as much wealth as possible for the firm while considering the overall welfare of all stakeholders.
- In Japan, companies form tightly knit, interlocking business groups called *keiretsu,* such as Mitsubishi, Mitsui, and Sumitomo, and the goal of the Japanese business manager is to increase the wealth and growth of the keiretsu.
  - As a result, they might focus on maximizing market share rather than stockholder wealth.
- In China, which is making a transition from a command economy to a market-based economy, there are sharp differences between state-owned companies and emerging private-sector firms.
  - The large state-owned companies have an overall goal that can best be described as maintaining full employment in the economy while the new private-sector firms fully embrace the Western standard of stockholder wealth maximization.

E. *Basic Principles Remain the Same*

- The basic principles of managerial finance remain the same whether a transaction is domestic or international.
  - The time value of money is not affected by whether a business transaction is domestic or international.
  - Likewise, the same models are used for valuing capital assets, bonds, stocks, and entire firms.

21.2 Foreign Exchange Markets

- The **foreign exchange market** is a group of international markets connected electronically where currencies are bought and sold in wholesale amounts.
- Foreign exchange markets provide three basic economic benefits:
  - A mechanism to transfer purchasing power from individuals who deal in one currency to people who deal in a different currency.
  - A way for corporations to pass the risk associated with foreign exchange price fluctuations to professional risk-takers.
  - A channel for importers and exporters to acquire credit for international business transactions.

A. *Market Structure and Major Participants*

- Participants are linked by telephone, telegraph, and cable.
- The major participants in the foreign exchange markets are multinational commercial banks, large investment banking firms, and small currency boutiques that specialize in foreign exchange transactions.
- In addition, the central banks, which intervene in the markets primarily to smooth out fluctuations in their exchange rates, also play a significant role.

B. *Foreign Exchange Rates and the Equilibrium Exchange Rate*

- A foreign exchange rate is the price of one monetary unit.
- One of two parties in a transaction will be forced to deal in a foreign currency and incur foreign exchange rate risk.
- Exhibit 21.4 shows the *equilibrium exchange rate,* which is at the point where the supply and demand curves intersect.
  - Equilibrium occurs at the price at which the quantity of the currency demanded exactly equals the quantity supplied.
  - In general, whatever causes U.S. residents to buy more or fewer foreign goods shifts the demand curve for the foreign currency.
  - Similarly, whatever causes foreigners to buy more or fewer U.S. goods shifts the supply curve for the foreign currency.

C. ***Foreign Currency Quotations***

- The **spot rate** is the cost of buying a foreign currency today, "on the spot."
  - o If the exchange rate is the price in dollars for a foreign currency, it is often called the *American* or *direct* quote.
  - o If the exchange rate is the price in foreign currency for a dollar, the quote is called a *European* or an *indirect* quote.
- Foreign exchange dealers quote two prices: *bid* and *ask* quotes.
  - o The *bid* quote represents the rate at which the dealer will *buy* foreign currency.
  - o The *ask* quote is the rate at which the dealer will *sell* foreign currency.
- When one is given two quotes of foreign exchange rates involving three currencies, it is possible to find the exchange rate between the third pair of currencies, and this is known as the *cross rate*.
- The forward rate is the rate that one agrees to buy or sell a currency at some future date.
  - o Note that the forward rate is established at the date on which the agreement is made and defines the exchange rate to be used when the transaction is completed in the future.
  - o By contracting now to buy or sell foreign currencies at some future date, businesses can lock in the cost of foreign exchange at the beginning of the transaction, and do not have to worry about the risk of an unfavorable movement in the exchange rate in the future.
- The difference between the forward rate and the spot rate is called the *forward premium* or *forward discount.*

21.3 International Capital Budgeting

- When a multinational firm wants to consider overseas capital projects, the financial manager faces the decision of which capital projects should be accepted on a company-wide basis.
- The decision to accept international projects with a positive NPV increases the value of the firm and is consistent with the fundamental goal of financial management, which is to maximize stockholder wealth.
- Although the same basic principles apply to both international and domestic capital budgeting, firms must deal with some differences.

A. ***Determining Cash Flows***

- A number of issues complicate the determination of cash flows from overseas capital projects.
- First, most companies find it more difficult to estimate the incremental cash flows for foreign projects.
- Second, problems with cash flows can arise when foreign governments restrict the amount of cash that can be repatriated, or returned, to the parent company.

B. ***Exchange Rate Risk***

- Financial managers have to deal with foreign exchange rate risk on international capital investments.
- To convert the project's future cash flows into another currency, we need to come up with projected or forecast exchange rates.
- One of the problems with obtaining currency rate forecasts for use in analysis of capital projects is that many projects have lives of 20 years or more.

C. ***Country Risk***

- Financial managers must also incorporate a country risk premium when evaluating foreign business activities.
- If a firm is located in a country with a relatively unstable political environment, management will require a higher rate of return on capital projects as compensation for the additional risk.
- At the extreme, a local government could take over the plant and equipment of the overseas operation without giving the company any compensation.
  - o This expropriation of assets is called *nationalization.*
- Once management has gauged a capital project's country risk, that risk must be incorporated into the capital budgeting analysis by, for example, adjusting the firm's discount rate for the additional risk.

21.4 Global Money and Capital Markets

A. ***The Emergence of the Euromarkets***

- A **Eurodollar** is defined as a U.S. dollar deposited in a bank outside the United States, primarily in Europe.
- The banks accepting these deposits are called *Eurobanks.*
- The Euromarkets are vast, largely unregulated money and capital markets with major financial centers in Tokyo, Hong Kong, and Singapore.

B. *The Eurocurrency Market*

- The *Eurocurrency market* is the short-term portion of the Euromarket.
- A **Eurocurrency** is a timed deposit of money held by corporations and governments in a bank located in a country different from the country that issued the currency.
- The most widely quoted Eurocurrency interest rate is the **London Interbank Offer Rate,** or **LIBOR**, which is the short-term interest rate that major banks in London charge one another.

C. *The Eurocredit Market*

- The international banking system gathers funds from businesses and governments in the Eurocurrency market and then allocates funds to banks that have the most profitable lending opportunities.
- These loans, which are short- to medium-term loans of a Eurocurrency to multinational corporations and governments of medium to high credit quality, are called **Eurocredits.**
- Eurocredits are denominated in all major Eurocurrencies, although the dollar is the overwhelming favorite.

D. *International Bond Markets*

- International bonds fall into two generic categories: foreign bonds and Eurobonds.
- **Foreign bonds** are long-term debt sold by a foreign firm to investors in another country and denominated in that country's currency.
  - o Foreign bonds may have colorful nicknames:
    - ▪ foreign bonds sold in the United States are called ***Yankee*** bonds, and
    - ▪ yen-denominated bonds sold in Japanese financial markets by non-Japanese firms are called ***Samurai*** bonds.
  - o Firms sell foreign bonds when they need to finance projects in a particular foreign country.
- Eurobonds are long-term debt instruments sold by firms to investors in countries other than the country in whose currency the bonds are denominated.
  - o Multinational firms can use Eurobonds to finance international or domestic projects.
  - o Eurodollar and other Eurocurrency bonds have a number of characteristics that differ from similar U.S corporate bonds.
  - o Eurobonds are bearer bonds and do not have to be registered.
  - o Eurobonds also pay interest annually.
  - o Historically, almost all Eurocurrency bonds were sold without credit ratings.
  - o Today, more than half of the Eurodollar bonds sold in Europe have credit ratings.

21.5 International Banking

- European governments fostered the growth of large international banks in their countries and viewed them as engines of territorial and economic expansion.
- To accommodate their customers' needs, large U.S. banks established networks of foreign branches and affiliates.

A. *Risks Involved in International Bank Lending*

- The principles of loan administration and credit analysis are similar for domestic and overseas loans.
- There are differences, however, including some additional risk exposures for overseas lending.
  - o Credit risk is the same whether a loan is domestic or international. However, it may be more difficult to obtain or assess credit information abroad.
  - o Bank loans that have foreign exchange risk will carry an additional risk premium.
  - o If an international loan or investment is expected to suffer some loss in value, the loan will carry an additional risk premium.

B. *Eurocredit Bank Loans*

- Eurocredits are short- to medium-term loans of a Eurocurrency to multinational corporations or governments.
- They can have a high degree of credit risk and may be too large for a single bank to handle.
- The lending banks often form a syndicate to spread the risk.
- The loan rate is equal to a base rate, such as LIBOR, which represents the bank's cost of funds, plus a markup.
- Eurocredits typically are floating-rate loans structured as "rollovers."

II. Suggested Approach to Material

This chapter begins with some background information about the globalization of the world economy, the rise of multinational corporations, and the key factors that distinguish domestic from international business transactions. Emphasis is placed on the fact that the basic principles of finance remain valid for international business transactions, even though some of the variables used to calculate financial models change. Two risks are introduced that are not present in domestic business transactions: foreign exchange risk and country risk.

The markets for foreign exchange are discussed next, and the authors explain how firms protect themselves from fluctuations in exchange rates. The discussion moves to how multinational firms manage their overseas capital investments and compute the NPV for these projects. Finally, the discussion turns to global money and capital markets. Particular attention is paid to the Euromarket, where large multinational companies adjust their liquidity, borrow short term from banks in the Eurocredit market, and borrow long term in the international bond markets. Finally, bank pricing and the structure of Eurocredits are discussed.

III. Chapter Glossary

Globalization	The removal of barriers to free trade and the integration of national economies.
Multinational corporation	A business firm that operates in more than one country.
Transnational corporation	A multinational firm that has widely dispersed ownership and that is managed from a global perspective.
Foreign exchange rate risk, or **exchange rate risk**	The uncertainty associated with future exchange rate movements.
Country risk	The political uncertainty associated with a particular country.
Foreign exchange market	International markets where currencies are bought and sold in wholesale amounts.
Spot rate	The exchange rate in the market at any given point in time.
Forward rate	A rate agreed on today for an exchange to take place at a specified date in the future.
Hedge	A financial transaction intended to reduce risk.
Repatriation of earnings restrictions	Restrictions placed by a foreign government on the amount of cash that can be repatriated, or returned, to a parent company by a subsidiary doing business in the foreign country.
Eurodollar	A U.S. dollar deposited in a bank outside the United States.
Eurocurrency	A time deposit owned by a corporation or government that is in a bank located in a country different from the country that issued the currency.
London Interbank Offer Rate (LIBOR)	The interest rate British-based banks charge each other for short-term loans. Also, commonly used as the base rate for Eurodollar loans that are not between two banks.
Eurocredits	Short- to medium-term loans of a Eurocurrency to multinational corporations and governments of medium- to high-credit quality.

IV. Summary of Key Equations

Equation	Description	Formula
21.1	Bid-ask spread	$\text{Bid-Ask Spread} = \dfrac{\text{Ask rate} - \text{Bid rate}}{\text{Ask rate}}$
21.2	Discount or forward premium	$\text{Forward premium (discount)} = \dfrac{\text{Forward rate} - \text{Spot rate}}{\text{Spot rate}} \times \dfrac{360}{n} \times 100$
21.3	Eurocredit pricing	$k = \text{BR} + \text{DRP} + \text{FXR} + \text{CR} + \text{GPMAR}$

V. True or False Questions

1. Consumers in many countries buy goods that are purchased from a number of countries, other than just their own.
   - a. True
   - b. False

2. The production of goods and services has also become highly localized.
   - a. True
   - b. False

3. Like product markets, the financial system has also become highly integrated.
   - a. True
   - b. False

4. A multinational corporation is a business firm that operates in more than one country but is headquartered or based in its home country.
   - a. True
   - b. False

5. Shell is a transnational corporation.
   - a. True
   - b. False

6. The risk that a firm's future cash flows will be affected by unexpected changes in the exchange rate is called foreign exchange rate risk.
   - a. True
   - b. False

7. Foreign exchange rate risk can affect a firm's future cash flows, but not the value of the firm.
   - a. True
   - b. False

8. Differences in legal systems and tax codes can also impact the way firms operate in foreign countries.
   - a. True
   - b. False

9. English is the world's social language.
   - a. True
   - b. False

10. An economic system determines how a country mobilizes its resources to produce goods and services needed by society, as well as how the production is distributed.
    - a. True
    - b. False

11. Nationalization is an extreme form of country risk.
    - a. True
    - b. False

12. Stockholder wealth maximization is the accepted goal for firms in countries like the United States, U.K., Canada, and Australia.
    - a. True
    - b. False

13. European firms outside of the United Kingdom focus on maximizing market share rather than stockholder wealth.
    a. True
    b. False

14. The foreign exchange market allows importers and exporters to acquire credit for international business transactions.
    a. True
    b. False

15. Tokyo is the largest foreign exchange trading center.
    a. True
    b. False

16. The major participants in the foreign exchange markets are multinational commercial banks, large investment banking firms, and small currency boutiques that specialize in foreign exchange transactions.
    a. True
    b. False

17. If the exchange rate is the price in dollars for a foreign currency, it is often called the direct quote.
    a. True
    b. False

18. The *bid* quote is the rate at which the dealer will *buy* foreign currency.
    a. True
    b. False

19. The difference between the forward rate and the spot rate is called the *forward premium* or *forward discount*.
    a. True
    b. False

20. The decision to accept international projects with a positive NPV increases the value of the firm and is consistent with maximizing stockholder wealth.
    a. True
    b. False

21. To convert the project's future cash flows into another currency, we need to use today's spot exchange rates.
    a. True
    b. False

22. Country risk can be incorporated into the capital budgeting analysis by adjusting the firm's discount rate.
    a. True
    b. False

23. The most widely quoted Eurocurrency interest rate is the **LIBOR.**
    a. True
    b. False

24. Yen-denominated bonds sold in Japanese financial markets by non-Japanese firms are called Samurai bonds.
    a. True
    b. False

25. Credit risk is the same whether a loan is domestic or international.
    a. True
    b. False

VI. Multiple-Choice Questions and Problems

1. Which **ONE** of the following statements about multinational firms is true?
   - **a.** A multinational corporation is a business firm that operates in more than one country but is headquartered or based in its home country.
   - **b.** Multinationals are owned by a mixture of domestic and foreign stockholders.
   - **c.** Multinationals may purchase raw materials from one country, obtain financing from a capital market in another country, and produce finished goods with labor and capital equipment from a third country.
   - **d.** All of the above.

2. Factors that can cause international business transactions to differ from domestic deals include
   - **a.** exchange rate risk.
   - **b.** legal systems.
   - **c.** country risk.
   - **d.** All of the above.

3. The official language of business globally is
   - **a.** English.
   - **b.** Spanish.
   - **c.** French.
   - **d.** None of the above.

4. Which one of the following statements is **NOT** true?
   - **a.** Stockholder value maximization is the accepted goal for firms in Canada.
   - **b.** Firms in the United Kingdom focus on maximizing corporate wealth.
   - **c.** Firms in France focus on maximizing corporate wealth.
   - **d.** Private-sector firms in China focus on maximizing firm value.

5. The largest foreign exchange market based on daily volume is
   - **a.** New York.
   - **b.** London.
   - **c.** Tokyo.
   - **d.** Zurich.

6. A foreign exchange rate is
   - **a.** the price of one monetary unit in terms of another currency.
   - **b.** the price at which two different currencies can be exchanged for a third one.
   - **c.** the price that certain governments will pay foreign citizens on transactions.
   - **d.** None of the above.

7. The spot rate is the cost of buying a foreign currency
   - **a.** a month from today.
   - **b.** today.
   - **c.** a year from today.
   - **d.** a year ago.

8. Which **ONE** of the following is a direct quote from an American perspective?
   - **a.** £0.5125/$
   - **b.** €0.6900/$
   - **c.** $1.5637/€
   - **d.** ¥115.23/€

9. If the foreign exchange rate is the price in dollars for a foreign currency, then the exchange rate quote is called
   a. a European quote.
   b. an indirect quote.
   c. a direct quote.
   d. a cross quote.

10. The forward rate is the rate that one buys or sells a currency
    a. today.
    b. immediately.
    c. at a future date.
    d. None of the above.

11. International capital budgeting projects are accepted if the NPV of the project is
    a. negative.
    b. below zero.
    c. positive.
    d. None of the above.

12. A Eurodollar is
    a. a petrodollar held in U.S banks.
    b. a dollar deposited by European investors in the United States.
    c. a U.S. dollar deposited in a bank outside the United States.
    d. None of the above.

13. The most widely quoted Eurocurrency interest rate is the
    a. prime rate.
    b. Fed funds rate.
    c. euro rate.
    d. LIBOR.

14. Bonds sold by foreign firms in the United States are called
    a. Yankee bonds.
    b. Bulldog bonds.
    c. Uncle Sam bonds.
    d. Confederate bonds.

15. Which one of the following statements about Eurocredit bank loans is **NOT** true?
    a. Eurocredits are short- to medium-term loans of a Eurocurrency to multinational corporations or governments.
    b. They can have a high degree of credit risk and may be too large for a single bank to handle.
    c. They can have a low degree of credit risk.
    d. The lending banks often form a syndicate to spread the risk.

16. Starling Corporation purchased some components from a Mexican manufacturer. They have to pay 70 million Mexican pesos for the goods today. The spot rate today is MP10.4640/$. What is the dollar cost of this payable? Round to the nearest dollar.
    a. $7,000,000
    b. $6,689,602
    c. $11,110,235
    d. $6,940,000

17. If the spot rate is quoted as \$0.009517/¥, what is the exchange rate in terms of yen per dollar?
    a. ¥0.009369/\$
    b. ¥0.936900/\$
    c. ¥105.0751/\$
    d. ¥160.7350/\$

18. Given that the spot rate is \$1.5276/€ and the 90-day forward quote is \$1.5174/€, we can say that
    a. the U.S. dollar is at a forward premium against the euro.
    b. the U.S. dollar is at a forward discount against the euro.
    c. the euro is at a forward premium against the U.S. dollar.
    d. the dollar is at neither a premium nor a discount against the euro.

19. Del Negro, Inc., purchased machinery from a Japanese firm and will have to pay ¥338.45 million in 90 days. The bank quotes a forward rate of ¥108.46/\$ to buy the required yen. What is the cost to Del Negro in U.S. dollars?
    a. \$3,120,459
    b. \$2,784,500
    c. \$2,936,534
    d. \$3,714,300

20. A local bank has requested foreign exchange quotes for the Danish krone from Citibank. Citibank quotes a bid rate of \$0.2052/DK and an ask rate of \$0.2087/DK. What is the bid-ask spread?
    a. 1.2%
    b. 2.1%
    c. 1.7%
    d. 0.6%

21. Bartman Corporation observes that the Swiss franc (SF) is being quoted at \$0.6164/SF, while the Swedish krona (SK) is quoted at \$0.1981/SK. What is the SK/SF cross rate?
    a. SK0.3214/SF
    b. SK3.1116/SF
    c. SK0.4183/SF
    d. SK2.1467/SF

22. The spot rate on the New York market was \$1.8939/£, while the 90-day forward rate was \$1.9234/£. What is the annualized forward premium or discount on the U.S. dollar for the period? Round to one decimal place.
    a. 6.2% premium
    b. 5.6% premium
    c. 5.2% discount
    d. 4.1% discount

23. Quintel Industries has purchased equipment from a German firm for a total cost of €1,272,500. The firm has to pay in 30 days. Citicorp has given the firm a 30-day forward quote of \$1.6123/€. Assume that on the day the payment is due, the spot rate is at \$1.6317/€. How much would Quintel save by hedging with a forward contract? Round to the nearest dollar.
    a. \$24,687
    b. \$803,838
    c. \$779,152
    d. \$31,278

24. Carrington Industries sold equipment to a Mexican firm. Payment of 41,275,000 pesos will be due in 30 days. Carrington has the option of selling the pesos at a 30-day forward rate of \$0.09739/peso. If it waits 30 days to sell

the pesos, the expected spot rate is \$0.09596/peso. How much additional dollar revenue will Carrington get by selling forward the pesos? Round to the nearest dollar.

a. \$24,687
b. \$83,838
c. \$59,023
d. \$31,278

25. Universal International can borrow \$7.5 million from HSBC at LIBOR plus a lending margin of 0.75 percent on a three-month rollover Eurocredit loan. Suppose that the prevailing LIBOR rate is 4.0 percent and that over the next three month period, the LIBOR rate is expected to increase to 4.25 percent. How much interest will Universal have to pay HSBC for the Eurocredit loan for the first six months?

a. \$89,062.50
b. \$93,750.00
c. \$182,812.50
d. \$178,125.00

Answers to True or False Questions

1. a	**2.** b	**3.** a	**4.** a	**5.** a
6. a	**7.** b	**8.** a	**9.** b	**10.** a
11. a	**12.** a	**13.** b	**14.** a	**15.** b
16. a	**17.** a	**18.** a	**19.** a	**20.** a
21. b	**22.** a	**23.** a	**24.** a	**25.** a

Answers to Multiple-Choice Questions

1. d	**2.** d	**3.** a	**4.** b	**5.** b
6. a	**7.** b	**8.** c	**9.** c	**10.** c
11. c	**12.** c	**13.** d	**14.** a	**15.** c
16. b	**17.** c	**18.** a	**19.** a	**20.** c
21. b	**22.** b	**23.** a	**24.** c	**25.** c

Solutions to Multiple-Choice Problems

16. Solution:

Cost of payables = MP 70,000,000
Spot rate = MP10.4640/\$
Dollar cost of payables = MP 70,000,000 / MP 10.4640/\$ = \$6,689,602.45

17. Solution:

Spot rate = \$0.009517/¥
Direct quote = 1/ \$0.009517/¥ = ¥105.0751/\$

18. Solution:

Since the forward quote of \$1.5174/€ implies that fewer dollars will be needed to purchase the euro compared to the spot rate of \$1.5276/€, we can say that the U.S. dollar is at a forward premium against the euro.

19. Solution:

Cost of machinery = ¥338.45 million

Forward rate = ¥108.46/\$

Cost of equipment in dollars = ¥338,445,000 / ¥108.46/\$= \$3,120,459.16

20. Solution:

$$\text{Bid-Ask Spread} = \frac{\text{Ask rate} - \text{Bid rate}}{\text{Ask rate}} = \frac{\$0.2087/\text{DK} - \$0.2052/\text{SK}}{\$0.2087/\text{SK}}$$
$$= 0.01677 = \mathbf{1.7\%}$$

21. Solution:

To find the SK/SF cross rate, divide the Swiss franc quote by the Swedish krona quote.

Cross rate = \$0.6164/SF / \$0.1981/SK = SK3.1116/SF

22. Solution:

$$\text{Forward premium (discount)} = \frac{\text{Forward rate} - \text{Spot rate}}{\text{Spot rate}} \times \frac{360}{n} \times 100$$
$$= \frac{1.9234 - 1.8939}{1.8939} \times \frac{360}{90} = \mathbf{6.23\%}$$

The U.S. dollar is at a forward discount of 6.23 percent against the British pound as it takes more dollars to buy a pound at the forward rate.

23. Solution:

Foreign currency payables = €1,272,500

Spot rate on payment date = \$1.6317/€

Dollar cost of payables = €1,272,500 × \$1.6317/€= \$2,076,338.25

30-day forward rate = \$1.6123/€

Cost if hedged at forward rate = €1,272,500 × \$1.6123/€= \$2,051,681.75

Cost savings = \$2,078,338.25 – \$2,051,681.75= \$24,686.50

24. Solution:

Foreign currency receivables = MP 41,275,000

Spot rate on payment date = \$0.09596/peso

Dollar revenues from receivables = MP 41,275,000 × \$0.09596/peso = \$3,960,749

30-day forward rate = \$0.09739/peso

Revenues if hedged at forward rate = MP 41,275,000 × \$0.09739/peso = \$4.019,772.25

Additional revenues received = \$4.019,772.25 – \$3,960,749 = \$59,023.25

25. Solution:

Amount Universal plans to borrow = \$7.5 million

Term of loan = 6 months

Interest rate for first 3 months = LIBOR + 0.75% = 4.000% + 0.75% = 4. 750%

Interest cost for first 3 months = \$7,500,000 × 0.0475 = (90/360) = \$89,062.50

Interest rate for next 3 months = LIBOR + 0.75% = 4.250% + 0.75% = 5.000%

Interest cost for next 3 months = \$7,500,000 × 0.0500 × (90/360) = \$93,750

Total interest cost for 6 months = \$89,062.50 + \$93,750

= \$182,812.50

Notes

Notes

Notes

Notes

Notes

Notes

Notes

Notes

Notes

Notes

Notes

Notes

Notes

Notes

Notes

Notes

Notes